THE EXISTENTIALISTS

Critical Essays on the Classics
Series Editor: Steven M. Cahn

The volumes in this series offer insightful and accessible essays that shed light on the classics of philosophy. Each of the distinguished editors has selected outstanding work in recent scholarship to provide today's readers with a deepened understanding of the most timely issues raised in these important texts.

THE EXISTENTIALISTS
Critical Essays on Kierkegaard, Nietzsche, Heidegger, and Sartre

Edited by
Charles Guignon

ROWMAN & LITTLEFIELD PUBLISHERS, INC.
Lanham • Boulder • New York • Toronto • Oxford

ROWMAN & LITTLEFIELD PUBLISHERS, INC.

Published in the United States of America
by Rowman & Littlefield Publishers, Inc.
A wholly owned subsidiary of The Rowman & Littlefield Publishing Group, Inc.
4501 Forbes Boulevard, Suite 200, Lanham, Maryland 20706
www.rowmanlittlefield.com

PO Box 317
Oxford
OX2 9RU, UK

British Library Cataloguing in Publication Information Available

Library of Congress Cataloging-in-Publication Data

The existentialists : critical essays on Kierkegaard, Nietzsche,
Haidegger, and Sartre / edited by Charles Guignon.
   p. cm.—(Critical essays on the classics)
   Includes bibliographical references and index.
   ISBN 0-7425-1412-9 (alk. paper)—ISBN 0-7425-1413-7 (pbk. : alk. paper)
   1. Existentialism. 2. Kierkegaard, Søren, 1813–1855. 3. Nietzsche,
Friedrich Wilhelm, 1844–1900. 4. Heidegger, Martin, 1889–5. Sartre,
Jean-Paul, 1905– 1. Guignon, Charles B., 1944– II. Series.
   B819.E9453 2004
   142'.78—dc21   2003011950

Contents

Acknowledgments

THE EDITOR AND PUBLISHER thank the authors and publishers of these essays for permission to print or reprint them in this volume.

Chapter 1, Robert Merrihew Adams, "The Knight of Faith," originally appeared in *Faith and Philosophy* 7, no. 4 (October 1990): 383–95. Reprinted by permission of the editor.

Chapter 2, Louis Dupré, "*The Sickness unto Death*: Critique of the Modern Age," originally appeared in *International Kierkegaard Commentary:* The Sickness unto Death, edited by Robert L. Perkins (Macon, Ga.: Mercer University Press, 1987), 85–106.

Chapter 3, Robert C. Solomon, "A More Severe Morality: Nietzsche's Affirmative Ethics," originally appeared in the *Journal of the British Society for Phenomenology* 16, no. 3 (October 1985).

Chapter 4, Alexander Nehamas, "How One Becomes What One Is," originally appeared in *The Philosophical Review* 92, no. 3 (July 1983): 385–417. Copyright © 1983 Cornell University. Reprinted by permission of the publisher and the author.

Chapter 5, Harrison Hall, "Intentionality and World: Division I of *Being and Time*," originally appeared in *The Cambridge Companion to Heidegger*, edited by Charles Guignon (Cambridge: Cambridge University Press, 1993), 122–40. Reprinted with the permission of the Cambridge University Press and the author.

Chapter 6, Charles Guignon, "Becoming a Self: The Role of Authenticity in *Being and Time*," has not been previously published.

Chapter 7, Thomas C. Anderson, "Sartre's Early Ethics and the Ontology of *Being and Nothingness*," is reprinted from *Sartre Alive,* edited by Ronald Aronson and Adrian van den Hoven, with permission of Wayne State University Press. Copyright © 1991 by Wayne State University Press, Detroit, Michigan.

Chapter 8, Dorothy Leland, "The Sartrean *Cogito*: A Journey between Versions," *Research in Phenomenology* 5 (1975): 129–41. Copyright © 1975 by Brill Academic Publishers, Leiden, Netherlands.

Introduction

Charles Guignon

What Is Existentialism?

THE ENDURING INTEREST EXISTENTIALISM has for students and philosophers can be explained by the fact that it seems to offer an alternative to the dominant approaches to philosophy on the scene today. Whereas mainstream philosophy generally sees its role as discovering universally valid truths about such topics as knowledge, reality, and value, existentialism addresses questions that arise for individuals in the course of actually living out their lives. The emphasis in existentialism, as its name suggests, is on the concrete nature of existence. An inquiry of this sort is needed, existentialists claim, because the standard way of thinking about human beings—the conception of humans as members of a species or instances of a natural kind—generally leaves out of account such dimensions of life as passion, integrity, authenticity, and commitment.

The feeling that mainstream approaches to human phenomena leave something important out of account was expressed by Søren Kierkegaard over 150 years ago. "To be a human being means to belong to a race endowed with reason, to belong to it as a specimen, so that the race or species is higher than the individual, which is to say that there are no more individuals but only specimens."[1] In Kierkegaard's view, the traditional philosophical conception of human beings as members of a species conceals something crucially important to understanding who and what we are. To counteract this concealment, we need to reflect on our own existence as individuals: "The first thing to keep in mind," Kierkegaard says, "is that every human being is an individual human being and is to become conscious of being an individual human being."[2] The interest in making people aware of the specific concerns associated with individuality continues to be a central theme in existentialism.

But even though existentialism remains of interest, it is not easy to say exactly which thinkers are to be counted as existentialists. The problem of determining the existentialist "canon" arises because the term *existentialism* did not come into use until the 1940s, and even then it was embraced as a label only by specific philosophers in France, primarily Jean-Paul Sartre and Simone de Beauvoir. Some important thinkers who might be grouped with the existentialists—for example, Albert Camus and Martin Heidegger—went out of their way to deny that they were existentialists. And the majority of thinkers whom one might want to identify as existentialists never even heard of the word.

In his helpful book, *Existentialism: A Reconstruction*, David E. Cooper lists as existentialists such figures as Karl Jaspers, Maurice Merleau-Ponty, José Ortega y Gasset, Gabriel Marcel, and Martin Buber. But he is inclined to exclude the nineteenth-century philosophers Søren Kierkegaard and Friedrich Nietzsche on the grounds that they are "precursors" of existentialism. Questions could be raised, however, about some of the figures Cooper includes on his own list. Jaspers called his own philosophy the "philosophy of existence" (*Existenzphilosophie*), and his thought was certainly influential for Heidegger and others. But Jaspers's own use of the word *existence* was derived from his readings of Kierkegaard, as Jaspers would be the first to admit. Similar points can be made about Ortegay Gasset, Merleau-Ponty, and Buber. Though they were influenced by seminal figures who also influenced existentialists (for example, the life-philosopher Wilhelm Dilthey in the case of Ortegay Gasset and the phenomenologist Edmund Husserl in the case of Merleau-Ponty), there is no firm basis for identifying them as existentialists. It would seem, then, that on any accounting most of those who come to be included in the ranks of "existentialists" will turn out to be conscripts rather than volunteers.

Instead of trying to be maximally inclusive in deciding whom to count as an existentialist, I have decided to cut the Gordian knot and simply focus on the four central figures whose works are so often included in college courses on existentialism: Kierkegaard, Nietzsche, Heidegger, and Sartre. Although the first two of this group predated the coinage of "existentialism" and the third denied he was an existentialist, they form a coherent group in an important sense. Certainly all existentialists go back to Kierkegaard's thoughts about the existing individual, just as they all tend to follow Nietzsche in abandoning any belief in a timeless, suprahuman source of information about reality and values. Nietzsche's suggestion that the belief in Absolutes is no longer tenable, together with Kierkegaard's claim that it is up to each individual to decide where he or she stands in defining his or her own life, are two of the core assumptions of existentialist philosophy. Moreover, the "analysis of existence" in Heidegger's major work, *Being and Time*, has played a crucial role in shaping the thought of Sartre and other existentialist thinkers. So it seems that, no matter how one interprets the notion of existentialism, one will have to come to terms with these four pivotal figures.

The Essays

The eight essays collected here are among the most insightful and carefully crafted works written by scholars who write on the four thinkers examined in this book. Though some of these essays are written by philosophers who would call themselves existentialists, others are written by outstanding English-language philosophers who would claim no special connection to existentialist philosophy. I have made a point of choosing essays with very different styles and points of view to try to show the range of scholarly work in this area. Some of the essays are written in a conversational style and are easy to grasp, whereas others are written at a level of sophistication requiring considerable concentration and prior knowledge. In what follows, I will try to provide some of the background information needed to understand the essays.

Kierkegaard

Born in 1813 to a well-to-do family in Copenhagen, Denmark, Søren Kierkegaard was given a strict upbringing in the official state religion. Although he first studied theology at the university, he later turned to philosophy and literature. His writings are intensely critical of both the dominant philosophy of the time—that of the German philosopher, G. W. F. Hegel—and the religious practices and beliefs of those who mindlessly followed the official religion, a form of life he called "Christendom." With an exceptional combination of literary skill and biting wit, Kierkegaard opposed all system-building and mindless conformism, and promoted a life of religious intensity and commitment of the sort he saw as characteristic of authentic "Christianity." His major works include *Either/Or* (1843), *Fear and Trembling* (1843), *Concluding Unscientific Postscript* (1846), and *The Sickness unto Death* (1849). Kierkegaard died in 1855 at the age of forty-two.

Kierkegaard frequently satirized the heavy sort of academic writing typical of the Hegelian authors of his time. Though he generally opposed Hegel, he did adopt from Hegelian thought a picture of human development as moving through various stages. According to this Hegelian coming-of-age story, one starts out in life preoccupied solely with immediate sensations and the instant gratification of desires. This first stage Kierkegaard calls the "aesthetic" (from the Greek word *aesthesis*, meaning "sensation"). As one grows up and becomes a mature person, one typically chooses to move beyond this childish state of immediacy to a standpoint of *mediation*, a stage in which one conceptualizes what is presented in sensory experience and uses moral principles to regulate and direct desires. In this stage, which is called the "ethical," life for the first time comes to have continuity, cohesiveness, and cumulativeness.

In Kierkegaard's view, each stage on life's way is a self-contained "sphere of existence" which has its own intelligibility and standards within itself but is, strictly speaking, incomprehensible from outside that sphere. Since there are no "higher" standards outside all particular spheres of existence that one could use in order to compare different spheres, movement from one sphere to another must always involve a radical choice: a *leap* of the will that is not based on a deliberation about options.

Kierkegaard read Hegel as saying that the ethical sphere is as high as anyone can go in life. In opposition to this view, he claims that there is a higher stage of development open to human beings, the stage of "faith." Faith involves an all-consuming, world-defining commitment to something that gives an individual's life its meaning. Because faith cannot be understood or described from outside its own sphere of existence, it is something that can only be alluded to and indirectly communicated. For this reason, most of Kierkegaard's writings are pseudonymous, written from the standpoint of someone who is outside faith and is trying to intimate (inevitably in a partial and inadequate way) what faith is.

"The Knight of Faith" by Robert Merrihew Adams attempts to clarify one important aspect of Kierkegaard's notion of faith, the notion that it involves a paradox and is "absurd." In a section of *Fear and Trembling* titled the "Preliminary Expectoration," Kierkegaard examines the story of Abraham, "the father of faith," who out of obedience to God's command set out to kill his only son Isaac and was under way in carrying out the order until God stayed his hand.

Kierkegaard (or, more precisely, the pseudonymous author of *Fear and Trembling*) suggests that there are two ways in which Abraham's inner condition could be interpreted in this story. On one interpretation, Abraham renounced the finite thing in the world that meant the most to him out of his total devotion to God. Doing this would involve what Kierkegaard calls "infinite resignation," and it is a fairly common sort of otherworldly religious stance that is familiar in many world religions. Kierkegaard claims, however, that genuine faith involves something more than mere renunciation. Abraham's faith is distinctive in that he both renounces the most precious thing in the finite realm and at the same time takes back and holds fast what he is giving up. Such a state involves what Adams calls a "practical contradiction": "The act is impossible to accomplish because the specification of the act contains contradictory directions." Yet it is precisely such an absurd and paradoxical condition that is, on Kierkegaard's account, the nature of authentic religious devotion. In Kierkegaardian faith, an intense interest in worldly goods can be combined with the most intense devotion to God. What Adams's account suggests is that a form of faith that is not only "otherworldly" but also "this-worldly" can be the richest and most fulfilling form of religious life. It might be noted that even though this account of faith focuses on the religious life, it can also illuminate what is involved in defining commitments of a non-religious sort, for example, to a loved one, to a political cause, or to a vocation.

Louis Dupré's essay on *The Sickness unto Death* illuminates a number of key themes in Kierkegaard's thought. Dupré first lays out Kierkegaard's diagnosis of the spiritlessness of "the present age"—a criticism of contemporary public life that seems as relevant today as it was in 1846.[3] According to Kierkegaard's critique, modern public life involves a "leveling down" of everything to a point where nothing really means much of anything to anyone anymore. The result of this leveling down is an incapacity for real passion or intensity. Where there is no ability to see anything as really mattering, life is characterized by a pervasive sense of emptiness and futility, and everyone comes to be blended into the shapeless mass of society.

To counteract this tendency toward spiritlessness in the present age, Kierkegaard envisions the possibility of a renewal in which individuals recover from their dispirited state and come to live as individuals with the passion and intensity that is characteristic of fully realized human existence. As a religious existentialist, however, Kierkegaard sees this renewal as requiring a transformation in our relationship with God. In his view, the condition of emptiness and spiritlessness characteristic of modern life—a condition he calls "despair"—should be seen as *sin*, a condition of disrelation between the self and the Power that constituted it. Only by coming face-to-face with despair or sin, he suggests, can people discover their being as individuals and so come to see what is truly at stake in life. This is what he means when he says that the "category of sin is the category of the individual," and that sin "splits men into individuals and holds every individual fast as a sinner."[4] The point is that it is only by facing up to our *distance* from God that we can encounter our true individuality, and it is only by becoming conscious of our individuality that we can come to achieve the right relation to God. Once again, though this description is cast in religious terms, it can help us understand the possibility of self-fulfillment and the achievement of intensity ("spirit") in life through nonreligious forms of commitment.

Nietzsche

Friedrich Nietzsche was born in Prussia in 1844, studied philology at the universities of Bonn and Leipzig, and became a professor of classical philol-

ogy at the University of Basel at the unheard-of age of twenty-four. Racked by
poor health, he stepped down from his position at Basel in 1879 and spent the
next ten years living on disability payments and writing the main body of his
life's work. He was forty-four years old when he suffered a complete mental
collapse, from which he remained an invalid until his death in 1900. His major
works include *The Birth of Tragedy* (1872), in which he drew his famous distinction between the Dionysian and Apollonian; *The Gay Science* (1882,
expanded in 1887); *Thus Spoke Zarathustra* (1883–85); *Beyond Good and
Evil* (1886); *Genealogy of Morals* (1887); and *Twilight of the Idols* and *The
Antichrist* (both of 1889).

Nietzsche is perhaps best known for his claim that "God is dead." To say that
God is dead is to say that the traditional belief in a transcendent basis for values is no longer credible in the modern world. The loss of an ability to believe
in Absolutes results in part from the insights that have arisen in recent scientific discoveries. If humans are in fact social animals that differ in degree but
not in type from other higher-order animals, then their perception and conception of reality will be shaped by their evolution and by their internalization
of prevailing social interpretations. But if that is the case, then the beliefs we
hold about reality and moral values are contingent constructions, products of
circumstances of historical development that could have been very different.
And if our beliefs are arbitrary constructions in this sense, there is no basis for
thinking we have ultimate knowledge of reality or of right and wrong. As
Nietzsche says, "we 'know' (or believe or imagine) just as much as may be useful in the interests of the human herd, the species; and even what is here called
'utility' is ultimately also a mere belief, something imaginary, and perhaps precisely that most calamitous stupidity of which we shall perish some day."[5] So
we have no access to True Reality or to The Good; we have access only to vary-
ing *perspectives* that seem "useful" relative to particular interests and needs we
may have in particular contexts.

The recognition that there are no Absolutes telling us what to believe and
how to act leads to *nihilism,* the complete disbelief in all traditional values.
Nietzsche suggests that there can be two different sorts of nihilism following
the death of God. The first, a *reactive* nihilism, springs from feelings of resentment and bitterness about the loss of something that seemed necessary to
life. Reactive nihilism will be characterized by a "monstrous logic of terror," a
long "sequence of breakdown, destruction, ruin, and cataclysm"[6] as people
discover that their gods had clay feet and that, without those gods, everything
seems to be permitted. But Nietzsche also sees the prospect of a different kind
of nihilism, a *positive,* yes-saying, life-affirming nihilism, in which people may
come to recognize that the loss of Absolutes brings with it "a new and scarcely
describable kind of light, happiness, relief, exhilaration, encouragement,

dawn."[7] For if there is no suprahuman source of instructions about what we ought to believe and how we ought to act, then the door is open for us to create our own tables of virtues, and so to define our own lives. The death of God points to the possibility of a new ideal for humanity, "the ideal of a spirit who plays naively—that is, not deliberately but from overflowing power and abundance—with all that was hitherto called holy, good, untouchable, divine." This is "the ideal of a human, superhuman, well-being and benevolence" that may follow on the recognition of the death of God.[8]

Nietzsche's conception of *playfulness* as a mark of the ideal Overman has led some readers to assume that he is promoting an "anything goes" moral relativism that paves the way to a deeply distressing *amoralism*. Robert C. Solomon's essay, "A More Severe Morality: Nietzsche's Affirmative Ethics," sets out to show that the rejection of traditional morality—where morality is understood as "a set of universal, categorical principles of practical reason"—does not necessarily undermine the possibility of ethics, where ethics is understood as a background of practices embodying a shared sense of what is worthwhile in life. Solomon argues that, appearances notwithstanding, Nietzsche's conception of ethics is similar to Aristotle's in that it sees the basis for moral action as lying not in rules and principles, but in "an ethics of *practice*, a description of an actual ethos" bound to a culture. As Solomon notes, however, there is a fundamental difference between Aristotle and Nietzsche. Whereas Aristotle could point to practices either currently existing in Greece or having existed in the not so distant past, Nietzsche has to try to recover and revive older, currently neglected values—the areteic values of masterly virtue.

Alexander Nehamas's "How One Becomes What One Is" deals with Nietzsche's picture of the most fulfilling life possible for individuals after the loss of Absolutes. The essay begins by noting how puzzling this idea of becoming what one is actually is. For Nietzsche holds that "the ego, construed as a metaphysical abiding subject, is a fiction," and so there is no such thing as a substantial self with pregiven attributes that one could strive to bring to realization. It is a consequence of Nietzsche's antiessentialism that humans are self-making or self-fashioning beings whose identity is constantly being composed throughout their lives. If this is the case, however—if there is nothing that one *is* in advance—then it is unclear how one can undertake the project of *becoming* what one is.

In addressing this puzzle, Nehamas offers an illuminating account of Nietzsche's view of the human self. Nietzsche's claim is not that there is some True Self given in advance that one must strive to realize and express. It is rather that the self that takes shape in ordinary life generally tends to be dispersed and manifold, so that there is a need to give unity and coherence to what initially lacks cohesiveness and unity. This is Nietzsche's point when he says that

"*One thing is needful*—To 'give style' to one's character," to "survey all the strengths and weaknesses of [one's] nature and then fit them into an artistic plan until every one of them appears as art and reason"[9] Nietzsche's ideal, then, is "creating one's life as a work of art." What he has in mind, according to Nehamas, is not a final state of being, but "a continual process of greater integration of one's character traits, habits and patterns of interaction with the world" with the goal of making "a unified character out of all one has done." In this process, one takes responsibility for oneself: one owns up to what one is as one comes into one's own. Self-enownment so conceived is an open-ended process that requires rigorous honesty about one's own traits as well as enough flexibility to let go of configurations that do not really work. The aim of this self-formation is not a static state, not Being with a capital *B*, but what Nietzsche calls "the innocence of becoming."

Heidegger

Martin Heidegger was born in 1889 in a small town on the edge of the Black Forest in Germany. Originally planning to enter the priesthood, he entered the Jesuit novitiate in 1909, but was forced by ill health to withdraw. His early intellectual development was influenced by Kierkegaard's newly translated works, the appearance of a full edition of Nietzsche's works, the life-philosophy of Wilhelm Dilthey, and the phenomenology of Edmund Husserl. Heidegger worked as an academic assistant to Husserl at the University of Freiburg, then taught for several years at Marburg University, and in 1928 returned to Freiburg to take the chair in philosophy formerly held by Husserl. His greatest work, *Being and Time*, was published in 1927, establishing him as one of the greatest philosophers of the twentieth century. When the Nazis came to power in 1933, he joined the party and became rector of the University of Freiburg. Although he resigned the rectorship a year later and became increasingly critical of the Nazis as the years passed, he continued his membership in the party until the end of World War II. He was banned from teaching after the denazification hearings of 1945 but was reinstated in 1950 and became professor emeritus at Freiburg a year later. His publications include "The Letter on Humanism" (1947), in which he distanced himself from Sartre's existentialism; *Introduction to Metaphysics* (1953); *On the Way to Language* (1959); and the two-volume work, *Nietzsche* (1961). He died in 1976.

Heidegger's *Being and Time* begins by asking one of the oldest questions of philosophy, the question about the Being of things in general: What is it to be an entity of any sort whatsoever? But it quickly shifts to asking about the Being of human existence (or "Dasein," the German word for existence, usually left untranslated). In asking the question, "What is human existence?"

Being and Time is firmly in the existentialist tradition. Heidegger insists that in inquiring into the Being of human existence, one must undertake a concrete *description* (phenomenology) of one's own "factical" life as it is being lived out in specific circumstances at a particular time in history. Moreover, he holds that what we should describe is not the way we are when we are engaged in theoretical reflection, but rather the way we are when we are engaged in average, everyday *agency* in a concrete lifeworld. His claim is that the traditional conception of the self as a subject or as a consciousness arises because philosophers have concentrated their attention on the way things show up when one is involved in theorizing. If we look at what shows up when we are caught up in practical affairs (i.e., equipment in use), we will see that we are "proximally and for the most part" not so much minds who happen to be related to objects, but are rather *being-in-the-world*, a unified phenomenon in which the distinction between subject and objects does not yet appear.

To be human, then, is to be inextricably bound up with a meaningful, purposive lifeworld—the world of academia, for example, or the business world. Heidegger points out that our lives as being-in-the-world always have a social dimension. As agents in familiar contexts, we generally do things as "one" is supposed to do such things according to the way these activities are interpreted in our social context. We are attuned through our upbringing to move along the guidelines of the norms and conventions that govern the forms of life of our culture. As a result, we exist as instances or exemplifications of what Heidegger calls the "they" or the "anyone" (*das Man*). In his words, "We take pleasure and enjoy ourselves as *they* take pleasure; we read, see, and judge about literature as *they* see and judge; likewise we shrink back from the 'great mass' as *they* shrink back; we find 'shocking' what *they* find shocking."[10] In his characterization of the "they," Heidegger carries forward a criticism of social existence developed in Kierkegaard's attack on the "public" and continued in Nietzsche's remarks about the "herd." But Heidegger is also acutely aware that social existence has a positive side. In his view, it is only because we have absorbed the shared understanding of an ongoing community that we have the kind of know-how and familiarity with things we need in order to be agents in the first place. Thus, Heidegger says that being the "they" is a "*primordial phenomenon* [and so] *belongs to Dasein's positive constitution.*"[11]

At the same time, however, Heidegger suggests that the need to fall into step with the crowd creates an inveterate tendency toward distraction and dispersal, and that it tempts us away from the need to take responsibility for our own lives. Dasein draws its possibilities of understanding itself and its world from the way things have been interpreted by the "they." This public interpretation gives us a window onto things, but it also leads to a leveling down of possibilities of understanding to "the range of the familiar, the attainable, the respectable—

that which is fitting and proper."[12] The only way to pull oneself back from this *falling* into conformism is through the experience of anxiety. In anxiety, one comes to see the contingency of all social interpretations, and one comes face-to-face with one's own responsibility for making something of one's own life as an individual. Anxiety reveals "naked Dasein as something that has been thrown into uncanniness [*Unheimlichkeit*, literally, 'not-being-at-home']."[13]

What we are anxious about in anxiety, Heidegger says, is our own finite existence, our *being-toward-death*. To say we exist as being-toward-death is not to say that some day, in the distant future, we will grow old and die. Instead, the existential concept of death refers to the fact that at every moment we face "*the possibility of the impossibility of any existence at all*," the ultimate nothingness of our Being.[14] Heidegger suggests that coming face-to-face with death so understood can transform our lives. Instead of drifting with the crowd and doing what "they" do, you can become *authentic* and resolutely face up to the task of realizing your life story in a way that is truly your own. This ideal of owning up to and owning one's life does not imply that one somehow escapes from social existence and achieves a condition unaffected by the contingencies of one's communal context. Instead, it means that one lives with *resoluteness* in taking a stand on the most meaningful possibilities of existence made accessible within one's historical culture.

Harrison Hall's "Intentionality and World: Division I of *Being and Time*" provides an especially clear and informative account of the conception of being-in-the-world laid out in the first half of *Being and Time*. Heidegger's picture of human existence draws on the account of *intentionality* developed by the founder of phenomenology, Edmund Husserl. To say that consciousness is intentional is to say that consciousness is directed *toward* something; it is the nature of consciousness to be *of* or *about* something (e.g., perceiving a house, being afraid of bees, loving Mary, believing in protons, raging against injustice). This *aboutness* or *directedness-toward* makes human existence different from that of other beings in nature. It means that human beings are not self-contained units but are always "outside themselves" in relating themselves to entities in the world.

Heidegger agrees that human agency must be understood in terms of "comportment towards. . . ," but he breaks with Husserl on two key points. First, he rejects Husserl's uncritical assumption that humans must be understood in terms of the notion of *consciousness*. Instead of speaking of Dasein as consciousness, Heidegger describes human existence in a way that avoids mentalistic vocabulary and instead shows how things show up in relation to our engaged agency, prior to all assumptions about the mind/body split. Second, Heidegger holds that, although Husserl gives a pretty good description of the sort of intentionality that is involved in theoretical observations of decontextualized objects, he misses another sort of intentionality, the sort that is characteristic of our practical dealings with things in everyday affairs. The kind of theoretical intentionality Husserl describes portrays us as related to objects that are simply "out there," merely *present-at-hand* for our inspection. In contrast, Heidegger argues that the theoretical modes of activity Husserl takes as primary are in fact possible only against a background of engaged agency in which our encounters with things have a very different structure. What we encounter in such practical affairs is not present-at-hand objects set over against a conscious mind, but holistic contexts of *ready-to-hand* equipment related to our purposes.

Heidegger claims that the readiness-to-hand of meaningful totalities of equipment cannot be understood in terms of the account of reality that arises within theoretical reflection. As Hall shows, ready-to-hand equipmental totalities are prior to, and a condition for the possibility of, the discovery of any present-at-hand entities in specialized theoretical modes of comportment. For this reason, Heidegger can say that practical intentionality (e.g., using equipment) is more primordial or more fundamental than theoretical activity (e.g., perceptually registering and thinking about objects).

The moral Heidegger draws from this account of our most basic relation to the world is that no clear line can be drawn between us and the world. Human existence is a *clearing* or *disclosedness* in virtue of which anything can show up at all. This is the starting point for my own contribution to this volume, "Becoming a Self: The Role of Authenticity in *Being and Time*." In this essay I try to show that Heidegger describes *being a self* (understood as being a fairly cohesive, self-contained, enduring unity) not as a given—something merely there from the outset—but rather as an accomplishment that is only realized through becoming authentic. As in the case of Nietzsche's view of the self, personal identity is accounted for not in terms of the enduring presence of some object called the "self," but through the continuity and coherence of an unfolding event: the "happening" of a life story "from birth to death."

Sartre

Born in Paris in 1905, Jean-Paul Sartre studied at the École Normale Supérieure, graduating in 1929. During his studies in Berlin in 1933–34, he discovered Husserlian phenomenology and wrote his early works, the novel, *Nausea*, and his first important philosophical work, *The Transcendence of the Ego*. His most important book, *Being and Nothingness*, appeared in 1943, and his defense of existentialism, "The Humanism of Existentialism," appeared three years later. Sartre was active in the Resistance during the war, and in the 1950s and 1960s was involved in a number of leftist political movements. In

1964, he refused to accept the Nobel Prize for literature on the grounds that such prizes tend to turn writers into institutions. He died in 1980.

Following in the footsteps of Husserl, Sartre contends that the proper starting point for philosophy must be the way things show up for us in our experience. Like Husserl, Sartre sees that the need to start from the *cogito* is the fundamental insight we have inherited from Descartes: as he says, "There can be no other truth to take off from than this: *I think, therefore, I exist.* There we have the absolute truth of consciousness becoming aware of itself."[15]

Sartre also agrees with Husserl in rejecting the idea that consciousness should be conceived of as a substance of any sort. Consciousness is first and foremost an *act*: it is an intentional directedness-toward objects, for "there is no consciousness which is not a *positing* of a transcendent object."[16] In contrast to Descartes, who would say that my perception of a table is mediated by my consciousness of a table-image inside my mind, Sartre claims that consciousness is always already out there, *with* the entities to which it is related, and so it always transcends inwardness. When I chase a bus, for example, my consciousness is there with the bus I am chasing, not inside my head. Sartre follows this line of thinking through to its logical conclusion when he claims that consciousness is not a container filled with representations. In fact, it is not a thing of any sort—it is a *no thing*, that is, a nothing, a nothingness.

Sartre maintains that consciousness, in knowing objects in the world, must also be conscious of itself. To defend this claim he presents a simple (though highly contentious) argument. When I know there is a table in front of me, he says, a necessary condition for this consciousness of an object is that consciousness be conscious of itself as being that knowledge. This is so because, "if my consciousness were not consciousness of being consciousness of the table, it would then be consciousness of that table without consciousness of being so. In other words, it would be . . . unconscious—which is absurd."[17] This argument might seem to suggest that there is a dualism built into consciousness, a distinction between, first, the consciousness one is conscious *of* in self-consciousness, and, second, the consciousness that is conscious of that first consciousness. But this is unacceptable: "Consciousness of self is not dual. If we wish to avoid an infinite regress, there must be an immediate, noncognitive relation to the self."[18] In other words, there must be a consciousness that is prior to and the basis for the kind of consciousness that is involved in cognitive activities, an immediate, "prereflective cogito which is the condition of the Cartesian cogito." This prereflective cogito "must be present to itself, not as a thing, but as an operative intention which can exist only as revealing-revealed."[19]

It follows that the fundamental nature of human existence, on Sartre's account, is to be a consciousness that it irreducibly *for itself, pour soi,* capable of self-awareness, and so always capable of having some understanding of what it is doing. Moreover, if it is the case that we know what we are doing, then we also must have some awareness that what we do *is our doing*, and hence that we could do otherwise if we chose to. It follows that at the heart of consciousness there is a fundamental self-awareness that shows that we always have *freedom* in the sense of being able to act otherwise than we do. What we do on any given occasion, therefore, must be seen as a matter of our own choice. And insofar as we are free to determine our own course of action through our choices, we are ultimately responsible for our own lives.

Seen in this light, humans are self-making or self-constituting beings. We define our own identities in the course of living out our active lives. Sartre sums up the significance of this insight in a couple of dramatic phrases. He says, first of all, that "a man is nothing else than a series of undertakings, . . . he is the sum, the organization, the ensemble of the relationships which make up these undertakings."[20] We just *are* what we *do* in the course of living out our lives. And, second, he says that "there is no determinism, man is free, man is freedom."[21] Though there are always the constraints of facticity—the force of circumstances that are beyond our control—it is also the case that it is up to us to decide what these circumstances *mean* to us. So even constraints are, in a sense, chosen by us. This is why Sartre says that "facticity is everywhere but inapprehensible; I never encounter anything except my responsibility."[22] Thus, we are condemned to be free: "I am responsible for everything, in fact, except for my very responsibility."[23] Even the fundamental values I adopt are chosen by me; I could always choose different values if I wished. In the end, there is no reason to accept any one set of values over another.

A common criticism of Sartre is that his views tend to undermine the possibility of ethics. It is often claimed that, since Sartre provides no basis for adopting one set of moral values over another, he seems to encourage an anything-goes relativism. The essay by Thomas C. Anderson, "Sartre's Early Ethics and the Ontology of *Being and Nothingness*," addresses objections of this sort while illuminating the ontology developed in Sartre's major work. Anderson first examines Sartre's claim that the fundamental project of humans is the "desire to be God," a desire to be the foundation of one's own being by being a *causa sui* (cause of itself), as God is supposed to be. Since we are always dependent on others, however, this desire to be God leads to a struggle with others that is summed up in Sartre's famous line, "Hell is the others." Next, he considers an apparent inconsistency between two claims Sartre makes: (1) the claim that human beings ought to strive for the ultimate goal of freedom, and (2) the claim that humans create all values, so that there is no reason to choose any one value over another. Finally, Anderson considers Sartre's suggestion that all human relations involve conflict. For each of these three issues, he shows that there is a way to soften or resolve the problematic dimensions of Sartre's early work by using ideas developed in Sartre's later writings.

Dorothy Leland's deep and thoughtful essay, "The Sartrean *Cogito*: A Journey between Versions," examines the claims Sartre makes about consciousness in *The Transcendence of the Ego* and in the opening pages of *Being and Nothingness*. As we have just seen, Sartre holds that there is a prereflective consciousness that is prior to the cognitive forms of consciousness thematized by Descartes, and that this consciousness is inherently and necessarily a self-consciousness. It is crucial to Sartre's account that self-consciousness be understood not in terms of two consciousnesses, one of which is aware of the other (as in Husserl's account of the relation between the transcendental ego and the empirical ego), but instead be understood in terms of consciousness's presence to itself "as the pre-cognitive foundation of all that is known to the reflecting cogito." This self-consciousness is "non-positional" in the sense that it does not posit something other than itself but is, rather, a consciousness of consciousness without being for itself an object. It is both "thetic" (from the Greek word *thesis*, meaning positing or placing something) insofar as it relates to an intentional object, and a non-positing self-awareness.

Closely examining the relevant texts, Leland tries to show that Sartre's view of prereflective consciousness is not tenable. In the course of her essay, a number of core ideas in Sartre's thought are clarified. Sartre holds that consciousness embodies a "lack" or "fissure" in virtue of the gap it presupposes between consciousness *of* consciousness and the consciousness of which one is conscious. This "'fissured' unity" is said to be the source of the "negativity" that appears in the world, a negativity that first introduces the distinctions, differentiations, and determinations that appear within being (our experience "of this, *not* that"). Sartre also holds that "bad faith" or self-deception is possible only because consciousness "is not what it is and is what it is not." Leland's account of consciousness helps to illuminate this and other mysterious phrases in Sartre's writings.

For help with the preparation of this volume, I wish to thank Kevin Aho, Indrani Bhattacharjee, and Chris Kirby. I owe a special debt of gratitude to Robert L. Perkins, who went out of his way to help me secure permission to use the essay by Louis Dupré appearing in this volume.

Notes

1. Søren Kierkegaard, *The Point of View for My Work as an Author*, trans. W. Lowrie (New York: Harper, 1962), 111 (slightly modified).

2. Søren Kierkegaard, *The Sickness unto Death*, trans. H. V. and E. H. Hong (Princeton, N.J.: Princeton University Press, 1980), 117, quoted in the essay by Louis Dupré in this volume.

3. For an especially insightful contemporary use of Kierkegaard's diagnosis of the modern world, see Hubert Dreyfus, *On the Internet* (London: Routledge, 2001).

4. Søren Kierkegaard, *Fear and Trembling*, trans. W. Lowrie (Princeton, N.J.: Princeton University Press, 1941), 250, 251, quoted in Richard Kearney, *The Poetics of Modernity: Toward a Hermeneutic Imagination* (Atlantic Highlands, N.J.: Humanities Press, 1995), 22.

5. Friedrich Nietzsche, *The Gay Science*, trans. W. Kaufmann (New York: Vintage Books, 1974), 354.

6. Nietzsche, *The Gay Science*, section 343.; all references to *The Gay Science* are to section numbers.

7. Nietzsche, *The Gay Science*, 343.

8. Nietzsche, *The Gay Science*, 382.

9. Nietzsche, *The Gay Science*, 290.

10. Martin Heidegger, *Being and Time*, trans. J. Macquarrie and E. Robinson (New York: Harper & Row, 1962), 164.

11. Heidegger, *Being and Time*, 167.

12. Heidegger, *Being and Time*, 239.

13. Heidegger, *Being and Time*, 394.

14. Heidegger, *Being and Time*, 307.

15. Jean-Paul Sartre, "The Humanism of Existentialism," trans. B. Frechtman, in *Existentialism: Basic Writings* (2d ed.), ed. C. Guignon and D. Pereboom (Indianapolis, Ind.: Hackett, 2001), 302.

16. Jean-Paul Sartre, *Being and Nothingness: An Essay on Phenomenological Ontology*, trans. H. E. Barnes (New York: Philosophical Library, 1956), li.

17. Sartre, *Being and Nothingness*, lii.

18. Sartre, *Being and Nothingness*, lii–liii.

19. Sartre, *Being and Nothingness*, liii

20. Sartre, "The Humanism of Existentialism," 300.

21. Sartre, "The Humanism of Existentialism," 296.

22. Sartre, *Being and Nothingness*, 556.

23. Sartre, *Being and Nothingness*, 555.

I
KIERKEGAARD

1

The Knight of Faith

Robert Merrihew Adams

O NE OF THE MANY ATTRACTIONS of Kierkegaard's *Fear and Trembling* is its tantalizing talk of "the absurd." "The movement of faith," we are told, "must continually be made by virtue of the absurd" (37).[1] The knight of faith "does not do even the slightest thing except by virtue of the absurd: "by faith," he tells the resigned lover of the unattainable princess, "by faith you will get her by virtue of the absurd" (50). What is "the absurd" by which all this is done? Is there a power in absurdity, wonderfully brought to light (or barely to the edge of light) by Kierkegaard? Is absurdity actually a ground of belief, contrary to our usual assumptions? And what indeed is absurd—not just strange, improbable, or tragic, but truly absurd—in the story Kierkegaard tells us about Abraham? What is it that Johannes de Silentio, the fictitious "author" of the book, thinks he cannot understand about Abraham?

I offer here a reading of the "Preliminary Expectoration" of *Fear and Trembling*, and some reflections on it, so read. I write, not as a Kierkegaard scholar (I do not know Danish, for example), but only as one who has lived with the book, and taught about it, for many years. And the present paper is about only a part of the book, a "preliminary" part. We shall not get to the famous "teleological suspension of the ethical." Our concern will be with "infinite resignation" and faith as forms of religious life. But I begin with the idea of the absurd.

1. The Absurd

What is absurd here? I ask again. The teleological suspension of the ethical will be presented as absurd (56); but that is not the focus of the "Preliminary Expectoration," and the movement of faith, which Abraham makes by virtue of the absurd (37), is not the movement by which he sacrifices Isaac but the movement by which he gets him back (49). Likewise it is not the resignation or sacrificing of Isaac that Johannes de Silentio finds hardest to understand. Though "the infinite movement of resignation" is difficult, says Johannes, "I can also perceive that it can be done. The next [movement] amazes me, my brain reels, for, after having made the movement of resignation, then by virtue of the absurd to get everything, to get one's desire totally and completely— that is over and beyond human powers, that is a marvel" (47f.). We may therefore be inclined to infer that "the absurd" is to be identified with Abraham's faith that he will keep Isaac in the end. This interpretation is supported by the statement that "it certainly was absurd that God, who required [the sacrifice] of him, should in the next moment rescind the requirement" (35f.).

There is an important objection to this reading, however. For we are assured that "the absurd . . . is not identical with the improbable, the unexpected, the unforeseen" (46). And 'improbable, unexpected, unforeseen' seem exactly the terms to describe the chain of events by which Abraham gets to keep Isaac, provided we accept the story's assumptions about a God who speaks, or sends angels, to Abraham. Perhaps Kierkegaard (or Johannes) supposes that the (real or apparent) inconsistency in God's commands to Abraham is not merely improbable, but an absolute impossibility, being inconsistent with the essential constancy of the divine nature. Perhaps; but this explanation of the absurdity fails to satisfy, for two reasons. (1) The apparent inconstancy is no more at variance with the background theology presupposed in the book than the initial command to sacrifice Isaac is. It therefore provides insufficient motivation for focusing on the *sparing* of Isaac as specially involving the absurd. (2) The claim of Genesis, that God was "tempting" or testing Abraham, which receives its emphasis in Kierkegaard's retelling of the story, offers an explanation in which both of the mutually contradictory commands serve a rational function in relation to an underlying unity of divine purpose. If such an explanation is accepted, as it seems to be by our author, God's rescinding of the command to sacrifice Isaac can hardly be more than improbable and unforeseen.

Of course Abraham, climbing Mount Moriah, does not know that God is only testing him.[2] Even if there is no inconsistency in what God must actually do if Isaac is to be spared, there may be contradiction in Abraham's beliefs. And in fact it is not hard to identify mutually contradictory beliefs that

Kierkegaard's Abraham appears to hold. We are told that "he had faith that God would not demand Isaac of him" (35). I have not found an explicit statement that he also (and inconsistently) believed that Isaac would really be demanded of him, that he would be deprived of Isaac; but we can hardly understand the story otherwise. Indeed Kierkegaard seems to think it important for Abraham to believe to the last possible moment that he is losing Isaac; why else would it be a disaster "if he had happened to spot the ram before drawing the knife" (22)? So there does seem to be a contradiction, and hence a real absurdity, in Abraham's system (or non-system) of beliefs. But why must it be so? Why is believing this contradiction essential to Abraham's role as knight of faith, as Kierkegaard (or Johannes) clearly believes it to be?

It should also be noted that it is Abraham's behavior, perhaps even more than this beliefs, that Johannes finds hard to understand (34–38). It is "the movements of faith" that Johannes cannot perform (37f.). And this seems to be something that he cannot *do*, much more than something that he cannot believe. "[B]y my behavior," he says, "I would have spoiled the whole story, for if I had gotten Isaac again, I would have been in an awkward position. What was easiest for Abraham would have been difficult for me—once again to be happy with Isaac!" (35).

This seems a strange thing for Johannes to say; yet I believe the main key to his conception of "the absurd" is to be found right at this point. Casting himself in the role of a "knight of infinite resignation" who has given up a princess whom he loves above all else in the world, Johannes declares that he would be unable to receive her back again:

> By my own strength I cannot get the least little thing that belongs to finitude, for I continually use my strength in resigning everything. By my own strength I can give up the princess, . . . but by my own strength I cannot get her back again, for I use all my strength in resigning. On the other hand, by faith, says that marvelous knight, by faith you will get her by virtue of the absurd. But this movement I cannot make. (49f.)

Why can't Johannes, in this imagined situation, make the movement of faith? Because his spiritual power is entirely, and "continually," employed in the opposite direction, making the movement of resignation. While he is using all his strength to give up the princess, it would be inconsistent to accept her back. That taking back of what one is still giving up with all one's force of decision is a practical rather than a theoretical contradiction. It is, I take it, "the absurd" by virtue of which the knight of faith says the princess is to be won (and by virtue of which Abraham gets Isaac back with joy). And Johannes cannot do it.

Other statements in the book confirm this reading:

> So I can perceive [declares Johannes] that it takes strength and energy and spir-
> itual freedom to make the infinite movement of resignation; I can also perceive
> that it can be done. The next [movement] amazes me, my brain reels, for, after
> having made the movement of resignation, then by virtue of the absurd to get
> everything, to get one's desire totally and completely—that is over and beyond
> human powers, that is a marvel. (47f.)

Here an impossibility is asserted that is absolute in relation to human powers.
And the main obstacle to the satisfaction of one's desires appears to be one's
own "movement of resignation"; no external obstacle is mentioned here, at
any rate. A similar view of what is astonishing about Abraham is expressed in
the statement that

> it is great to give up one's desire, but it is greater to hold fast to it after having
> given it up; it is great to lay hold of the eternal, but it is greater to hold fast to the
> temporal after having given it up. (18)

There is an essential point, however, which is not reflected in the two passages
I have just quoted, inasmuch as they speak of getting or holding the temporal
after giving it up.[3] For if one first gives up something and then later takes it
back, there is no paradox in this sequence of "movements." Johannes locates
"the absurd" more precisely when he declares that he cannot take back the
princess because he "continually" uses all his strength in resigning. The absurd
enters the picture because the movement of faith does not end the movement
of resignation, but must be made simultaneously with it. That this is part of
the conception of faith in the book is confirmed by the statement that the
knight of faith "has made and at every moment is making the movement of
infinity" (40)—by which, in the context, is clearly meant the movement of infinite resignation. Why this must be so, will be explored more fully below; here
we may say simply that if Abraham stopped making the movement of resignation in order to make the movement of faith, he would nullify his sacrifice.

   We can now explain why Abraham must believe a contradiction. Believing
"that God would not demand Isaac of him" is essential to the movement of
faith. But believing that he would in fact be deprived of Isaac is seen as important to making the movement of resignation fully real. The contradiction
in belief, however, can hardly be more than an *expression* of what is fundamentally "the absurd." It cannot be the essence of it. For after they have sacrificed the ram and descended the mountain, Abraham can hardly have continued to believe that he would be deprived of Isaac; but Kierkegaard surely does
not conceive of him as ceasing at that point to make the movement of infinite
resignation. That would spoil everything. The practical contradiction in life
orientations must therefore continue after the contradiction in beliefs ceases.

If this interpretation is correct, then in these introductory portions of *Fear and Trembling* Kierkegaard is concerned with a problem that arises as a serious issue about the religious life in more than one tradition. For some sort of detachment from "the world," or from finite things, or even (for Buddhism) from everything, is an important goal for many religious traditions. Yet it is difficult to see how a human being can even live without some interests in finite things. The question therefore arises how detachment can be combined with interests in finite things. This, or some similar question, seems to have been among Kierkegaard's lifelong preoccupations. The answer it receives in *Fear and Trembling* is in terms of the movements of infinite resignation and faith.

2. Infinite Resignation

More than one reason has been given for aspiring to detachment, and more than one motive was at work in Kierkegaard's thought on this point. But the dominant motive in *Fear and Trembling* is that detachment, or "resignation," is seen as important for devotion to God. Attachments to finite things may be seen as incompatible with total devotion to God, and hence idolatrous. The language of 'idolatry' does not play an important part in Kierkegaard's thought, but has been used by many Christian thinkers to express a concern very similar to his. A more Kierkegaardian way of speaking of the issue would note that an orientation of life toward finite objects of interest—objects that one wishes to enjoy, and that are not totally within the control of one's will—is characteristic of the "aesthetic" way of life that he opposes to the ethical and religious ways of life.[4] If one is to live a religious life, one must "dethrone" the aesthetic, shake oneself free of it, detach oneself from its interests.

The strategy of "infinite resignation" proposed in *Fear and Trembling* differs from many other strategies of detachment (for instance Buddhist strategies) in that it is *not* meant to involve extinction of desire. Kierkegaard emphatically denies that the knight of infinite resignation will "forget" the princess when he gives her up. On the contrary, he keeps his love for her "young" (43–45, 50). It continues to absorb him, in a way that contributes to his religious life, as we shall see. Resignation is not indifference.[5]

God is the one who demands absolute love. Anyone who in demanding a person's love believes that this love is demonstrated by his becoming indifferent to what he otherwise cherished is not merely an egotist but is also stupid. . . . For example, a man requires his wife to leave her father and mother, but if he considers it a demonstration of her extraordinary love to him that she for his sake became an indifferent and lax daughter etc., then he is far more stupid than the stupid. (73)

Indeed the strategy of infinite resignation involves intensification, or at any rate concentration, of desire rather than extinction of desire. The movement of resignation must involve an "interest in which an individual has concentrated the whole of reality." In the case described, "a young lad falls in love with a princess, and this love is the entire substance of his life" (41). This is the first thing that is required of a knight of infinite resignation:

> In the first place, the knight will then have the power to concentrate the whole substance of his life and the meaning of actuality into one single desire. If a person lacks this concentration, this focus, his soul is dissipated in multiplicity from the beginning, and then he never manages to make the movement; he acts as shrewdly in life as the financiers who put their resources into widely diversified investments in order to gain on one if they lose on another—in short, he is not a knight. (42f.)

The comment about a soul "dissipated in multiplicity" is significant. Kierkegaard was persistently concerned for the unification of the self through focused willing. Such unification was characteristic, in his view, of the ethical and religious ways of life, as contrasted with the aesthetic life, oriented toward enjoyment, which he sees indeed as dissipated in multiplicity. It is interesting, therefore, that in *Fear and Trembling* the focusing of the self is accomplished, not first in the religious movement of resignation, but in the knight's concentration of desire in love for the princess, which is not a religious movement, and not clearly ethical rather than aesthetic. Though not itself religious, the concentration of selfhood in the desire for the one finite object is seen as desirable, or even essential, for the religious movement.

This may be explained by the negative character of resignation. The scope and importance of a resignation depend on the scope and importance of the desire that is resigned. If one's interests in the finite (like the financiers' investments) are as numerous and as replaceable as the hydra's heads, then it seems that in cutting them off one by one by separate acts of resignation, one will never reach a comprehensive (or in Kierkegaard's terms "infinite") resignation; one will never have resigned them all. On the other hand, a general or generic resignation of them all might seem to Kierkegaard too vague, too indefinite to be trusted, or even to be fully real. If religious devotion is to define itself by resignation, it may therefore be advantageous to religion if desire for the finite presents itself concentrated in one head that can be severed by a single stroke of resignation, so to speak.

What is said about resignation here foreshadows an important point in the dialectic of despair in *The Sickness unto Death*, the distinction between "despair over the earthly" and "despair over something earthly."[6]

When the self in imagination despairs with infinite passion over something in this world, its infinite passion changes this particular thing, this something, into the world in *toto*. . . . The earthly and the temporal as such consist precisely of particular things, and some particular thing may be regarded as the whole. The loss or deprivation of every earthly thing is actually impossible. . . . Consequently, the self infinitely magnifies the actual loss and then despairs over the earthly *in toto*.[7]

Here we have, explicitly articulated, a problem for any strategy of giving up the earthly, a problem that is left implicit in *Fear and Trembling*: the earthly consists of particular things, which cannot all be actually lost (while one lives, at any rate). We find also the same type of solution of the problem as in *Fear and Trembling*: the concentration of one's whole passion for the earthly on a particular finite object. And, as in *Fear and Trembling*, this concentration marks "a genuine advance in consciousness of the self."[8] In effect, it prepares the way for a transition from an aesthetic to a religious consciousness, if in despair one gives up the earthly as a whole—though the religious consciousness to which one may pass at this point in *The Sickness unto Death* is much less at peace with its relation to the eternal than the "infinite resignation" portrayed by Johannes de Silentio.

In *Fear and Trembling* the movement of resignation, the sacrifice of the finite object of concentrated passion, is seen as constituting devotion to God. "[W]hat I gain in resignation is my eternal consciousness," declares Johannes, and "my eternal consciousness is my love for God" (48). And in this constitution of religious devotion the persistence of the knight's love for the princess, transfigured now, plays an essential part. "His love for that princess would become for him the expression of an eternal love, would assume a religious character, would be transfigured into a love of the eternal being" (43). His love for God thus appears to draw some of its substance—presumably its concentration—from his love for the princess. There are undoubtedly autobiographical echoes in this passage. Walter Lowrie quotes Kierkegaard as saying of Regine Olsen, "My engagement to her and the breaking of it is really my relation to God, my engagement to God, if I may dare to say so."[9]

If we may interpret *Fear and Trembling* in the light of the *Concluding Unscientific Postscript*, this reliance on love for a finite good, and its renunciation, to give substance to a love for God has deep reasons in Kierkegaard's conception of religiousness, or of the possibilities of a human relationship with God. In view of the transcendent otherness of God, there is no possible positive content of a human life that Kierkegaard sees as inherently suited to express the divine.[10] A negative expression seems more possible. "The first genuine expression for the relationship to the absolute *telos* is a total renunciation" of relative ends.[11]

The strategy of constituting devotion to God through "infinite resignation," as presented in *Fear and Trembling*, is liable to important objections. The most obvious objections are ethical. Since the finite objects most apt to engage our love are persons, and since "sacrificing" a person is apt to be harmful to the person sacrificed, the strategy seems only too likely to lead to the sort of conflict of the ethical with the religious that forms the agonizing heart of *Fear and Trembling*. Nor can we expect it to be harmless to other persons. If you have concentrated the *whole* meaning of your life in your son, for example, the position of your spouse or your daughter is surely unenviable (though less so than your son's, if he will be sacrificed).

A less obvious objection may be even more serious, because it questions the religious as well as the ethical acceptability of the strategy of infinite resignation. We may suspect that, contrary to Kierkegaard's intention, the outward renunciation of the finite beloved does not abolish but shelters the "knight's" idolatry of her—shelters it from the vicissitudes and ordinariness of real relationships—so that it can retain exaggerated proportions. It still crowds out interests in other finite things and defines the possibility (or rather impossibility) of happiness for him (50). Religiously, however, the most offensive feature of this pattern is that (as we have seen) the knight's passion for his "princess" serves to define, by its continuing concentration, the meaning of his life and specifically its religious character as devotion to God. Martin Buber's comment on Kierkegaard's similar interpretation of his own sacrifice of his engagement with Regine Olsen is a telling thrust, in my opinion. "God as Regina's successful rival? Is that still God?" asks Buber.[12] This may be classified as an idolatry that can remain in the organization of the heart even when God is voluntarily preferred to the idol.

3. Faith

It is, of course, not the knight of infinite resignation but the knight of faith who is the hero of *Fear and Trembling*. The portrait of the knight of faith (in the "Preliminary Expectoration," at any rate) can be seen as one of a number of attempts Kierkegaard made to understand, or imagine, how devotion to God could coexist with pursuit and enjoyment of finite goods, how one can "maintain an absolute relation to the absolute *telos* and at the same time participate like other men in this and that" or "exist in relative ends," as the *Postscript* puts it. The general formula of the *Postscript* would surely be accepted in *Fear and Trembling* too, that one is to do it "by making the relationship to the absolute *telos* absolute, and the relationship to the relative ends relative."[13] But that contributes more to setting the problem than to solving it; it defines the task whose accomplishment Kierkegaard labors to understand.

By the end of his life, to be sure, Kierkegaard seems to have rejected the task, coming to the conclusion that, from a Christian point of view, it is a mistake to try to combine the enjoyment of finite goods with devotion to God. "A witness to the truth," he declared, "is a man whose life from first to last is unacquainted with everything which is called enjoyment." Specifically with reference to family relationships, which provide the central cases of enjoyment of the finite for *Fear and Trembling*, he implied in his last writings that marriage and the begetting of children are displeasing to God. In a passage with obvious echoes of *Fear and Trembling* he seems to identify the Christian path with what he had earlier characterized as infinite resignation rather than as faith:

> The Christianity of the New Testament would be: in case that man were really able to love in such a way that the girl was the only one he loved and one whom he loved with the whole passion of a soul (yet such men as this are no longer to be found), then, hating himself and the loved one, to let her go in order to love God.[14]

But I shall leave Kierkegaard's later conclusions on one side here, both because our present concern is with *Fear and Trembling* and because its dialectical tensions seem to me more interesting than the unambiguous world-rejection of the *Attack Upon Christendom*.

The ideal that Kierkegaard was trying to understand in *Fear and Trembling* is vividly expressed by the image of a ballet dancer who not only executes the upward leap (the movement of infinity) with artistic perfection, but also returns to earth so gracefully "that instantaneously one seems to stand and walk, to change the leap into life into walking, absolutely to express the sublime in the pedestrian" (41). There is also the famous description of a knight of faith as a very ordinary man who "looks just like a tax collector." Here the account of his interest in finite things is very vivid, but (except for the point that he will not be disturbed that his wife has not made him the nice supper he imagined) we are not given enough detail of his inner life to make very real to us the idea that "this man has made and at every moment is making the movement of infinity" and "drains the deep sadness of life in infinite resignation" (38–41).

Other images of combining a relative relationship to relative ends with an absolute relationship to the absolute *telos* are offered to us in the *Postscript*, though not under the heading "knight of faith." Two passages may be quoted here:

> Let the world give him everything, it is possible that he will see fit to accept it. But he says: "Oh, well," and this "Oh, well" means the absolute respect for the absolute *telos*. If the world takes everything from him, he suffers no doubt; but he says again:

"Oh, well"—and this "Oh, well" means the absolute respect for the absolute *telos*.
Men do not exist in this fashion when they live immediately in the finite. . . .
   An adult may very well whole-heartedly share in the play of children, and may
even be responsible for really bringing life into the game; but he does not play as
a child. One who understands it as his task to exercise himself in making the absolute distinction sustains just such a relationship to the finite.[15]

The "Oh, well" hardly seems serious enough for a morally satisfying appreci-
ation of finite goods, but the analogy of an adult playing a children's game
may well express the spirit of what would be, at least in many contexts, a religiously desirable detachment.

   The main resolution of the problem offered by *Fear and Trembling*, however, is a strategy that incorporates the devotional strategy of infinite resignation. It is characterized in the book as a two-movement strategy, but in fact
it involves three "movements." The first, which Johannes does not explicitly
count as a separate movement, either in infinite resignation or in faith, but
which is essential to both, is the concentration of desire on a single finite object. That this applies to the knight of faith, and not just to the knight of infinite resignation, is made explicit: "First and foremost, then, the knight of
faith has the passion to concentrate in one single point the whole of the ethical that he violates" (78). And this is not just a preliminary step; the passion
must be maintained. "The absolute duty . . . can never lead the knight of faith
to stop loving." In the moment of sacrifice (in which he is making the movements of both resignation and faith) Abraham "must love Isaac with his
whole soul" (74).

   The second movement, of course, is the movement of infinite resignation, by which the knight gives up, or sacrifices, the beloved. And the third
is the movement of faith itself, by which he receives the beloved again. And
these movements must be made simultaneously, or at any rate the knight
must still be making the movement of resignation when he makes the
movement of faith. He not only "has made" but also "at every moment is
making the movement of eternity" (40). Since the movement of concentration on the finite object must continue while the movement of resignation
is made, the knight of faith must make all three movement at once. But it
is making the second and third movements (resignation and faith) at once
that constitutes "the absurd"; Johannes thinks the combination of the first
two movements is difficult but humanly possible.

   Why must the movements of resignation and faith take place simultaneously? Why can't they be sequential? In reading Genesis is a natural to assume
that Abraham receives Isaac back only after the movement of sacrificing him
is finished. A hint of the answer to this question may be found in the statement that "Faith is therefore no aesthetic emotion, but something far higher,

exactly because it presupposes resignation; it is not the immediate inclination of the heart but the paradox of existence."[16] If Abraham's resignation ceased when Isaac's life was spared, he would fall back, in Kierkegaard's view, into an "aesthetic" way of life, one oriented to the enjoyment of finite goods. The resignation must continue because it still is what constitutes the knight of faith's devotion to God.

Another question will detain us longer. Why is the third movement the object of Johannes's extremist admiration? Not everything difficult is admirable, after all. Why is it important for faith to accept the finite back? Of course it is nice to be able to enjoy the finite; but that consideration seems to appeal to an aesthetic point of view. And obviously it is desirable not to kill Isaac; but that consideration seems to appeal to an ethical point of view. What we want to understand here is the *religious* value that *Fear and Trembling* assigns to the third movement by identifying it as the movement of faith.

My answer to this question is somewhat speculative as an interpretation of Kierkegaard. In faith, we may suppose, one trusts in God, and that implies that one consciously, believingly, willingly depends on God for something. In infinite resignation, however, one does not in this way depend on God. For one has resolved to live solely for one's relationship of love to God. And I take it the knight of infinite resignation sees this relationship as constituted sufficiently by his own voluntary resignation (48f.). In relation to what he lives for, therefore, he does not depend on anything outside the control of his own will. Hence the knight of infinite resignation has no occasion for trusting God; and faith, in the sense of trust, plays no essential part in his religion. The knight of faith, on the other hand, does willingly depend on God for something outside the control of his own will. But if he depends thus on God for it, he must surely accept it when given, and must be prepared to accept it.

For Kierkegaard, however, depending on something outside the control of one's own will is a mark of the aesthetic life, and serves to distinguish it from both the ethical life and the sort of religiousness exemplified by the knight of infinite resignation.[17] So faith ends up in the same boat with the aesthetic in this respect; and Kierkegaard is faced with the problem of finding some other way of differentiating faith, as a religious form of life, from the aesthetic.[18] The solution proposed in *Fear and Trembling*, as I have already indicated, is that faith is to incorporate a continuing infinite resignation, and is to be distinguished from the aesthetic by accepting and enjoying the finite only while simultaneously giving it up.

There is another direction in which we might seek a solution. We might wonder whether there are not some distinctively religious, and not aesthetic, goods that are outside the power of our wills and that might be sought, in faith, from the hand of God. The most obvious candidates for this role may be religious experiences. I think it is clear, however, that Kierkegaard regarded an interest in any sort of experience as such, specifically including mystical experience, as essentially aesthetic. In *Either/Or* he argues that because an interest in mystical experience is an interest in something that is in principle complete in a "moment," or at any rate in a short period of time, it lacks the concern for history and continuity that characterizes an ethical interest (and, in the *Postscript*, a religious interest) as understood by Kierkegaard.[19]

Might there be some other sort of specifically religious good for which we could depend on God? Perhaps every form of this idea presents difficulties for Kierkegaard, since he insists that explicitly religious features of a human life are no less finite than more obviously mundane goods as objects of interest.[20] Explicit religiosity is no protection against idolatry. On the other hand, it may be argued that in the *Philosophical Fragments* and the *Postscript* Kierkegaard develops a conception of Christianity in which the believer does depend on God for specifically religious goods that are not within the power of the believer's own will—namely for the enactment of God's love in a historical existence (the Incarnation), and for the "condition" without which one cannot have faith. Kierkegaard might have regarded that as rendering obsolete for Christians the type of faith "for this life" that he had ascribed to Abraham—a type of faith that is no longer featured, at any rate, in the *Philosophical Fragments* and *Postscript*.

In *Fear and Trembling*, however, an interest in mundane goods is viewed as important for the trusting character of faith in God. I have no quarrel with that view. It is the book's account of the movements of concentration and infinite resignation, not the movement of faith, that seem to me most liable to objection. I have tried elsewhere to give a more adequate account of the nature of religious devotion, in relation to other interests;[21] and I hope to try again, but not here.[22]

Notes

1. Parenthetical page references in this essay are to Søren Kierkegaard, *Fear and Trembling*, edited and translated (with Kierkegaard's *Repetition*) by Howard V. and Edna H. Hong (Princeton, N.J.: Princeton University Press, 1983).

2. Cf. The scorn expressed (p. 37) for one who "deludes himself into thinking he may be moved to have faith by pondering the outcome of the story."

3. I cannot check this point against the Danish original, but the expression of temporal sequence is the same in the translation of Walter Lowrie (Princeton, N.J.: Princeton University Press, 1970, pp. 58, 33) and Alastair Hannay (Harmondsworth, U.K.: Penguin Books, 1985, pp. 75, 52).

4. Kierkegaard's first and fullest development of his conception of the "aesthetic" way of life is in *Either/Or*, but it plays a part in several of his works, notably in the *Postscript*.

5. Cf. T. S. Eliot, *Four Quartets*, "Little Gidding," III: *The Complete Poems and Plays, 1909–1950* (New York: Harcourt, Brace, 1952), p. 142: "There are three conditions which often look alike / Yet differ completely, flourish in the same hedgerow: / Attachment to self and to things and to persons, detachment / From self and from persons; and, growing between them, indifference / Which resembles the others as death resembles life . . ." I do not mean to assimilate Eliot's conception of detachment to Kierkegaard's idea of resignation.

6. A similar distinction is implied, with a similar relation to the possibility of a transition (or choice) out of the aesthetic life, in Kierkegaard's *Either/Or*, Part II, edited and translated by Howard V. and Edna H. Hong (Princeton, N. J.: Princeton University Press, 1987), pp. 194, 208.

7. Søren Kierkegaard, *The Sickness unto Death*, edited and translated by Howard V. and Edna H. Hong (Princeton, N. J.: Princeton University Press, 1980), p. 60.

8. Ibid., p. 60.

9. Walter Lowrie, *A Short Life of Kierkegaard* (Princeton, N. J.: Princeton University Press, 1965), p. 147.

10. I take this to be a theme of the section on "the essential expression" of religiousness in Søren Kierkegaard, *Concluding Unscientific Postscript*, translated by David F. Swenson and Walter Lowrie (Princeton, N. J.: Princeton University Press, 1941), pp. 386–468. A related theme is the abstractness of the conception of an eternal happiness (ibid., pp. 351ff., 382).

11. *Postscript*, p. 362.

12. Martin Buber, *Between Man and Man*, translated by Ronald Gregor Smith and Maurice Friedman (New York: Macmillan, 1965), p. 57.

13. *Postscript*, pp. 365, 363.

14. Kierkegaard's *Attack Upon Christendom*, translated by Walter Lowrie (Boston: Beacon Press, 1956), pp. 7, 220, 223, 163. There is doubtless some anticipation of this viewpoint in the *Postscript* (p. 160f.), where Johannes Climacus raises the question, "whether the ghost of paganism does not still haunt the institution of marriage." Climacus's stance, however, is one of raising "difficulties," rather than outright rejection of marriage.

15. *Postscript*, pp. 368, 370.

16. I quote from Alastair Hannay's translation of *Fear and Trembling*, p. 76. Walter Lowrie's translation (p. 58) agrees in essentials. The Hongs' translation (p. 47) has resignation as "antecedent" rather than presupposed. That may be linguistically correct, for all I know; but it obscures the point that the resignation must continue during the faith, a point for whose presence and importance in the work I have already argued.

17. See *Either/Or* (Part II, pp. 179ff.) and *Postscript* (pp. 121, 494). In this respect (though not in every respect) Religiousness A is the analogue, in the *Postscript*, of infinite resignation in *Fear and Trembling*.

18. The *Postscript* (pp. 494, 498) makes this point about Religiousness B, which is in some ways the analogue there of faith in *Fear and Trembling*. There is a further analogy between the two books on the solution to this problem; for Religiousness B is to be distinguished from the aesthetic by being paradoxically combined with Religiousness A, as faith is to be distinguished from the aesthetic in *Fear and Trembling* by being paradoxically combined with infinite resignation.

19. *Either/Or*, Part II, p. 2442f. I believe this argument reflects Kierkegaard's own views. It is associated, in the text, with the criticism that mysticism is too individualistic, which is more plausibly ascribed to Judge William, the fictitious author, than to Kierkegaard.

20. *Postscript*, 359–71; the point is developed in a discussion of monasticism.

21. Robert Merrihew Adams, "The Problem of Total Devotion," in Robert Audi and William J. Wainwright, eds., *Rationality, Religious Belief, and Moral Commitment* (Ithica, N.Y.: Cornell University Press, 1986), pp. 169–94.

22. I have profited from discussing *Fear and Trembling* with many people over the years. Particular thanks are due here to Van A. Harvey, under whose guidance I first developed some of the ideas contained in the present essay; and to the participants in the NEH summer institute in philosophy of religion at Western Washington University in 1986, for their comments on another version of the material.

2

The Sickness unto Death: Critique of the Modern Age

Louis Dupré

KIERKEGAARD CONSIDERED *The Sickness unto Death* one of his two best works (the other being *Fear and Trembling*) and Guardini regarded it as the most appropriate introduction to his thought. Which qualities justify the particular significance attached to a work that lacks the brilliance and literary grace of the earlier writings? One major attribute of the later treatise is, I believe, a speculative depth attained through several layers of meaning. *The Sickness unto Death* may be read as a philosophic-theological anthropology based on a penetrating analysis of despair. But it also develops an original theology of sin, far more mature than the one contained in the earlier *Concept of Anxiety*. Especially noteworthy here is that sin is treated as an existential attitude, not as a single act or as an inherited state. Finally, it contains a critique of modern culture. Much of what Kierkegaard refers to as despair corresponds to the passionless, noncommittal attitude of the mass society that has replaced individual responsibility with historical awareness.

The three meanings are connected. Precisely because of the decline of individual responsibility, the sense of sin has vanished from our cultural horizon, and the reduction of both has distorted the modern vision of man. The concept that unites the three meanings is that of the *individual*. I shall restrict my comments to Kierkegaard's critique of demise of authentic individuality in modern culture, which, for him, is the cause of its anthropological and theological inadequacy. This critique appears mostly in the second part of *The Sickness unto Death*.

(A) The Diagnosis

From the beginning the Western mind has been allured by the temptation to define existence within the limits of theoretical awareness. "The Greek mind posits an intellectual categorical imperative."[1] Socrates qualified this attitude without abolishing it. In the intellectualist tradition, he attributed evil to ignorance. But at the same time his irony exposed the comic deficiency of theory unrelated to existence. Not only is pure speculation sterile, it fails intellectually as well. "When someone does not do what is right, then neither has he understood what is right" (SUD, 92).

Ignoring Socrates' warning, modern thought tends to reduce being to thinking. Descartes's principle, *Cogito, ergo sum,* expresses a freely chosen rationalization of the real, rather than a necessary rule of thought. At the cost of ethical seriousness, modern philosophy articulates the mentality of an age that subsumes the concrete responsibility of the individual under the abstract category of the universal. This would eventually generate the *homo sociologicus,* whose entire existence coincides with the function he fulfills in the *universale* of society. Modern anthropology reduces the subject to its objective creations and subordinates the individual to the group.

In a perverse dialectic, the culture of self-consciousness has created the exact opposite of the pure subjectivity from which it started. Exalted to being the sole source of meaning and value, the subject soon loses its own identity in the function of exhaustively constituting objectivity.

The subordination of the individual to the group follows from the same unconditional autonomy of the subject. In this work, as in others, Kierkegaard relates one to the other without attempting to justify their connection. Only in the group does the subject attain the *universal* meaning that it alone still recognizes. The accepted significance of the person has increasingly come to consist in the parts he plays in the various social units (political, economic, professional, religious) to which he belongs. More and more our situation is moving toward the condition described in Robert Musil's *The Man without Qualities.* The person is forced to live his existence on various, separate levels. On each one he expresses himself differently according to the particular demands of his function; in none does he engage himself unconditionally. Existence withdraws behind a variety of social masks. Kierkegaard has exercised his mordant wit on this comic separation between a shrinking personal existence and an ever-expanding social front. To be sure, the actor of the multiple parts remains unaware of the comic effect of his life. In this respect his attitude differs from that of the deliberate aestheticism of the young man in *Either/Or,* or of Constantin Constantius in *Repetition.* Indeed, the most serious danger lies precisely in the person's inadequate awareness of his situation. As in Ronald Laing's description of the schizophrenic mind, the real self—hidden behind these social masks—slowly shrivels into nothingness. When social functions take the place of authentic personhood, the *mass* with its characteristic lack of responsibility and its refusal of commitment becomes "the truth."

The problem of mass culture had constantly preoccupied Kierkegaard during the period immediately preceding his writing of *The Sickness unto Death* and strongly emerges also in the entire second part of that work. In *The Present Age* (1846) he had described the contemporary mentality in terms reminiscent of his earlier analyses of the aesthetic attitude. Apropos of Thomasine Gyllembourg's novel *Two Ages* (*To Tidsaldre*), he compared the age of revolution (surprisingly relegated to the recent past) to the present "age of reflection." The former was determined by mass movements: vulgar, nonreflective, but passionate. The present age has become purely reflective, steeped in moral apathy and noninvolved speculation. In both epochs the individual has yielded to the mass, but in the latter he has lost even that last quality of individual involvement—passion.

> The individual does not belong to God, to himself, to the beloved, to his art, to his scholarship; no, just as a serf belongs to an estate, so the individual realizes that in every aspect he belongs to an abstraction in which reflection subordinates him. . . . The idolized positive principle of sociality in our age is the consuming demoralizing principles that in the thralldom of reflection transforms even virtues into *vitia splendida* [glittering vices].[2]

Our contemporaries attempt to find in universal objectivity a substitute for the individual's eternal responsibility in time. Even if some succeed in breaking loose from the bonds of reflection, they still remain imprisoned in a reflective environment. Only religious inwardness allows them to escape from this second imprisonment.

Hence, for Kierkegaard, the problem of contemporary culture is essentially a religious one. Only in the confrontation with God can man become an individual. Yet the conditions for such a confrontation are lacking today. Man has too much lost the sense of distance that a confrontation with God requires: God has become yet another human idea.

Kierkegaard stresses the need for a preliminary awareness of the chasm that separates God from man. In the Lutheran tradition he has presented this as a separation caused by sin. Thus the repentant consciousness becomes a necessary condition for a correct conception of God. But the problem is that, to be possible, such a consciousness already presupposes a correct conception of God. Only *before God* can man attain a genuine consciousness of sin. Through a reflection on the experience of despair Kierkegaard intends to prepare the modern mind to understand again the language of revelation concerning God

and sinfulness. To analyze this experience from its first, only half-conscious refusal to allow the spirit to emerge, to the final, fully God-conscious sin against
the Holy Spirit, was the project of the first part of *The Sickness unto Death*.

Yet the impact of the mass mentality itself upon the religious consciousness
needed to be reevaluated. In *Two Ages* Kierkegaard had severely underestimated
its potential. As late as 1846 he had considered a revolution unthinkable.

It is hard to believe that any informed person could have reached such a conclusion only two years before a major revolution would topple entire political
systems and undermine the social structures of France and much of Germany
and Austria. Denmark itself would pass through an enormous political turmoil
over the Schleswig-Holstein question and over the introduction of a constitu-
tional monarchy. These expressions of a new social awareness were far more
powerful than Kierkegaard had deemed possible. (Social consciousness may
still remain below the spiritual level, yet it is far more than the gossip of public
opinion.) Here was a new force at work far more powerful than anything that
preceded it. Kierkegaard came to understand that it would threaten the individual more than he had suspected. A new sense of urgency left its impact upon
all his writings during the months following the 1848 revolution.

In *The Point of View of My Work as an Author* (published after Kierkegaard's
death by his brother, Peter Christian, in 1859) contempt has made place for
concern, and perhaps fear. The diagnosis of the leveling tendencies he had de-
nounced in his earlier writings takes on a precision that it had lacked before.
The preface to the *Addendum* entitled "The Individual," written in 1848 (the
main text contains fragments dating back to 1846–1847), begins with the declaration: "In these times all is politics."[3] To this view Kierkegaard now opposes
the religious one as being radically different: one is all "practical," the other totally unpractical. Yet religion alone is able to *realize* the new political dream of
human equality. Only religiously understood *Menneskelighed* (humanity) entails *Menneske-lighed* (equality of men). Politics wrongly assume that truth
consists in the agreement of the majority.

> There is a view of life which conceives that where the crowd is, there also is the
> truth, and that in truth itself there is need of having the crowd on its side. There
> is another view of life which conceives that wherever there is a crowd there is un-
> truth, so that (to consider for a moment the extreme case), even if every indi-
> vidual, each for himself in private, were to be in possession of the truth, yet in
> case they were all together in a crowd . . . untruth would at once be in evidence.
> (PV, 110)

Only the individual can establish an essential relation to God and thereby introduce the element of eternity needed to provide the equality that modern society vainly pursues through political means. "What the age *needs* in the deep-

est sense can be said fully and completely with one single word: it needs eternity" (PV, 108). Instead our society has become purely temporal. "Where there is a multitude, a crowd, or where decisive significance is attached to the fact that there is a multitude, *there* it is sure that no one is working, living, striving for the highest aim, but only for one or another earthly aim" (PV, 112). Truth can reach the mass only after it has been broken down into individuals.

> A crowd is untruth. And I could weep, or at least I could learn to long for eternity, at thinking of the misery of our age, in comparison even with the greatest misery of bygone ages, owing to the fact that the daily press with its anonymity makes the situation madder still with the help of the public, this abstraction which claims to be the judge in matters of "truth." (PV, 118)

Kierkegaard's main objective following 1846 was to reestablish the category of the *individual*, as a precondition for returning a religious basis to our culture.

(B) The Sinful Individual

The idea of the *individual*, used since 1843, did not originate with Kierkegaard. Hamann's impact is clear and well established. That of Max Stirner's *Der Einzige und sein Eigentum* (1845) is less certain, but some influence of a work that stirred up so much controversy would seem to be almost inevitable. The simultaneous appearance of the idea in disparate places reflects that first inventory of the gains and losses of modernity made around the turn of the nineteenth century. Inspired by the awareness that an existence detached from the given, cosmic order must henceforth provide its own meaning, the idea of the *individual* hardly seemed qualified to play a decisive role in reawakening the religious consciousness of our age. Even Kierkegaard's Christian reinterpretation of it still bears traces of the Promethean idea, both proud and tragic, that henceforth man must bear the sole responsibility for his fate in an indifferent world. Still, the use of the category of the individual for defining man's dependence on God was no hasty adaptation of a modern concept to a traditional worldview. Underneath Kierkegaard's often biased evaluation of contemporary culture we detect a keen perception of the profound changes Europe had undergone in a few years. In the short period since the beginning of the nineteenth century the romantic consciousness, with its initial emphasis on the individual, had given way to an objective-scientific one dominated by objective universality and a new social consciousness in which the group would hold priority over the individual. Thus a wholly new threat emerged: the individual came to be identified with its social *persona*. Kierkegaard clearly perceived the issue and declared the salvation of the individual to be dependent on a revived religious consciousness. Only *before God* can man regain the solitude that enables him to exist as an individual. In the second part of *The Sickness unto Death* Kierkegaard states the dilemma of modern life:

> If order is to be maintained in existence . . . then the first thing to keep in mind is that every human being is an individual human being and is to become conscious of being an individual human being. If men are first permitted to run together in what Aristotle calls the animal category—the crowd—then this abstraction, instead of being less than nothing . . . comes to be regarded as being something—then it does not take long before this abstraction becomes God. (SUD, 117–18)

This idolatry had, in fact, already taken place. For Strauss and the early Left-Hegelians, the God-man had been reduced to a mythical expression of the unlimited aspirations of the human race. For Kierkegaard, such a social reduction heralds—beyond the demise of the Christian faith—the utter degradation of the existence itself. In thus divinizing the race, that is, the multitude, man has turned to adore what is less than himself. To such a debasing equation of God and the mass Kierkegaard opposes the individual's solitary confrontation: "Christianity teaches that . . . this individual human being exists *before God*" (SUD, 85). To recover his dignity, man has to reestablish his relation to God. However, unless he approaches God in the repentant awareness of his infinite distance, the speculative equation soon regains its foothold. In thus making the category of the individual dependent upon his permanent adoption of the attitude of a *sinner before God*, Kierkegaard moves it from philosophical speculation to a religious obedience.

Are we not arguing in a circle? How could a generation that has lost the very precondition for true religion, namely, being an individual, be able to use religion itself as a means to regain the individuality that is its precondition? Kierkegaard's strategy in dealing with this problem is complex and perhaps not entirely successful. Recognizing that one is a sinner-before-God is, indeed, the only way to become an authentic individual, but since this recognition itself is not available, Kierkegaard presents his argument by describing a state with which modern man is *at least partly* acquainted—despair. Next, in the second part of *The Sickness unto Death*, "Despair is Sin," he identifies this state of consciousness with the theological category of sin. This transition, crucial for Kierkegaard's strategy, creates serious problems. The reader, abruptly introduced into a new territory, will not likely find his way back to the beginning. Does despair, understood in the very wide sense of the preceding description, always coincide with sin as the title suggests? Even if it does, does it follow that all sin, after the first, is an act of despair as the argument seems to imply? Kierkegaard calls sin "despair qualitatively intensified" (SUD, 100). But Christian theology hardly recognizes itself in such a close link between sin and despair. It reserves the term despair to one particularly acute state of sin. Of course, Kierkegaard would point out that despair is *implicitly* present in all forms of sinfulness, and at the slightest occasion it will be fully activated. Such a theory may not necessarily be incompatible with Christian orthodoxy, but, then, what does it mean that sin is "despair . . . intensified"? Kierkegaard himself was not unaware of some of the difficulties. However, before discussing his response, we must first turn to the problems inherent in the modern understanding of sin itself.

Hegelian philosophy and theology had emptied sin of its ethico-religious content by declaring it a necessary moment in the development of consciousness. This speculative move merely rationalizes the actual attitude of society itself. If a deed condemned in principle becomes sufficiently accepted by "public opinion" it ceases to provoke feelings of guilt and rapidly loses even the name of sin.

> Experience teaches us, that when there is a mutiny on a ship or in an army there are so many who are guilty that punishment has to be abandoned, and when it is the public, the esteemed cultured public, or a people, then there is not only no crime, then, according to the newspapers . . . it is God's will. . . . It is nonsense, an antiquated notion, that the many can do wrong. What many do is God's will. (SUD, 123)

For the idea of sin to be at all meaningful, the sense of personal responsibility must first be restored; and this requires that sin be reunited with its religious origins. Originally sin consists in a failure in one's duty toward God, not in a failure in moral perfection. "Very often it is overlooked that the opposite of sin is by no means virtue. In part this is a pagan view, which is satisfied with a merely human criterion and simply does not know what sin is, that all sin is before God. No, the opposite of sin is faith" (SUD, 82). Beyond restating the Augustinian-Lutheran doctrine, Kierkegaard here attempts to restore the essential, religious dimension to the idea of sin.

Another issue concerns the relation of despair with the awareness of the transcendent dependence essential to full selfhood. From the first part of *The Sickness unto Death* it would appear that despair is, in fact, accompanied by an implicit or explicit—but always negative—God-consciousness. This would seem to bring it close to the attitude of the repentant sinner-before-God with respect to the kind of self-awareness needed for constituting a true *individual*. Early in part two, Kierkegaard summarizes his conclusions about despair:

> Despair is intensified in relation to the consciousness of the self, but the self is intensified in relation to the criterion for the self, infinitely when God is the criterion. In fact the greater the conception of God, the more self there is; the more self, the greater the conception of God. Not until a self as this specific single

individual is conscious of existing before God, not until then is it the infinite self, and this self sins before God. (SUD, 80)

Kierkegaard asserts two theses here: (1) Despair intensifies with self-consciousness; and (2) self-consciousness increases with God-consciousness. Does this only mean that a greater God-consciousness creates the possibility of a more intensive despair? Or does it also imply the contrary thesis that, as despair intensifies, a stronger self-consciousness—and hence also a clearer (though negative) consciousness of God—develops? To be sure, the latter does not follow *logically* from the quoted statement; but several indications suggest that it may have been present in Kierkegaard's mind. God-consciousness itself is conditioned by the individual's awareness of his own sinfulness. But being a sinner-before-God would seem to imply a previous acquaintance with despair (= sin). Only in the light of the second thesis does Kierkegaard's emphasis on the intensive self-consciousness of the demonic mind become fully intelligible. For that and other reasons I am inclined to interpret the strong self-consciousness, and consequently the clear God-consciousness, as resulting *either* from the individual's repentance before God, *or* from an intensified (and intrinsically sinful) despair. Both despair and repentance appear to be possible agents in the intensification of self-consciousness as well as in the process of becoming an "individual."

Of course, modern society renders both equally difficult. "How in the world can an essential sin-consciousness be found in a life that is so immersed in triviality and silly 'aping' of 'the others' that it can hardly be called a sin . . .?" (SUD, 101). The problem is not merely that the concept of sin has become theologically empty, but that the very *experience* of despair has become impossible. Most men and women are, by Kierkegaard's norm, simply "too spiritless" to qualify for despair. That, however, does not make them immune to despair; for despair is not simply a mode of consciousness intrinsically clear to the person who despairs. It is a negative state of being of which only the more intensive forms become directly conscious. The "lower" forms of despair consist precisely in a state of *unawareness* about one's spiritual identity in which the person *feels* nothing negative about himself. Such a condition removes the person further from spirit (and consciousness of himself as an individual) than the higher ones which, admittedly, are further from salvation. Hence we must not interpret the first part of *The Sickness unto Death* as a mere description of what is familiar to everyone, in contrast to the theological theory of the second part that has become unintelligible to the modern mind. No, despair itself remains to a great extent latent, and Kierkegaard considered it his first task to bring the reality of despair to the surface of consciousness. He himself felt by no means assured of success in this basic enterprise.

The theme of unconscious despair once again introduces the complex relation between sin and despair. To what extent do they coincide? I would be inclined to connect the unconscious despair with the largely unexplained concept of original sin. If *every* person is a sinner-before-God, every person must
have been touched with despair. The two concepts appear to be at least co-
extensive. The largely Pelagian interpretation that appears in *The Concept of
Anxiety*—each person commits his own "original sin," but the moral climate in
which Adam's descendants enter is infested by an ever-increasing anxiety-
toward-sin—is not repeated or implied in *The Sickness unto Death*. Kierkegaard
merely indicates that the dogma of hereditary sin is "the *prius* in which sin presupposes itself" (SUD, 89). An intriguing footnote explains that original sin
"splits men up into single individuals and holds each individual fast as a sinner,
a splitting up that in another sense is both harmonized with and teleologically
oriented to the perfection of existence" (SUD, 120). I interpret this to mean that
the objective condition of original sin predisposes man to become an *individual*, both through the consciousness of despair and through that of repentance.
In spite of the essential differences between the despair and repentance, with respect to the development of the person both are preferable to ignoring one's sinful condition, which is in fact unconscious despair.

The relation between original sin and sin has become even more obscure
than in *The Concept of Anxiety*. Whatever theories Kierkegaard may have en-
tertained about original sin at the time he wrote *The Sickness unto Death*,
however, they resist a simple equation with despair. Despair remains a category of freedom, of choice—even at its lowest level where man refuses to become spirit. A condition that merely overcomes man—that he suffers pas-
sively like sickness and death—cannot be called despair (SUD, 16). Hereditary
sinfulness does not result from choice. In view of these complexities, it is not
surprising that Kierkegaard decided to remove from his text the allusions to
the dogma of hereditary sin that originally appeared in chapter 2. "What is appropriately stated about sin . . . is not said with respect to the doctrine of
hereditary sin"(Supplement to SUD, 156).

Yet even after omitting the problems of original sin, those problems inherent in the equation of despair with sin remain. Earlier I mentioned the reference to sin as "despair qualitatively intensified." Kierkegaard himself reports
other discrepancies. The sin of *offense* (despairing of the forgiveness of sins)
displays characteristics that deviate from the phenomenological description of
despair in the first part.

Ordinarily weakness is: in despair not to will to be oneself. Here [in the sin of of-
fense] this is defiance, for here it is indeed the defiance of not willing to be oneself, what one is—a sinner—and for that reason wanting to dispense with the

forgiveness of sins. Ordinarily defiance is: in despair to will to be oneself. Here this is weakness, in despair to will to be oneself—a sinner—in such a way that there is no forgiveness. (SUD, 113)

The same argument would seem to apply to *all* sins which have God as explicit object.

Sin is revealed—it does not come "from within." But as a category of faith, sin would seem to exclude a full equation with despair which consists in a free choice.

Perhaps we should consider despair a particular aspect of all sin, but one that becomes fully manifest only when *revealed* as sinfulness. I mean the aspect of *continuity* that, although inherent in the sinful drive itself, is mostly ignored by the sinner. The sinner recognizes only actual sins, not a continuous state. To him sin is "specifically the discontinuous" (SUD, 105). In this common, purely negative idea, the sinful act constitutes an intermittent negation in a positive state of being. Christianity regards such a purely negative idea as inadequate. Sin fundamentally changes the self's *ontological relation* to God, whether the sinner is conscious of this change or not. Indeed, since it affects consciousness itself (cf. *Philosophical Fragments*), the consciousness of sin alone is no reliable index of one's sinfulness. Socrates' definition of sin as ignorance (the prototype of all later "negative" theories of sin) makes sin not only discontinuous: it eliminates it altogether. "If sin is ignorance, then sin really does not exist, for sin is indeed consciousness" (SUD, 89). Kierkegaard himself here refers to sin as conscious, not, however, in order to *equate* sin with a state of consciousness, but merely to indicate that directly or indirectly (for example, through revelation) sin must be accessible to consciousness. If consciousness belong to the definition of sin, sin would not exist in those who live outside the revelation. "Neither paganism nor the natural man knows what sin is" (SUD, 89). Nevertheless, revelation itself teaches that *their* condition is sinful. Ignorance does not render them incapable of sinning, but merely creates an obstacle to redemption. Christian revelation must begin by teaching the believer that he or she is indeed a sinner. Hence the Christian conception of sin defines both itself *and* the (ignorant) pagan sinfulness.

Essential to the Christian conception is that it treats sin as a continuous state rather than a discontinuous act. In doing so it introduces into human existence a dimension of eternity—which consists in "essential continuity"—a precondition for the very possibility of becoming spirit. In ordinary, spiritless existence, continuity is no more than the repetitiousness of identical moments of succession, the interval between discontinuous "events" and experiences.

Most men probably live with all too little consciousness of themselves to have any idea of what consistency is; that is, they do not exist *qua* spirit. Their lives—

either in a certain endearing childish naiveté or in shallow triviality—are made
up of some action of sorts, some incidents, of this and that; now they do something good, and then something stupid, and then they begin all over again. . . .
They are always talking among themselves about the particular, particular good
deeds, particular sins. (SUD, 107)

Life "in spirit" takes the opposite attitude; it possesses a consistency lacking in
ordinariness. In stressing the continuous character of sin, Christianity brings
out the spiritual character of existence. Indeed, the revelation of the "state" of
sinfulness may be the first, and for many the only, way in which the person
discovers his spiritual nature. The awareness of spirit consists in an awareness
of an eternal dimension in human temporality. Acts thereby come to be
viewed as part of a totality rather than as isolated decisions.

According to Kierkegaard, next to the believer, the demonic person is the
only one to have developed this spiritual consistency. Even as the believer fears
to change the entire spiritual nature of existence by yielding even once to temptation, so the demonic person fears to be tempted to take one step beyond his
chosen path. In this attitude he merely follows the internal dynamism of sin itself which, as a spiritual state, tends toward continuity. This drive to persist in
being expresses itself in despair which, in one form or another, always accom-
panies the sinful deed. On the least reflective level, that implicit despair may
simply consist in a desire to repeat the original deed. More reflectively it turns
to a refusal to believe in the possibility of change—"an effort to survive by
sinking even deeper" (SUD, 110). In explicitly Christian terms this may take the
form of despair of the forgiveness of one's sins, or an outright rejection of the
doctrine of salvation; but all religious forms of despair clearly manifest that
"sin has become or wants to be internally consistent" (SUD, 109).

The sinful act introduces a state of diminished selfhood. Kierkegaard describes this condition with Macbeth's words after the murder: "From this instant there's nothing serious in mortality: all is but toys." The self feels itself ir-
resistibly sliding down on a declining surface. "He has also lost himself; he
cannot even keep on going by himself" (SUD, 110). The only concern of the
person who thus loses hold of himself is to preserve at least the new reality ini-
tiated by his deed. Thus he tends to freeze its actuality in the permanence of
an attitude. What survives is the state, not the original self, and despair gives
"stability and interest to sin as a power" (SUD, 110).

(C) A Critical Conclusion

Having explored Kierkegaard's notion of the individual and its relation to the
consciousness of sin, we are now in a better position to evaluate the critique

of modern culture it implies. What is sick is not only the individual: he or she participates in the despair of an entire culture. The "sickness unto death" here consists in having lost the sense of ultimate responsibility which, according to Kierkegaard, defines *existence* itself—ultimate in the sense that to *exist* for Kierkegaard means being in time yet acknowledging responsibility for eternity. It is essentially a dynamic mode of being in which the individual freely actualizes his or her own selfhood.

There is no need once again to analyze the well-known description of selfhood with which *The Sickness unto Death* begins. Here I shall only point out the specific form of self-awareness it implies. Kierkegaard is not referring to the self-consciousness whereby I experience myself as *this* particular embodied individual. Such an empirical awareness, for him, is merely an epiphenomenon of genuine selfhood. If selfhood were no more than the perspectival center and principle of continuity of all perception—as Hume and the empiricist school of psychology describe it—it would itself be an *object* of observation. Yet neither is Kierkegaard's self that *transcendental ego* of Kant, Fichte, and Husserl—the universal structuring principle of experience which itself never becomes a direct object of experience. Such a principle, as Jaspers has pointed out, is a condition for *existence*, but does not constitute it.[4] For Kierkegaard, existence is rather the dynamic center of responsible self-assertion. It relates itself to itself, but also to its own constituting transcendent principle. This second relation distinguishes it from a purely temporal act of free self-realization (as in atheistic existentialism). The person who realizes himself in time is also responsible for his relation to *eternity*. Only through a full awareness of this eternal element does the self become *spirit*, the decisive condition for achieving authentic selfhood.

We find, of course, precedents to Kierkegaard's analysis of selfhood as an act of self-realization. Aristotle, whose influence here is certain though hard to circumscribe, views man as a being that brings itself from potency to act in accordance with a self-directed teleology. Endowed with rational potencies, the human agent determines his existence by deliberate choice. Kierkegaard's definition of the person on the basis of freedom, then, does not introduce an irrational innovation but reaffirms Aristotle's idea.[5] This dependence in no manner diminishes his originality because Aristotle's self has little in common with the strictly *individual* concept of the person. As his *Ethics* shows, he is concerned with an essentially social being, a universal *species*; in the characteristics of its individual specimens he takes little interest. Moreover, that being is essentially oriented toward theoretical activity. Kierkegaard's emphasis upon the individual self is new in a manner in which only a thinker of the modern epoch could have conceived novelty. Theory for him does not belong to the highest level of self-realization. Indeed, a person who fails to surpass the theoretical attitude remains within that "aesthetic" stage of existence that prevents him from achieving authentic selfhood. Above all, the primary task of the developing self consists not in social integration, but rather in becoming an *individual*. Both of these characteristics are inconceivable without the antecedents of the modern mind. Nevertheless, Kierkegaard's entire theory of the self must be seen not as continuing the trend *actually followed* by modern thought, but as an attempt to reverse it. He abandoned, of course, the Humean empiricist approach to self-hood that would determine all of nineteenth-century psychology. But, closer to home, he also head-on opposed the idealist current that had begun with Descartes's *self* as exclusive principle of intelligibility and was completed with Hegel's theory of Spirit. (In that sense Kierkegaard's approach is new and revolutionary to an extent that we, who all have been influenced by it, seldom realize.) Yet when Kierkegaard equated existence with the realm of the strictly individual, he limited his newborn concept within the lines drawn by the same modern thought that he criticized so severely.

First we should observe that his "individual" has little in common with the kind of narcissistic psychology and ego-mystique to which our time has become more and more accustomed. The self-centered attitude belongs to the "aesthetic" order, described in *Either/Or*, that precedes the sphere of existence proper or is an escape from it. On the other hand, Kierkegaard's idea of the "individual's" self-realization shows unexpected affinities with a line of thought that runs from Stirner to Nietzsche. At first sight no two contemporaries could have been further apart than the philosopher of ultimate responsibility and the intellectual anarchist who rejected *any* kind of responsibility as pseudo-religion. Yet a closer look reveals that much of what Kierkegaard dismisses as "the crowd" includes the social relations, for the omission of which we now blame Stirner. Perhaps, as Buber suggests,[6] Kierkegaard's "narrow pass" leads us into the open country of egoism and eventually despair—the very territory of Stirner's *self* (SUD, 72). Of course, Kierkegaard moves on to a realm of transcendence high above selfish desires and secular finitude, but not above social isolation. In contrast to Stirner's "single one," Kierkegaard's *individual* remains infinitely open—but only in a vertical sense. The social as such contributes nothing to its existential relationship: it remains a distracting "crowd."

It is not difficult to see here, as Kierkegaard himself occasionally did in the private reflection of his diary, the result of personal problems—the incurable melancholy, the inability to communicate with others except through his writings, themselves mostly pseudonymous. Yet more significant to us is the connection between this individualism and the very culture that Kierkegaard attacks. The concept of the *individual* owes much of its prominence in the modern age to two factors, one negative and one positive. The disintegration of philosophical and social *universals* in the late Middle Ages made possible the emergence of the individual as a moral and aesthetic ultimate in the Italian Renaissance. Never before had the single person held the center state of

attention. The breakdown of the traditional social structure in late antiquity
may have led to an experience of individual isolation. All indications are that it
actually did. Already Hegel attributed the dissolution of the organic city-states
into unstructured masses to the collapse of the existing political units and the
formation of the huge empires of the Hellenistic and the Roman periods. Precisely when social structures disintegrate, persons become singularized. The
breakdown into single units resulted in such positive effects as the development of personal rights and the appearance of private law indispensable for the
full emancipation of the individual. But as long as the concept of person remained primarily a juridical unit, the time of the individual had not arrived. It
did not begin until the disintegration of the *res publica christiana* and the medieval structures of thought created a new vacuum that the outburst of individual creativity in the Renaissance filled with a wholly new concept of man.

Kierkegaard himself was not aware of the difference between the modern
age and the "touching naiveté" of the medieval mind in which the individual
remains submersed in the universal. In the same diary entry where he mentions the difference he also points at the connection in the modern age between the dominance of the masses and the exclusive claims of the individual.
What led to the emergence of the individual eventually caused his deperson-
alization. "Alas in our time things are often turned around: it is quite definite
that it is *this* human being who speaks, and yet there is no human being who
speaks."[7] Kierkegaard rarely connects the notion of individual with the ill effects of modernity, but here he clearly views the individual, himself a product
of the mass society, threatened to be reabsorbed by it.

The *mass* epitomizes the dehumanization of modern life. While Pascal had
still been frightened by the isolation of man lost in an infinite space,
Kierkegaard fears the endless masses of human beings, "these countless millions and millions of men" that surround him like an animal species "with their
teeming duplicated specimens in the millions" (JP, 2:2010). This fear of the
mass drives him to distrust *all* social organisms. Derived from the individual's
needs, they constantly stand ready to squeeze him out. Thus the all-
encompassing social entity of modern life, the State, is no more than "egoism
in its wider dimensions constituted in such a clever and ingenious way that the
egoism of individuals cancel and correct each other" (JP, 4:4238). While Hegel
considered the State the concrete universal and, hence, the higher truth of the
individual, for Kierkegaard the single individual is higher than the universal.
The Hegelian position in his interpretation subordinates the individual to the
race, thus lower in men to the status of "an animal race endowed with reason"
(JP, 2:1614). For him, the foundation of the individual's superiority (and the
only solid one!) consists in his exclusive kinship with God. "God is spirit and it
would be bestial for him to be in kinship with a race. He can be in kinship only

with the single individual" (JP, 2:2024). The person's *spiritual* determination lies in his individuality, while his social character, based upon a plurality of individuals in one race, belongs to his *animal* quality (JP, 2:2082).

Here we touch on the heart of the problem. Kierkegaard attempted to rescue the transcendent dimension of human existence that he rightly considered to be jeopardized in modern life. To succeed in this task he felt it was necessary first to force the person to confront his strictly individual responsibility before God. This may well have been a correct practical maneuver for eliminating the ready temptation of escaping into the mass. Yet elevated into a theoretical principle it leads to a distorted vision both of the person and of his relation to the transcendent. If it is severed from its social context, that relation turns into an abstraction without any content of its own. Detached from the total realities of life, the ultimate relation of existence loses it concreteness. But did Kierkegaard not, more than anyone in his time, insist on the concrete ethical obligations implied in the person's relation to God? Undoubtedly, but if this obligation is itself not built upon a preexisting reality in its own right, it lacks the dense social texture that alone conveys a real content. In the *Works of Love*, Kierkegaard emphatically declares the duty to others essential in a person's relation to God; but he fails to provide the social obligation with any concrete determination of its own. As he presents it, the duty to one's fellow man remains part of the vertical relation to God—it lacks a genuinely horizontal dimension. All his life Kierkegaard insisted on the ethical commitment required by that relation and cautioned against the mystic's impatience in attempting to achieve a more "direct" approach to God. Having depleted the ethical injunction of any internal structure, he may have left the religious attitude no alternative but to attempt a direct relation to God. While stressing ethical responsibility, Kierkegaard appears to have dangerously loosened the bonds through which alone the individual becomes ethically "concrete."

Kierkegaard's insistence on the single individual has affected the relation to God in yet another respect. As a means to attain that singularity, he chose what is indeed the most isolating religious experience—the consciousness of being a sinner. But this approach not only "isolates": if taken exclusively it renders the religious attitude predominantly negative, and exposes it to the risk of rapidly degenerating into a morbid disposition toward life. Ironically, precisely because of his emphasis on the single individual, Kierkegaard was incapable of dealing adequately with what in Christian dogma constitutes the basis of man's sinful condition—original sin. While Christian doctrine declares the human race *as a whole* guilty, Kierkegaard's treatment of it in *The Concept of Anxiety* never moved beyond a Pelagian interpretation, according to which each person becomes guilty only through his or her own freely committed sin. The difficulties inherent in the idea of corporate guilt reemerged when he started writing *The Sickness unto Death* to a point where Kierkegaard eventually was forced to omit it from his argument. A few months later he suggests that racial solidarity itself implies a fallen state.

> In eternal life the race will cease. This will be of great significance with respect to the entire doctrine of original sin. . . . In a Christian sense man sighs under being "race." By the synthesis he is constrained in and with the race, must assume all the concretions given thereby as his task, participate as an accomplice in the guilt of the race, and by his own guilt increase the guilt of the race. (JP 2:2433)

This text nearly identifies the *species* quality of human existence with a diminished, or even a sinful, state of being.

The issue is not, of course, whether the consciousness of sin and the concomitant experience of isolation form an integral part of the Christian experience. They clearly do. Nor should we dispute the need for an awareness of man's lonely state in his quest for transcendence. But to declare the prerequisite solitude as the very essence of the religious attitude is to build the relation to the transcendent on one of the principal obstacles for establishing it in our time, namely, the exclusive emphasis upon the individual as a source of meaning and value. Despite his unique religious sensitivity, Kierkegaard was not able to overcome the "egocentric" predicament of the modern age. Kierkegaard may have acted correctly in attacking the state church; but toward the end of his life it became ever clearer that the affiliation with the Danish State was not the main problem. It was the existence of "Christendom" and, indeed, of the Church as such. Not only did he exclude all acculturation, but, ultimately, he was unable to justify any kind of social or ritual practice in other than an educational function. "God sees only the individual" (JP 4:4281). Increasingly, Christianity for him became a religion of total isolation. "Back to the monastery out of which Luther broke—that is the truth—that is what must be done" (JP 4:4454). That "monastery," needless to say, was not a common ground for spiritual encounter. With the traditional monastic life Kierkegaard's ideal shares only celibacy and removal from the world.

No more than the category of the *individual* does that of *subjectivity* escape the restrictions of modern thought. Kierkegaard correctly identified the objectivism that culminated in the nineteenth century as the principal obstacle to a genuine understanding of transcendence. Once reality becomes reduced to objectivity, as had gradually happened after Descartes, the very idea of God becomes contradictory.[8] Kierkegaard countered the objectivist trend by swinging the pendulum in the opposite direction. Yet the exclusive emphasis upon the subject derives from the same source as objectivism itself. Indeed, critics of the modern age frequently refer to the so-called "objectivist" slant of modern thought as "subjectivist" (e.g., Max Horkheimer in *Eclipse of Reason*). The reduction of reality to objectivity follows directly from a turn to the subject, whereby it becomes the sole source of meaning and value. In the process of fulfilling its exclusive function of constituting reality, the subject loses all specific content of its own. It becomes an empty "transcendental subject."[9] This was precisely the tragic failure of the romantic reaction: the subject to which it so desperately wished to return remained only the empty shell. Kierkegaard was no romantic, and in his very first writing had exposed the flaw of romantic subjectivism. Through an ethico-dialectical (rather than a sentimental) relation to the transcendent, he fully intended to overcome the inherent weakness of that subjectivism. Nevertheless his thinking remained caught in the subject-object opposition responsible for both extremes of modern thought.

As is so often true of Kierkegaard, however, his basic insight was right, however questionable its philosophical expression. The theological categories within which Kierkegaard attempted to contain the experience of despair may not have suited the purpose. The universal claims made for the experience were definitely inflated. But beyond the general, theoretical categories, Kierkegaard correctly intuited despair as the ultimate consequence of the modern attitude. The reason why his analyses of despair and of dread so uniquely fascinated the twentieth-century mind was, of course, not their theological merit—which in both cases remains dubious—but their sure grasp of the modern predicament. Nietzsche would later refer to it as the nihilism of European culture—a nihilism that had become manifest only at the end of the modern age. What Kierkegaard described as a disease, the possibility of which is inherent in the human condition as such, has in fact become the actual, though mostly latent, sickness of our own age.

At the beginning of this essay I wrote that *The Sickness unto Death* contains a critique of an entire epoch as much as of a particular individual attitude. In my conclusion I wish to strengthen that claim. Kierkegaard never wrote a treatise on despair as one of the possible attitudes an individual could adopt that would have theological implications. Constant allusions to the condition of his own contemporaries reveal that he was writing about the sickness of his own epoch. The phenomenological analysis of the first part and the theological discussion of the second are anything but abstract speculations. They provide the theoretical foundations, by their very nature universal, for an understanding of his own age. Hence *The Sickness unto Death* must be read as one of the most incisive contributions to a critique of modernity. In this respect it confirms, completes, and anticipates analyses written by Marx, Nietzsche, and Freud. As in their work, Kierkegaard's critique remains *within* the ideological restrictions of the period it criticizes. It offers no prophetic message, no magic formula for curing the ills of the time. Indeed, as a critique it is remarkably un-self-conscious. But as in all great works of art and of thought, therein may lie its greatest strength. It forces the reader to go through the whole critical process himself. What Jaspers wrote about Nietzsche applies eminently to the Kierkegaard of *The Sickness unto Death*:

> He does not show us the way, he does not teach us a faith, he gives us nothing to stand on. Instead, he grants us no peace, torments us ceaselessly, hunts us out of every retreat, and forbids all concealment. It is precisely by plunging us into nothingness that he wants to create for us the vastness of space. It is precisely by showing us a fathomless world that he wants to enable us to grasp the ground we sprang from.[10]

In his own indirect way, then, Kierkegaard awakens each reader personally to the consciousness of his age and urges him critically to examine its unquestioned assumptions. In taking this critical distance from current ideologies, the reader is forced to become an *individual*. Thus, performatively, he will restore truth to a category that, taken by itself, is no more than a consequence of modernity.

Notes

1. Søren Kierkegaard, *The Sickness unto Death*, trans. H. V. and E. H. Hong (Princeton, N. J.: Princeton University Press, 1980), p. 90, hereafter cited in the text as SUD.

2. Søren Kierkegaard, *Two Ages: The Age of Revolution and the Present Age*, trans. H. V. and E. H. Hong (Princeton, N. J.: Princeton University Press, 1978), pp. 85–86.

3. Søren Kierkegaard, *The Point of View for My Work as an Author*, trans. W. Lowrie (London: Oxford University Press, 1939), p. 107, hereafter PV.

4. Karl Jaspers, *Philosophy* 1 (1932), trans. E. B. Ashton (Chicago: University of Chicago Press, 1969), pp. 54–57.

5. Cf. George J. Stack, "Kierkegaard's Concept of Existential Possibility," *The New Scholasticism* 46 (1972): 159.

6. Martin Buber, "The Question to the Single One," in his *Between Man and Man*, trans. R. G. Smith (New York: Macmillan, 1963), pp. 60-81.

7. Søren Kierkegaard, *Søren Kierkegaard's Journals and Papers*, trans. H. V. and E. H. Hong (Bloomington: Indiana University Press, 1967–78), vol. 2, p. 2005, hereafter cited by volume and page as JP.

8. Restrictions of space do not allow me to develop this important point. But I have done so on several occasions, e.g., in *Transcendent Selfhood* (New York: Seabury Press, 1976) and *The Other Dimension* (New York: Seabury Press, 1979).

9. This was one of Hegel's main objections against Kant's theory of practical reason—"how this empty unity as practical reason is nonetheless supposed to become constitutive again, to give birth out of itself and give itself content." *Faith and Knowledge*, trans. W. Cerf and H. S. Harris (Albany: State University of New York Press, 1977), p. 81.

10. Karl Jaspers, *Nietzsche and Christianity*, trans. E. B. Ashton (Chicago: Henry Regnery, 1961), p. 104

II
NIETZSCHE

3

A More Severe Morality: Nietzsche's Affirmative Ethics

Robert C. Solomon

> She told me herself that she had no morality,—and I thought she had, like myself, a more severe morality than anyone.
>
> —Nietzsche, in a letter to Paul Rée, 1882

A MAD DOG, FOAMING AT THE MOUSTACHE and snarling at the world; that is how the American artist David Levine portrays Friedrich Nietzsche in his well-known caricature in *The New York Review of Books*. It is not so different in its malicious intent, nor further wrong in its interpretation of Nietzsche, than a good number of scholarly works. This is indeed the traditional portrait: the unconsummated consummate immoralist, the personally gentle, even timid, archdestroyer. Of course, Nietzsche himself made adolescent comments about his own destructiveness not infrequently—throughout *Ecce Homo*, for example. Nevertheless, these give a false impression of his intentions as well as of the good philosophical sense to be made of his works.

In recent years, we have been treated to a rather systematic whitewashing of Nietzsche. Gone is the foam and the snarl; indeed, what has come to replace the "revaluation of all values" has become so tame that, a certain impatience for scholarship aside, one of these new Nietzsches (perhaps not the French one) would find himself very much at home on most university campuses. This new Nietzsche, founded by Walter Kaufmann and now promoted by Richard Schacht, is the champion of honesty against the forces of hypocrisy.[1] Or, more recently, he is Harold Alderman's benign Californish guru, urging us simply to "be ourselves," preferably by reading Heidegger.[2] This picture is no less false than the first, but it has the undeniable virtue of welcoming Nietzsche, belatedly, back to the fold of professional philosophers. Better respectable than rabid, one might suppose, though I would guess Nietzsche himself would opt for the latter.

The new French Nietzsche, on the other hand, enjoys the *philosophe* at the extremes, almost beyond the limits of the imaginable, an adolescent implosion of forces dancing on the edge of nothingness. He is, accordingly, a thoroughly playful Nietzsche. He is the "anti-Oedipe" as well as the "anti-Christ," a deconstructionist, a Derridian, a Dada-ian, before his time. He does not destroy but rather revels in the destruction we have already inflicted upon ourselves. He is a burst of energy rather than a philosopher, an explosion instead of a visionary. Most of all, he plays, and reminds us of the importance of dancing and the unimportance of serious scholarship and Truth. And, we are assured (for example, by David Allison in his introduction to *The New Nietzsche*[3]) that Nietzsche is wholly outside of that somber and intellectually fraudulent onto-theological tradition that he so playfully attacks, but in which we less imaginative and playless scholarly souls are still enmired.

Perhaps. But of all the authors in German history, Nietzsche must surely be the most historical and even "timely," as well as one of the most solemn (as opposed to bourgeois "serious"). He was, from all evidence, incapable of even the uptight version of dancing propounded by his Zarathustra. His playfulness seemed largely limited to the scholarly joke. Lou Andreas Salomé once described him (in 1882):

> a light laugh, a quiet way of speaking, and a cautious, pensive way of walking . . . He took pleasure in the refined forms of social intercourse. . . . But in it all lay a penchant for disguise. . . . I recall that when I first spoke with him his formal manner shocked and deceived me. But I was not deceived for long by this lonesome man who only wore his mask as unalterably as someone coming from the desert and mountains wears the cloak of the worldly-wise.[4]

Playful, indeed. And as for "the tradition," as it has come to be called, Nietzsche as philosopher can be understood only within it, despite his unselfcritical megalomania about his own "untimely" and wholly novel importance.

It is decidedly *within* that somber philosophical tradition, typically traced in misleading linear fashion back to Socrates, that I want to try to understand Nietzsche's ethics. His reputation as archdestroyer and philosophical outlaw has so enveloped Nietzsche's notorious "reputation," largely at his own bidding, that the kernel of his moral philosophy—and I do insist on calling it that—has been lost. There is in Nietzsche, unmistakably, an ethics that is considerably more than nihilism or academic good fellowship or playfulness, an ethics that is very much part of "the tradition." It is, however, a brand of ethics that had and has been all but abandoned in the wake of Kant and the anal compulsiveness of what is now called rationality in ethics. It is this other brand of ethics, for which Nietzsche quite properly failed to find a name, that I would like to indicate in this essay.

Nietzsche's Nihilism, and Morality

Nietzsche's novelty is to be found, in part, in his energetic descriptions of what he calls "nihilism." It is, first of all, a cultural experience, a profound sense of disappointment, not only, as some ethicists would have it, in the failure of philosophy to justify moral principles, but in the fabric of life as such, the "widespread sensibility of our age" more sympathetically described by Camus half a century later. It is also, Nietzsche keeps reminding us, a stance to be taken up as well as a phenomenon to be described. Zarathustra, in one of his more belligerent moments, urges us to "push what is falling" and, in his notes, Nietzsche urges to promote "a complete nihilism," in place of the incomplete nihilism in which we now live (*WP* 28).[5] Here again we note Nietzsche's self-conscious "timeliness," and his devotion to a tradition dedicated to completeness in ethics.

"Nihilism," obvious etymology aside, does not mean "accepting nothing." Like most philosophical terms, subsequently raised to an isolated and artificial level of abstraction, this one does its work in particular contexts, in specific perspectives, often as a kind of accusation. Some traditional but much-in-the-news Christians use the term as a more or less crude synonym for "secular humanism," on the (false) assumption that a man without God must be a man without Christian values as well. (The dubious argument by Ivan Karamazov: "if there is not God, then everything is permitted.") But note that I say "Christian" values, for the accuser might well allow, indeed insist, that the nihilist does have values—subjective, self-serving, and secularly narrow-minded though they be. (Brother Mitya, perhaps: hardly a paragon if virtue.) Similarly, an orthodox Jewish friend of mine refers to as "nihilists" any people without a self-conscious if not obsessive sense of tradition, assuming that others must lack in their experience what he finds so essential in his own. Marxists use the term (sometimes but not always along with "bourgeois individualism") to indict those who do not share their class-conscious values. Aesthetes use it to knock the philistines, and my academic colleagues use it to chastise anyone with "looser" standards and higher grade averages than themselves. Stanley Rosen attacks nihilism at book length without ever saying exactly what's wrong with it, except that it falls far short of his own rather pretentious search for Hegelian absolute truth.[6]

If Nietzsche made us aware of anything in ethics, it is the importance of *perspectives*, the need to see all concepts and values *in context*. How odd, then, that the key concepts of Nietzsche's own ethics have been so routinely blown up to absolute—that is, nonperspectival—proportions. Nihilism is an accusation, in context. Outside of all contexts, it is nothing (which, of course, leads to some quaint and cute Parmenidean wordplay.) As Blanchot has written, nihilism is a particular achievement of a particular sort of society.[7] It becomes a world-hypothesis only at the expense of losing what is most urgent and cleansing in Nietzsche, the attack on the transcendental pretension of understanding the world "in itself" on the basis of our own limited and limiting moral experience.

Nietzsche's nihilism is an accusation *within* the context of traditional ethics (what other kind of ethics could there be?). It points to a tragic or at any rate damnable hollowness in "the moral point of view," which we might anticipate by asking why moral philosophers ever became compelled to talk in such a peculiar fashion. Indeed, it is part and parcel of the whole history of ethics that morality is emphatically *not* just "a point of view"; it is necessary and obligatory. Such talk already betrays a fatal compromise; "perspectivism" and Morality are warring enemies, not complementary theses. What is morality, that it has been forced and has been able to hide behind a veneer of pluralism, to search for "reasons" for its own necessity which—successful or not—leave the acceptance of morality unchallenged?

What is morality? This, perhaps more than any other question, guided Nietzsche's ethics. It is the concept of morals that intrigues Nietzsche: How morals ever became reduced to Morality, how the virtues ever got melted together into the shapeless form of Virtue. But, as I shall argue shortly, there are many meanings of "morality" just as there are many different sorts of morals. (It is the terms themselves—but not just the terms—that are most in question here.) The definition of "morality" that preoccupies Nietzsche, and which I shall be employing here, is the definition provided by Kant: a set of universal, categorical principles of practical reason. "Morals," on the other hand, is a term much less precise, and I shall be using that term much as Hume used it in his *Enquiry:* morals are those generally agreeable or acceptable traits that characterize a good person—leaving quite open the all-important nonconceptual question what is to count (in what context) as a good person. Ethics, finally, I take to the be the overall arena in which morality and morals and other questions concerning the good life and how to live it are debated. Morality in its Kantian guise may not be all that essential to ethics; indeed, one might formulate Nietzsche's concern by asking how the subject of ethics has so easily been converted into Moral Philosophy, that is, the philosophical analysis of Morality *à la Kant* rather than the somewhat pagan celebration of the virtues *à la Hume* (which is not to say that Nietzsche would have felt very much at home with the Scot either, whatever their philosophical affinities).

In his recent book, *After Virtue*,[8] Alasdair MacIntyre has attacked Nietzsche and nihilism together, as symptoms of our general decay ("decadence" would be too fashionable and thus too positive a term for our moral wretchedness). But in doing so, he has also rendered Nietzsche's own thesis in admirably contemporary form; morality is undone, hollow, an empty sham for which philosophers busily manufacture "reasons" and tinker with grand principles if only to convince themselves that something might still be there. What philosophers defensively call "the moral point of view" is a camouflaged retreat. It serves only to hide the vacuousness of the moral prejudices they serve. Morality is no longer a "table of virtues" but a *tabula rasa*, for which we are poorly compensated by the insistence that it is itself necessary. Or, in Hume's terms, morality is the repository of those "monkish" virtues, whose degrading, humiliating effects are disguised by the defenses of reason.[9] For Hume, as for Nietzsche, "some passions are merely stupid, dragging us down with them." And this will be the area where an adequate understanding of morals will emerge, in the realm of passion rather than reason. The good person will emphatically not be the one who is expertly consistent in universalizing maxims according to the principles of practical reason.

Nietzsche, Kant, and Aristotle

Nihilism is not a thesis; it is a reaction. It is not a romantic "nay-saying" so much as it is a feature of good old Enlightenment criticism in the form of a critical phenomenology or a diagnostic hermeneutics. Indeed, in Germany romanticism and *Aufklärung* were never very clearly distinguished, except in rhetoric, and so too beneath the bluster of nihilism a much more profound and, dare I say, reasonable Nietzsche can be discerned. In fact, I want to argue that Nietzsche might best be understood, perhaps ironically, in the company of that more optimistic decadent of ancient times, Aristotle, and in close contrast to the most powerful moral philosopher of modern times—Immanuel Kant. They were hardly nihilists; indeed, they remain even today the two paradigms of morality, the two great proponents of all-encompassing ethical worldviews. Next to them, the contemporary fiddling with so-called "utilitarianism" seems, as Hegel complained in the *Phenomenology*, rather petty and devoid of anything deserving the honorific name "morality."[10]

It has always seemed to me perverse to read Aristotle and Kant as engaged in the same intellectual exercise, that is, to present and promote a *theory* of morality. They were, without question, both moralists; that is, they had the "moral prejudices" that Nietzsche discovers beneath every philosophical theory. This, of course, would not bother them (except perhaps the word "prejudices").

They were both also, Nietzsche would be the first to argue, *reactionaries*, try-ing to prop up with an ethics an *ethos*—an established way of life—that was already collapsing. To do so, both ethicists appealed to an overriding (if not absolute) *telos* of reason and rationality, the suspicious status of which Nietz-sche deftly displays vis-à-vis Socrates in *Twilight of the Idols*.[11] Both philoso-phers too saw themselves as defenders of "civilized" virtues in the face of the nihilists of their time, though Aristotle displays ample affinity with Protago-ras and Kant had no hesitation about supporting Robespierre. But, neverthe-less, there is a profound difference between these two great thinkers that too easily gets lost in the need to sustain the linear tradition that supposedly be-gins with Socrates, ignoring the dialectical conflict that is to be found even within Socrates himself. Aristotle and Kant represent not just two opposed ethical theories, "telelogical" and "deontological" respectively, synthesized by the *telos* of rationality. They represent two opposed ways of life.

Aristotle may be a long way from the Greece described by Homer, but the form of his ethics is still very much involved with the Homeric warrior tradi-tion. The virtue of courage still deserves first mention in the list of excellences, and pride is still a virtue rather than a vice. It is an ethics for the privileged few; though Aristotle, unlike Nietzsche, had no need to announce this in a preface. But most important, it is an ethics that is not primarily concerned with rules and principles, much less *universal* rules and principles (i.e., *categorical imper-atives*). Indeed, Aristotle's much-heralded discussion of the so-called "practical syllogism" in Book VI of the *Nicomachean Ethics*, in which something akin to principles universal in form (and as ethically invigorating as "eating dry foods is healthy") is quite modest—hardly the cornerstone of his ethics, as some re-cent scholars have made it out to be.[12] Aristotle's ethics is not an ethics of prin-ciples, categorical or otherwise. It is an ethics of *practice*, a description of an ac-tual ethos rather than an abstract attempt to define or create one. Ethos is by its very nature bound to a culture; Kantian ethics, by its pure rational nature but much to its peril, seems not to be. Of course, any philosopher can show how a practice is *really* a rule-governed activity, and proceed to formulate, ex-amine, and criticize the rules.[13] Indeed, one might even show that children playing with their food follow certain rules, but to do so clearly is to misde-scribe if not also misunderstand their activity.[14] But what is critical to an ethics of practice is not the absence of rules; it is rather the overriding importance of the concept of *excellence* or virtue (*aretê*). What Aristotle describes is the ideal citizen, the excellent individual who is already (before he studies ethics and learns to articulate principles of any kind) proud of himself and the pride of his family and community. He is surrounded by friends; he is the model of strength, if not only the physical prowess that was singularly important to Achilles (who was far from ideal in other virtues). He may have been a bit too "civilized" already for Nietzsche's Homeric fantasies, but he represents a moral type distinctively different from that described by Kant, two thousand years later. His ethics are his virtues; his excellence is his pride.

Kant, on the other hand, is the outstanding moralist in a very different tradition. The warrior plays no role and presents us with no ideal; individual talents and the good fortune of having been "brought up well," which Aristotle simply presupposes, are ruled out of the moral realm from page one.[15] Kant's ethics is the ethics of the categorical imperative, the ethics of universal rational principles, the ethics of obedient virtue instead of the cultivation of the virtues. It is an ethics that minimized differences and begins by assuming that we all share a common category of "humanity" and a common moral faculty of reason. The good man is the man who resists his "inclinations" and acts for the sake of duty and duty alone. This extreme criterion is qualified in a number of entertaining ways: for example, by suggesting that the rule that one should cultivate one's talents is itself an example of the categorical imperative and that one has a peculiar duty to pursue one's own happiness, if only so that one is thereby better disposed to fulfill one's duties to others.[16]

What I want to argue here should be, in part at least, transparent. Nietzsche may talk about "creating new values," but—as he himself often says—it is something of a return to an old and neglected set of values—the values of masterly virtue—that most concerns him. There are complications. We do not have the ethos of the *Illiad*, nor even the tamer *ethê* of Homer or Aristotle, nor for that matter even the bourgeois complacency of Kantian Königsberg with its definitive set of practices in which the very idea of an unconditional imperative is alone plausible. There is no context, in other words, within which the new virtues we are to "create" are to be virtues, for a virtue without a practice is of no more value than a word without a language, a gesture without a context. When Nietzsche insists on "creating new values," in other words, he is urging us on in a desperate state of affairs. He is rejecting the mediocre banality of an abstract ethics of principles, but he has no practice upon which to depend in advancing his renewed ethics of virtue. No practice, that is, except for the somewhat pretentious and sometimes absurd self-glorification of nineteenth-century German romanticism, which Nietzsche rebukes even as he adopts it as his only available context.[17] This is no small point: Nietzsche is not nearly so isolated nor so unique as he needs to think of himself. Dionysus, like "the Crucified," is an ideal only within a context, even if, in *Der Fall Nietzsche*, it seems to be a context defined primarily by rejection.

Nietzsche's nihilism is a reaction against a quite particular *conception* of morality, summarized in modern times in the ethics of Kant. Quite predictably, much of Judeo-Christian morality—or what is often called "Judeo-Christian morality"—shares this conception. It too is for the many, not just a few. It too treats all souls as the same, whether rational or not. It too dwells on abstractions, whether such categorical imperatives as "the Golden Rule" or the universal love called *agapê*, which applies to everyone and therefore to no one in particular. Hegel was not entirely wrong when, in an early essay, he had Jesus on the Mount deliver a sermon taken straight from *The Critique of Practical Reason*.[18] Nor was Kant deceiving himself when he looked with pride on his moral philosophy as the heart of Christian ethics, interpreting the commandment to love as well as the desire to be happy as nothing more nor less than instantiations of the categorical imperative, functions of practical reason rather than expressions of individual virtues and exuberance for life.[19]

Aristotle and Achilles versus Kant and Christianity. It is not a perfect match, but it allows us to explain Nietzsche's aims and Nietzsche's problems far better than the overreaching nonsense about "the transvaluation of *all* values" and "Dionysus versus the Crucified." On the other hand, it is not as if Kant and Nietzsche are completely opposed. It is Kant who sets up the philosophical conditions for the Nietzschean reaction, not only by so clearly codifying the central theses to be attached but also by conceptually undermining the traditional supports of morality. The (*Aufklärung*) attack on authority ("heteronom") and the emphasis of "autonomy" by Kant is a necessary precondition for Nietzsche's moral moves, however much the latter presents himself as providing a conception of morality which precedes, rather than presupposes, this Kantian move. It is Kant, of course, who so stresses the importance of the Will, which is further dramatized (to put it mildly) by Schopenhauer and which, again, Nietzsche attacks only by way of taking for granted its primary features. (Nietzsche's attacks on "the Will," especially "free will," deserve some special attention in this regard. "Character" and "will to power" are not the same as "willpower.") It is Kant who rejects the support of morality by appeal to religion—arguing instead a dependency of the inverse kind—and though Nietzsche's now-tiresome "God is dead" hypothesis may be aimed primarily at the traditional thesis, the bulk of his moral arguments presuppose the Kantian inversion: religion as a rationalization, not the precondition, of moral thinking.

Meanings of Morality

It was Kant too, perhaps, who best exemplified the philosophical temptation to suppose that "morality" refers to a single phenomenon, faculty, or feature of certain, if not all, societies. Moral theories and some specific rules may vary, according to this monolithic position, but Morality is that one single set of basic moral rules which all theories of morality must accept as a given. This is stated outright by Kant, at the beginning of his second *Critique* and his *Grounding of the Metaphysics of Morals.*[20] Every society, one might reasonably suppose, has some "trump" set of rules and regulations which prohibit certain kinds of actions and are considered to be absolute, "categorical." Philosophers might argue whether there is a single rationale behind the variety of rules (a "utility principle" or some principle of authority). Others might challenge the alleged universality and disinterestedness of such principles, but morality everywhere is assumed to be the same, in form if not in content, or in at least intent, nevertheless. Indeed even Nietzsche, in his later works, is tempted by the monolithic image; his pluralistic view of a "table of virtues hanging over every people" is explained by his familiar exuberant account: "it is the expression of their Will to Power!" In his repeated "campaign against morality," he too makes it seem too much as if morality is a monolith rather than a complex set of phenomena whose differences may be as striking as their similarities.

What is in question and what ethics is about, according to moral philosophers since Kant, is the *justification* of moral principles, and along with this quest for justification comes the search for a single *ultimate* principle, a *summum bonum*, through which all disagreements and conflicts can be resolved. The question "What is morality?" gets solved in a few opening pages; the search for an adequate answer to the more troublesome challenge, "Why be moral?" becomes the main order of business. The question, however, is not entirely serious. "But there is no reason for worry," Nietzsche assures us (*BGE* 228);[21] "Things still stand today as they have always stood: I see nobody in Europe who has (let alone *promotes*) any awareness that thinking about morality could become dangerous, captious, seductive—that there might be any *calamity* involved" (ibid.). Thus today we find a nearly total moral skepticism (nihilism?) defended in such centers of Moral Standards as Oxford and Yale, under such nonprovocative titles as "prescriptivism" and "emotivism." But, whatever the analysis, these folks still keep their promises and restrain themselves to their fair share of the high table pie. The quest for justification is not a challenge to the monolith; it is only an exercise.

In fact, it is the phenomenon or morality itself that is in question. More than half a century before Nietzsche issued his challenge to Kant, a more sympathetic post-Kantian, Hegel, attacked the Kantian conception of "morality" in terms that would have been agreeable to Nietzsche, had he been a bit more receptive to the German *Geist*. Hegel too treated the Kantian conception of morality as a monolith, but he also saw that it was surrounded by other conceptions that might also be called "moral" which were, in the *telos* of human development, both superior and more "primitive." One of these was *Sittlichkeit*, or the morality of customs (*Sitten*).[22] It is what we earlier called a morality of *practice*, as opposed to a morality of principles. Hegel proposed not just a different way of interpreting and justifying moral rules (though this would be entailed as well); he defended a conception of morals that did not depend upon rules at all—in which the activity of justification, in fact, became something of a philosophical irrelevancy, at best. The need to justify moral rules betrays an emptiness in those rules themselves, a lack of conviction, a lack of support. Since then, Hegel has mistakenly been viewed as lacking in his concern for the basic ethical question, leading several noted ethical commentators (Popper, Walsh)[23] to accuse him of a gross amorality, conducive to if not openly inviting authoritarianism. It is as if rejecting the Kantian conception of morality and refusing to indulge in the academic justification game were tantamount to abandoning ethics—both the practice and the theory—altogether.

If we are to understand Nietzsche's attack on Morality, we must appreciate not so much the breadth of his attack and the all-out nihilism celebrated by some of his more enthusiastic defenders but rather the more limited precise conception of Morality that falls under his hollow-seeking hammer. We can then appreciate what some have called the "affirmative" side of Nietzsche's moral thinking, the sense in which he sees himself as having "a more severe morality than anybody." In *Beyond Good and Evil* he boasts, "WE IM-MORALISTS!— . . . We have been spun into a severe yarn and short of duties and CANNOT get out of that—and in this we are men of duty, we too . . . the dolts and appearances speak against us saying, 'These are men *without* duty.' We always have the dolts and appearances against us" (*BGE* 226). To write about Nietzsche as a literal "immoralist" and the destroyer of morality is to read him badly, or it is to confuse the appearance with the personality. Or, he would say, it is to be a "dolt."

For Nietzsche, as for Hegel, and as for Aristotle, morality does not consist of principles but of practices. It is *doing*, not willing, that is of moral significance, an expression of character rather than a display of practical reason. A practice has local significance; it requires—and sets up—a context; it is not a matter of universal rule; in fact, universality is sometimes argued to show that something is *not* a practice. (For example, sociobiologists have argued that incest and certain other sexual preferences are not sex practices because—on the basis of their alleged universality—they can be shown to be genetically inherited traits.)[14] Some practices are based upon principles, of course, but not all are; and principles help define a practice, though they rarely if ever do so alone. Hegel and Aristotle, of course, emphasize *collective* social practices, in which laws may be much in evidence. Nietzsche is particularly interested in the "genealogy" of social practices in which principles play a central if also devious role, but he too quickly concludes that there is but one such "moral type" and one alternative "type," which he designates "slave" ("herd") and "master" moralities, respectively. In fact, there are as many moral "types" as one is willing to distinguish, and to designate as "master morality" the histor-ical and anthropological gamut of relatively lawless (as opposed to lawless) so-cieties is most unhistorical as well as confusing philosophically.

The monolithic image of morality, divorced from particular peoples and practices, gives rise to the disastrous disjunction—common to Kant and Nietz-sche at least—it is either Morality or *nothing*. If Nietzsche often seems to come up empty-handed and obscurely calling for "the creation of new values," it is because he finds himself rejecting principles without a set of practices to fall back on. If only he had his own non-nihilistic world—something more than his friends and his study and his images of nobility—where he could say, "Here is where we can prove ourselves!" But what he finds instead is the hardly heroic world of nineteenth-century democratic socialism. In reaction, he celebrates self-assertion and "life." This is poor stuff from which to reconstruct Nietz-sche's "affirmative philosophy." Add a synthetic notion, "the will to power," and Nietzsche's ethics is reduced to a combination of aggressive banality and ener-getic self-indulgence. (Would it be unfair to mention Leopold and Loeb here? They were not the least literate of Nietzsche's students.) What we find in ap-pearances, accordingly, is not an "affirmative" philosophy at all. Having given us his polemical typology of morals, the rejection of Morality—misinterpreted as a broad-based rejection of *all* morality (for example, by Philippa Foot, who is one of Nietzsche's more sensitive Anglo-American readers)—seems to lead us to nothing substantial at all.[25] The banality of Zarathustra.

"What is morality?" The very question invites a simple if not simpleminded answer. But "morality" is itself a morally loaded term which can be used to designate and applaud any number of different *ethê* and their justificatory contexts. Nietzsche famously insisted that "there are no moral phenomena, only moral interpretations of phenomena." I would add that there are only moral interpretations of "morality" too. Indeed, I would even suggest that Nietzsche might mean the very opposite of what his aphorism says, that there are *only* moral phenomena, in precisely the sense that Kant denied, especially regarding the supposedly neutral word "Morality" itself.

Areteic Ethics: Nietzsche and Aristotle

In *After Virtue*, Alasdair MacIntyre gives us a choice, *enten-eller*: Nietzsche *or* Aristotle.[26] There is, he explicitly warns us, no third alternative. MacIntyre sees Nietzsche's philosophy as purely destructive, despite the fact that he praises the archdestroyer for his insight into the collapse of morals that had been increas-ingly evident since the Enlightenment. MacIntyre chooses Aristotle as the posi-tive alternative. Aristotle had an *ethos*: Nietzsche leaves us with nothing. But

Nietzsche is nevertheless the culmination of that whole tradition—which we still refer to as "moral philosophy" or "ethics"—which is based on a tragic and possibly irreversible error in both theory and practice. The error is the rejection of ethos as the foundation of morality with a compensating insistence on the rational justification of morality. Without a presupposed ethos, no justification is possible. Within an ethos, none is necessary. (Nietzsche: "not to *need* to impose values") And so after centuries of degeneration, internal inconsistencies, and failures in the Enlightenment project of transcending mere custom and justifying moral rules once and for all, the structures of morality have collapsed, leaving only incoherent fragments. "Ethics" is the futile effort to make sense of the fragments and "justify" them, from Hume's appeal to the sentiments and Kant's appeal to practical reason to the contemporary vacuity of "metaethical" theory. Here is the rubble that Nietzsche's Zarathustra urges us to clear away. Here is the vacuum in which Nietzsche urges us to become "legislators" and "create new values." But out of what are we to do this? What would it be, "to create a new value"?

MacIntyre, by opposing Nietzsche and Aristotle, closes off to us the basis upon which we could best reconceive of morality: a reconsideration of Aristotle through Nietzschean eyes. Nietzsche, of course, encourages the antagonistic interpretation. But the opposition is ill conceived, and the interpretation is misleading. MacIntyre, like Philippa Foot, takes Nietzsche too literally to be attacking *all* morality. But quite the contrary of rejecting the ethics of Aristotle, I see Nietzsche as harking back to Aristotle and the still warrior-bound aristocratic tradition he was (retrospectively) cataloging in his *Nicomachean* (Neo-McKeon) *Ethics*. Whatever the differences between Greece of the *Illiad* and Aristotle's Athens, there was a far vaster gulf—and not only in centuries—between the elitist ethics of Aristotle and the egalitarian, bourgeois, Pietist ethics of Kant. Nietzsche may have envisioned himself as Dionysus versus the Crucified; he is better understood as a modern-day Sophist versus Kant, a defender of the virtues against the categorical imperative.

When I was in graduate school an embarrassing number of years ago, my professor Julius Moravscik began his lectures on Aristotle with a comparison to Nietzsche. They were two of a kind, he said, both functionalists, naturalists, "teleologists," standing very much opposed to the utilitarian and Kantian temperaments. Moravscik never followed this through, to my knowledge, but his casual seminar remark has stuck with me for all of these years, and the more I read and lecture on both authors, so different in times and tempers, the more I find the comparison illuminating. Nietzsche was indeed, like Aristotle, a self-proclaimed functionalist, naturalist, teleologist, and, I would add, an elitist, though on both men's views this would follow from the rest. Nietzsche's functionalism is most evident in his constant insistence that we *evaluate* values, see what they are *for*, what role they play in the survival and life of a people. He never tires of telling us about his "naturalism," of course, from his flatly false declaration that he is the first philosopher who was also a psychologist (MacIntyre here substitutes sociology) to his refreshing emphasis on psychological explanation in place of rationalizing justification. Nietzsche often states this in terms of the "this-worldly" as opposed to the "other worldly" visions of Christianity, but I think that this is not the contrast of importance. Indeed, today it is the very "this-worldly" activity of some Christian power blocks that is a major ethical concern, and there is much more to naturalism (as opposed, for example, to Kant's rationalism) than the rejection of heaven and hell as the end of ethics. (Kant, of course, would agree with that too).

Nietzsche's teleology is at times as cosmic as Aristotle's, especially where the grand *telos* becomes "the will to power." But on the strictly human (if not all-too-human) level, Nietzsche's ethics like Aristotle's can best be classified in introductory ethics readers as an ethics of "self-realization." "Become who you are" is the slogan in the middle writings: the *telos* of the *Übermensch* serves from *Thus Spake Zarathustra* on. Indeed, who is the *Übermensch* if not Aristotle's *megalopsychos*, "the great-souled man" from whom Nietzsche even borrows much of his "master-type" terminology. He is the ideal who "deserves and claims great things." He is the man driven by what Goethe (the most frequent candidate for *Übermensch* status) called his "daemon" (the association with Aristotle's "*eu-daimonia*" is not incidental).

Aristotle's teleology begins modestly, with the *telos* of the craftsman, the physician, the farmer. Each has his purpose, his own criteria for excellence, his own "good." But such modest goods and goals are hardly the stuff of ethics, and Aristotle quickly turns to "the good for man," by which he means the ideal man, and the "function of man," by which he means man at his best.[27] There is no point to discussing what we banally call today "the good person," who breaks no rules or laws, offends no one, and interests no one except certain moral philosophers. There is no reason to discuss *hoi polloi*, who serve their city-state well and honor their superiors appropriately. It is the superiors themselves who deserve description, for they are the models from whom the vision of humanity is conceived. What sort of insanity, we hear Aristotle and Nietzsche asking in unison, can explain the idea that all people are of equal value, that everyone and anyone can serve as an ideal, as a model for what is best in us? With leaders like Pericles, who needs the categorical imperative? ("What are morals to us sons of God?") With leaders like our own, no wonder we are suffocating with laws.

To reject egalitarian ethics and dismiss the banal notion of "the good person" as no ethical interest is not to become an "immoralist." It does not mean breaking all the rules. It does not result in such inability as suffered by Richard Hare, a temporary incapacity to morally censure Hitler for any rational reasons.[28] Or, if we want an "immoralist," he might be at worst the sort of person that André Gide created in his short novel of that name, a man who senses his own morality and luxuriates in his own bodily sensations, amused and fascinated by the foibles of people around him.[29] This is not, of course, the man whom Aristotle has in mind. The Stagirite was concerned with statesmen, philosopher-kings, the flesh-and-blood *Übermenschen* who exist in actuality, not just in novels and philosophical fantasies and Zarathustra's pronouncements. But Nietzsche too, when it comes down to cases, is concerned not with a phantom but with real-life heroes, the "great men" who justify (I use the word advisedly) the existence of the society that created them—and which they in turn created. But though he may shock us with his military language, the *Übermenschen* more near to his heart are for the most part his artistic comrades, "philosophers, saints and artists."[30] The rejection of bourgeois morality does not dictate cruelty but rather an emphasis on excellence. The will to power is not *Reich* but *Macht* and not supremacy but superiority, Nietzsche urges us to create values, but I believe that it is the value of creating as such—and having the strength and the *telos* to do so—that he most valued. The unspoken but always present thesis is this: It is only in the romantic practice of artistic creativity that modern excellence can be achieved.

Elitism is not itself an ethics. Indeed, I think both Aristotle and Nietzsche might well object to it as such. It is rather the presupposition that people's talents and abilities differ. It is beginning with what is the case. (Compare John Rawls: "It is upon a correct choice of a basic structure of society . . . that justice . . . depends.")[31] The purpose of an ethics is to maximize people's potential, to encourage the most and the best from all of them, but more by far from the best of them. It is also the recognition that any universal rule—however ingeniously formulated and equally applied—will be disadvantageous to someone, coupled with the insistence that it is an enormous waste as well as unfair (both authors worry more about the former than the latter) for the strong to be limited by the weak, the productive limited by the unproductive, the creative limited by the uncreative. It will not do to mask the point by saying that elitism does not treat people unequally, only differently. It presumes inequality from the outset, and defends it by appeal to the larger picture. Aristotle by appeal to the well-being of the city-state and the natural order of things, Nietzsche by a more abstract but very modern romantic appeal to human creativity. Of course, Nietzsche refuses to be so Kantian as to appeal to "humanity" as such, and so he appeals to a step beyond humanity, to *über*-humanity. But what is the *Übermensch* but a projection of what is best in us, what Kant called "dignity" but Nietzsche insists is "nobility." The difference, of course, is that Kant thought that dignity was inherent in every one of us; Nietzsche recognizes nobility in only the very few.

What is essential to this view of ethics—let us not call it elitist ethics but rather an ethics of virtue, *areteic* ethics—is that the emphasis is wholly on excellence, a teleological conception. What counts for much less is obedience to rules, laws, and principles, for one can be wholly obedient and also dull, unproductive, and useless. This does not mean that the "immoralist"—as Nietzsche misleadingly calls him—will kill innocents, steal from the elderly, and betray the community, nor even, indeed, run a car through a red light. The *Übermensch* character is perfectly willing to act "in accordance with morality," even in a qualified way, "for the sake of duty," that is, if it is a duty that fits his character and his *telos*. In a much-debated passage, Nietzsche even insists that the strong have a "duty" to help the weak, a statement that is utterly confusing on the nihilist interpretation of Nietzsche's ethics.[32] What the *Übermensch*-aspirant does not recognize are categorical imperatives, commands made impersonally and universally, without respect for rank or abilities. As a system of hypothetical imperatives useful to his purposes, however, the *Übermensch* might be as moral as anyone else. (Why Philippa loves Friedrich, and how the spirit of Sils Maria finally comes to Oxford.)

MacIntyre's diagnosis of our tragic fate turns on his recognition that the singular *ethos* upon which a unified and coherent ethics might be based has fragmented. We no longer have a culture with customs and an agreed upon system of morals; we instead have pluralism. Our insistence on tolerance and our emphasis on rules and laws are a poor substitute, more symptoms of our malaise rather than possible cures. But Nietzsche is something more than the pathologist of a dead or dying morality. He is also the champion of that sense of integrity that MacIntyre claims we have lost. The question is, "How is integrity possible in a society without an *ethos* or, in more positive terms, in a pluralist society with many *ethê*, some of them admittedly dubious?" Does it make sense in such as society to still speak of "excellence," or should we just award "achievement" and recognize limited accomplishments in cautiously defined subgroups and professions? Or should we rather express the atavistic urge to excellence with an intentionally obscure phrase: "will to power"?

Nietzsche's Problem

In Aristotle, two convening ideals made possible his powerful teleological vision: the unity of his community and the projected vision of the *telos* of man (which not incidentally coincided with the best images of his community). We no longer have that unified community—although those are not the grounds on which Nietzsche rejects bourgeois morality. (Indeed, sometimes it is the small-mindedness of small communities that he most violently reacts against.) It is not difficult to see Nietzsche's provocative ethics as precisely the expression of a rather distinctive if ill-circumscribed community, namely the community of disaffected academics and intellectuals, but this in not an *ethos* that Nietzsche could recognize as the basis for his rather extravagant claims for a new ethics. Nevertheless, Nietzsche, like Aristotle, held on to the vision of an overriding human *telos*, and enormous sense of human *potential*, a hunger for excellence that is ill-expressed by his monolithic expression, "will to power."

Depending on one's view of Aristotle (some rather priggish Oxford ethicists have called him a "prig"), this view of Nietzsche may or may not be considered another case of Anglo-American whitewash. After all, Aristotle may have retained some of the warrior virtues, but most of his virtues are distinctively those of the good citizen, concerned with justice and friendship and getting along together. There is little of the fire and ice that Nietzsche talks about, certainly no emphasis on cruelty and suffering. Aristotle was hardly the lonely wanderer in the mountains and desert whom Nietzsche sometimes resembled and celebrated in *Zarathustra*. However aristocratic they may be, Aristotle's virtues seem too genteel, too much in the spirit of party life to be comparable to Nietzsche's severe moral strictures (see Zarathustra's "party" in part IV). It would be an unforgivable historical mistake to call Aristotle's virtues "bourgeois," but, nevertheless, they surely lack the cutting edge of Nietzsche's pronouncements.

The problem, however, is that Nietzsche's affirmative instructions are often without substantial content. It is all well and good to talk about the glories of solitude, but Nietzsche's own letters and friendships show us that he himself lived by his friends, defined himself in terms of them. Zarathustra, Biblical bluster aside, spends most of his time looking for friends. "Who would want to live without them?" asked Aristotle rhetorically in his *Ethics*. Surely not Nietzsche. And he was, by all accounts, a good friend, an enthusiastic friend. And if he remained lonely, that is a matter for psychiatric, not ontological, diagnosis. As for the warrior spirit, the cutting edge of cruelty, the fire and ice, there is little evidence that we have that Nietzsche either displayed or admired them, Lou's description of the glint in his eyes notwithstanding. His own list of virtues included such Aristotelean traits as honesty, courage, generosity, and courtesy (*Daybreak* 556).[33] And, at the end, didn't he collapse while saving a horse from a beating?

One needn't ask whether Aristotle lived up to his own virtues. But Nietzsche leaves so much unsaid, and gives us so much hyperbolically, that an ad hominem hint is not beside the point. One can grasp the struggle with morality that is going on in the man, so readily expressed in the murderous language of adolescence, without confusing the rhetoric with the ideals. There are different warriors for different times. Achilles suited the *Iliad*. Our warrior today is Gandhi.

Nietzsche's problem is that he sees himself as a destroyer, not a reformer or a revisionist. ("On the Improvers of Mankind" in *Twilight of the Idols*, for example.)[34] He sees the Judeo-Christian tradition and the Morality that goes with it as a single historical entity, against which there is no clearly conceived alternative. Consequently, he gives us two very different prescriptions for our fate, which includes the moral collapse that has been so systematically described by MacIntyre.

First, he urges us to recapture a sense of "master" morality, a morality of nobility, insofar as this nobility is still possible, after two thousand years of Christianity. The war-torn pre*polis* world of the *Iliad* is gone, and it is never clear what Nietzsche intends to replace it with. Democracy and socialism have rendered the aristocratic virtues unacceptable, even where these coincide exactly with the good bourgeois virtues (courtesy, for instance). The foundation is gone; human equality has become an a priori truth. If "Christianity is Platonism for the masses," then democratic socialism is Christianity for the middle class.

That is on the one side—an impossible nostalgia, not unlike the American (and European) fantasy about the American West, "where men were men" (but were in fact unwashed and hungry refugees eking out a difficult living). But if there is no warrior *ethos* to which we can return, then what? "The creation of values!" Nietzsche says. But what is it to "create a value"? Not even Nietzsche suggests one—not even *one*! What he does is to remind us, again and again, of old and established values which can be used as an ethical Archimedean point, to topple the professions of a too abstract, too banal morality that fails to promote the virtues of character. He appeals to weakness of will (not by that name) and resentment—what could be more Christian vices? He charges us with hypocrisy—the tribute that even "immoralists" pay to virtue. He points out the cruelty of Tertullian and other Christian moralists. He chastises the Stoics for emulating wasteful nature. He attacks Spinoza for being too in love with "his own wisdom." He attacks Christianity as a whole as a "slave" morality, a "herd instinct" detrimental to the progress of the species as a whole. New values?

Ethics is an expression of an *ethos*. There is no such things as "creating new values" in Nietzsche's sense. It is not like declaring clam shells as currency and it is not, as in MacIntyre's good example, Kamehameha II of Hawaii declaring invalid the "taboos" whose function had long ago been forgotten. Nietzsche does not reject morals, only one version of Morality, which has as its instrument the universalizable principles formalized by Kant, the ancestries of which go all the way back to the Bible. But, as Scheler says in defense of Christianity, the diagnosis is not complete. Indeed, it would not be wrong (as Lou Salomé observed) to see Nietzsche as an old-fashioned moralist, disgusted with the world around him but unable to provide a satisfactory account of an alternative and unable to find a context in which an alternative could be properly cultivated.

None of this is to deny that Nietzsche is, as Kaufmann calls him, a moral revolutionary, or that he has an affirmative ethics. He is indeed after something new and important, even if it is also very old and something less than the creation of new values. He is, as MacIntyre puns, after virtues, even if he would prefer to think of them in Homeric rather than Aristotelean form. And in his writings and his letters, the focus of that alternative is as discernible as the larger concept of Morality he attacks. It is Aristotle's ethics of virtue, an ethics of practice instead of an ethics of principle, an ethics in which *character*, not duty or abstract poses of universal love, plays the primary role. "To give style to one's character. A rare art."[35] In that one sentence, Nietzsche sums up his own ethics far better than in whole books of abuse:

> One more word against Kant as a *Moralist*. A virtue must be *Our Own* invention, *Our* most necessary self-expression and self-defense; any other kind of virtue is a danger. . . . "Virtue," "duty," the "good in itself," the good which is impersonal and universally valid—chimeras and expressions of decline, of the final exhaustion of life, of the Chinese phase of Königsberg. The fundamental laws of self-preservation and growth demand the opposite—that everyone invent *his own* virtue, his *own* categorical imperative. A people perishes when it confuses *Its* duty with duty in general. . . . ANTI-Nature as instinct, German decadence as philosophy—*THAT IS KANT* (A 11).[36]

Notes

1. Walter Kaufmann, *Nietzsche: Philosopher, Psychologist, Antichrist*, 4th ed. (Princeton, N.J.: Princeton University Press, 1974).

2. Richard Schacht, *Nietzsche* (London: Routledge and Kegan-Paul, 1983).

3. David Allison, ed., *The New Nietzsche* (Columbus: Ohio University Press, 1980).

4. Lou Salomé (1882) quoted in Karl Jaspers's *Nietzsche* (Tucson: University of Arizona Press, 1965), pp. 37-B, and in R. C. Solomon, ed., *Nietzsche* (New York: Doubleday, 1963), p. 8.

5. Nietzsche, *The Will to Power*, trans. and ed. by Walter Kaufmann (New York: Random House, 1968). All references are to paragraph numbers.

6. Stanley Rosen, *Nihilism*. Cf. His more recent *G. W. F. Hegel: An Introduction to His Science of Wisdom* (New Haven, Conn.: Yale University Press, 1974).

7. Maurice Blanchot, "The Limits of Experience: Nihilism," *L'etretien infini*, reprinted in Allison, op. cit., pp. 121–28.

8. Alasdair MacIntyre, *After Virtue* (Notre Dame, Ind.: University of Notre Dame Press, 1981).

9. David Hume. *A Treatise of Human Nature* (Oxford: Oxford University Press, 1978), bk. II, esp. pp. 297ff.

10. G. W. F. Hegel, *The Phenomenology of Spirit*, trans. by A. W. Miller (Oxford: Oxford University Press, 1977). See esp. paras. 559–62 and Hegel's attack on the Enlightenment emphasis on "the Useful" ("an abomination" and "utterly detestable").

11. Nietzsche, *Twilight of the Idols*, trans., by Kaufmann in *The Portable Nietzsche* (New York: Viking, 1954), pp. 473–79 and 479–84.

12. See, for example, G. E. M. Anscombe in *Intention* (Oxford: Blackwell, 1957), esp. pp. 58–66, and John Cooper's rebuttal in his *Reason and Human Good in Aristotle* (Cambridge, Mass.: Havard University Press, 1975).

13. E.g., William Frankena, *Ethics*, 2d ed. (Englewood Cliffs, N.J.: Prentice-Hall, 1973), pp. 62–67.

14. The delightful use of this example is in MacIntyre, op. cit., contrasting descriptive reports of practices with prescriptive rules.

15. Immanuel Kant, *Grounding for the Metaphysics of Morals* (Indianapolis, Ind.: Hackett, 1983), pt. 1, p. 7.

16. Ibid, pp. 12.

17. E.g., "At first, I approached the modern world . . . *hopefully.* I understood . . . the philosophical pessimism of the nineteenth century as if it were the symptom of a greater strength of thought, of more daring courage, and of a more triumphant fullness of life. . . . What is romanticism? Every art and every philosophy may be considered a remedy and aid in the service of growing and struggling life, but there are two kinds of sufferers: first those who suffer from an *overfullness of life* . . . and then there are those who suffer from the *impoverishment of life.* . . . To this dual need of the *latter* corresponds all romanticism. . . .

The will to *eternalize* also requires a dual interpretation. First, it can come from gratitude and love. . . . But it can also be that tyrannic will (i.e. *ressentiment*) of one who is seriously ailing, struggling, and tortured" (*Gay Science* 370).

Cf. Novalis: "The world must be made more romantic. Then once more we shall discover its original meaning. To make something romantic . . . the lower self becomes identified with the higher self."

18. G. W. F. Hegel, *The Life of Jesus* (1795), trans. by Peter Fuss (Notre Dame, Ind.: University of Notre Dame Press, 1984).

19. Kant, op. cit. p. 12.

20. Kant, op. cit, and the second *Critique*, trans. by L. W. Beck (Indianapolis, Ind.: Bobbs-Merrill, 1956).

21. Nietzsche, *Beyond Good and Evil*, trans. by Kaufmann (New York: Random House, 1966). All references are to paragraph numbers.

22. Hegel, *System der Sittlichkeit* (1802) and *The Phenomenology*, pt. C (AA), ch. VI ("Spirit"), esp. paras. 439–50.

23. Karl Popper, *The Open Society and Its Enemies* (London: Routledge and Kegan-Paul, 1954); W. H. Walsh, *Hegel's Ethics* (New York: St. Martin's, 1969).

24. Edward O. Wilson toys with this argument, for example, in the infamous twenty-seventh chapter of his *Sociobiology* (Cambridge, Mass.: Harvard University Press, 1978).

25. Philippa Foot, "Nietzsche: The Revaluation of Values," in Solomon, ed., op. cit., pp. 156–68.

26. MacIntyre, op. cit., pp. 103ff.

27. Aristotle, *Nicomachean Ethics*, trans. by H. Rackham (Cambridge, Mass.: Harvard University Press, 1946), bk. 1, ch. ii.

28. Richard Hare, *Freedom and Reason* (Oxford: Clarendon, 1963), e.g., p. 172.

29. André Gide, *The Immoralist* (New York: Vintage, 1954).

30. Alexander Nehemas has completed one long-needed bit of empirical research in this regard: in *Beyond Good and Evil*, he has found that better than three-quarters of the candidates for *Übermensch* are writers. See his forthcoming *Nietzsche: Life as Literature* (Cambridge: Harvard University Press, 1986).

31. John Rawls, *A Theory of Justice* (Cambridge, Mass.: Harvard University Press, 1971).

32. "When the exceptional human being treats the mediocre more tenderly than himself and his peers, this is not mere courtesy of the heart—it is simply his duty." Nietzsche, *The Antichrist*, trans. by Kaufmann in *Portable Nietzsche*, op. cit., para. 57.

33. Nietzsche, *Daybreak*, trans. by R. J. Hollingdale (Cambridge, Mass.: Cambridge University Press, 1982). References are to paragraph numbers.

34. Nietzsche, *Twilight of the Idols*, trans. by Kaufmann in *Portable Nietzsche*, op. cit.

35. Nietzsche, *The Gay Science*, trans. by Kaufmann (New York: Random House, 1974), para. 290.

36. Nietzsche, *The Antichrist*, op. cit.

4

How One Becomes What One Is

Alexander Nehamas

People are always shouting they want to create a better future. It's not true.
The future is an apathetic void, of no interest to anyone. The past is full of life,
eager to irritate, provoke and insult us, tempt us to destroy or repaint it. The
only reason people want to be masters of the future is to change the past.

—Milan Kundera, *The Book of Laughter and Forgetting*

BEING AND BECOMING, according to Nietzsche, are not at all related as we
commonly suppose. "Becoming," he writes, "must be explained without
recourse to final intentions. . . . Becoming does not aim at a final state, does
not flow into 'being'."[1] One of his many criticisms of philosophers ("humans
have always been philosophers") is that they have turned away from what
changes and have only tried to understand what is: "But since nothing *is*, all
that was left to the philosopher as his 'world' was the imaginary."[2] His thinking is informed by his opposition to the very idea of a distinction between appearance and reality.[3] In "How the 'True World' Finally Became a Fable," one
of his most widely read passages, he concludes: "The true world—we have
abolished. What world remains? The apparent one perhaps? But no! With the
true world we have also abolished the apparent one."[4] The contrast itself is not
sensible: "The apparent world and the world invented by a lie—this is the antithesis"; and the pointlessness of the antithesis implies that "no shadow of a
right remains to speak here of appearance."[5]

Nietzsche does not simply attack the distinction between reality or things
in themselves on the one hand and appearance or phenomena on the other.

He also claims that this distinction is nothing but a projection onto the external world of our unjustified belief that the self is a substance, somehow set
over and above its thoughts, desires and actions. Language, he writes:

> everywhere . . . sees a doer and doing; it believes in will as *the* cause; it believes in
> the ego, in the ego as being, in the ego as substance, and it projects this faith in
> the ego-substance upon all things—only thereby does it first *create* the concept
> of a "thing" . . . the concept of being follows, and is a derivative of, the concept
> of ego.[6]

This is, to say the least, a very obscure view. Why should we suppose that a
particular construction of the self precedes, and is projected onto, our construction of the external world? Nietzsche should be particularly concerned
with this question since he consistently insists on the social nature of consciousness and therefore appears committed to the idea that the concepts of
self and object develop in parallel to each other. In *The Gay Science*, for example, Nietzsche offers what for his time may indeed have been "the perhaps
extravagant surmise . . . that consciousness has developed only under the pres-
sure of the need for communication" and connects this development with the
evolution of language.[7] In *The Will to Power*, to cite just one other instance, he
writes that consciousness

> is only a means of communication: it is evolved through social intercourse and
> with the view to the interests of social intercourse—"Intercourse" here under-
> stood to include the influences of the outer world and the reactions they compel
> on our side; also our effect upon the outer world.[8]

What concerns me on this occasion, however, is not Nietzsche's problematic "psychological derivation of the belief in things" itself. Rather, I want to
focus on the close analogy he finds to hold between what is true of the world
in general and what is true of the self in particular, independently of the question of which is modelled upon which. We have already seen him write that
"Becoming . . . does not flow into 'being'." But if this is so, how are we to account for that most haunting of his many haunting philosophical aphorisms,
the phrase "How one becomes what one is" (*Wie man wird, was man ist*),
which constitutes the subtitle of *Ecce Homo*, Nietzsche's intellectual autobiog-
raphy and, with ironic appropriateness, the last book he ever was to write?[9]

I

It could be, of course, that the phrase "How one becomes what one is" was
simply a very clever piece of language that happened to catch (as well it

might have) Nietzsche's passing fancy. But this is not true. The idea appears elsewhere in *Ecce Homo*,[10] and we can find it present in all the stages of his philosophical career. It appears as early as *Schopenhauer as Educator*, the third of Nietzsche's *Untimely Meditations*: "The man who would not belong to the mass needs only to cease being comfortable with himself; he should follow his conscience which shouts at him: 'Be yourself [*sei du selbst*]; you are not really all that which you do, think, and desire now'."[11] The formulation is simplified to an aphorism in *The Gay Science*: "What does your conscience say?—You must become who you are."[12] In the same book Nietzsche claims that, in contrast to "moralists," he and the sort of people with whom he belongs "want to become those we are."[13] Finally, in the late works, we find Zarathustra saying of himself: "*That* is what I am through and through: reeling, reeling in, raising up, raising, a raiser, cultivator, and disciplinarian, who once counseled himself, not for nothing: Become who you are! [*Werde, der du bist!*]"[14] In short, and as I shall try to show, this aphorism leads us if not to the center at least through the bulk of Nietzsche's thought.

As a consequence, in tracing its significance, we shall have to raise many more questions than we can answer. In addition, we shall be often confronted by the obstacles that commonly face such explorations of Nietzsche: on many occasions we shall find our path blocked by ideas that are at least seemingly inconsistent with our aphorism; and, just as we manage to interpret them appropriately, we shall find him denying them in directions that take us even farther afield.

We have already remarked on the problem posed for our aphorism by Nietzsche's view of the relation between becoming and being. But the interpretation of the phrase "Become who you are" is also made difficult by Nietzsche's vehement conviction that the very idea of the self as subject is itself an invention, that there is no such thing as the self. As he writes, for example, in *On the Genealogy of Morals*,

> there is no such substratum; there is no "being" behind doing, effecting, becoming: "the doer" is merely a fiction added to the deed—the deed is everything. The popular mind in fact doubles the deed; when it sees the lightning flash, it is the deed of a deed: it posits the same event first as cause and then a second time as its effect.[15]

In reducing the agent self to the totality of its actions, Nietzsche is applying his doctrine of the will to power, part of which consists in a general identification of every object in the world with the sum of its effects on every other thing.[16] This immediately raises the question of how we can determine which actions to group together as belonging to one self, the question of *whose* deed is the deed that is "everything." But even before we can turn to that, we are stopped by the following passage from *The Will to Power*:

> The "spirit," something that thinks—this conception is a second derivative of that false introspection which believes in "thinking": first an act is imagined which simply does not occur, "thinking," and secondly a subject-substratum in which every act of thinking, and nothing else, has its origin: that is to say, *both the deed and the doer are fictions*.[17]

Let us leave this further twist for later consideration. What we must do now is to see Nietzsche's original reduction of each subject to a set of actions in the context of his denial of the distinction between appearance and underlying reality: "What is appearance to me now?" he asks in *The Gay Science*; "Certainly not the opposite of some essence: what could I say about any essence except to name the attributes of its appearance!"[18] For this connection immediately blocks an obvious interpretation of the aphorism.

Such an interpretation would proceed along Freudian lines. We could try to identify the self that one is and that one must become with that set of thoughts and desires which, for whatever reason, have been repressed and remain hidden and which constitute the reality of which one's current self is the appearance. Such a view would allow for the reinterpretation of one's thoughts and desires as a means to realizing who one is. To that extent, I think, it would be congenial to Nietzsche, who wrote in *The Gay Science*: "There is no trick which enables us to turn a poor virtue into a rich and overflowing one; but we can reinterpret its poverty into a necessity so that it no longer offends us when we see it and we no longer sulk at fate on its account."[19] This passage raises questions about self-deception which we must also leave aside until later. The point I want to make now is that despite this parallel, the common or "vulgar" Freudian idea that the core of one's self is always there, formed to a great extent early on in life and waiting for some sort of liberation, is incompatible not only with Nietzsche's view of the self as fiction, but also with his attitude toward the question of the discovery of truth:

> "Truth" is . . . not something there, that might be found or discovered—but something that must be created and that gives a name to a process, or rather to a will to overcome that has in itself no end—introducing truth, as a *processus in infinitum*, an active determining—not a becoming conscious of something that is in itself firm and determined.[20]

In fact, Nietzsche goes so far as to write that he wants to "transform the belief 'it *is* thus and thus' into the will 'it shall become thus and thus.'"[21] In general, he vastly prefers to speak of creating rather than of discovering truth, and exactly the same holds of his attitude toward the self. We have seen him praise, in *The Gay Science*, those who want to become those they are: they are, he continues, "human beings who are new, unique, incomparable, who give themselves laws, who *create* themselves." Both the hero of *Thus Spoke Zarathustra* and his disciples are constantly described as "creators"; and the book revolves around the idea of creating one's own self or (what comes to the same thing) the *Übermensch*. Goethe was one of Nietzsche's few true heroes; and Nietzsche paid him his highest compliment when he wrote of him that "he created himself."[22]

Yet, again, we have the inevitable doubling. Despite his attack on the notion that there are antecedently existing things and truths, waiting to be discovered, despite his almost inordinate emphasis on the importance of "creating," Zarathustra at one point enigmatically says, "Some souls one will never discover, unless one invents them first,"[23] and expresses the same equivocal view when he tells his disciples that "you still want to create the world before which you can kneel."[24] and though Nietzsche writes that "the axioms of logic ... are ... a means for us to *create* reality," it still remains the case that "rational thought is interpretation according to a scheme that we cannot throw off."[25] Making and finding, creating and discovering, imposing laws and being constrained by them are involved in a complicated, almost compromising relationship.[26] It seems then that the self, even if it is to be discovered, must first be created. We are therefore faced with the question how that self can be what one is before it comes into being itself, before it is itself something that is. How could (and why should) that be one's proper self, and not some (or any) other? Why not, in particular, one's current self, which at least has over all others the advantage of existing?

Let us stop for a moment to notice that, however equivocal, Nietzsche's emphasis on the self's creation blocks another obvious interpretation of his aphorism. This interpretation would hold that to become what one is would be to actualize all the capacities for which one is inherently suited; it might be inaccurate but not positively misleading to call such an interpretation "Aristotelian."[27] Appealing to actuality and potentiality may account for some of the logical peculiarities of Nietzsche's phrase, since one (actually) is not what one (potentially) is. But this view faces two difficulties. The first is that if one actualizes one's capacities, one *has* become what one is; becoming has now ceased, it has "flowed into being" just in the sense that we have seen Nietzsche deny that this is possible. The second is that construing becoming as realizing inherent capacities makes the creation of the self be more like the uncovering of what is already there. Yet Nietzsche seems to be trying to undermine precisely the idea that there are antecedently existing possibilities grounded in the nature of things, even though (as on the view we are considering) we may not know in advance what they are. The problem therefore remains of explaining how a self that truly must be created and that does not appear in any way to exist can be considered as that which an individual is. Nietzsche's view, to which we keep returning, that becoming does not aim at a final state, constitutes yet another obstacle on our way. He holds that constant change characterizes the world at large: "If the motion of the world aimed at a final state, that state would have been reached. The sole fundamental fact, however, is that it does not aim at a final state."[28] And he holds that the same is also true of each individual. In *The Gay Science*, for example, he praises brief habits, which he describes as "an inestimable means for getting to know many things and states."[29] Later on in the same book he uses a magnificent simile involving will and wave, expressing his faith in the inevitability (and the ultimate value) of continual change and renewal:

> How greedily this wave approaches, as if it were after something! How it crawls with terrifying haste into the inmost nooks of this labyrinthine cliff! It seems that something of value, high value, must be hidden there.—And now it comes back, a little more slowly but still quite white with excitement; is it disappointed? Has it found what it looked for? Does it pretend to be disappointed?—But already another wave is approaching, still more greedily and savagely than the first, and its soul, too, seems to be full of secrets and the last to dig up treasures. Thus live waves—thus live we who will—more I shall not say.[30]

The idea of constant change is one of the central conceptions of *Thus Spoke Zarathustra*, where Nietzsche writes:

> All the permanent—that is only a parable. And the poets lie too much. . . . It is of time and becoming that the best parables should speak: let them be a praise and a justification of all impermanence . . . there must be much bitter dying in your life, you creators. Thus are you advocates and justifiers of all impermanence. To be the child who is newly born, the creator must also want to be the mother who gives birth.[31]

But if Nietzsche, as such passages suggest, advocates continual and interminable change, if, indeed, there is only becoming, what possible relation can there be between becoming and being? The most promising way to reach an answer to this question is to turn to an examination of his notion of being. Our hope will be that what Nietzsche understands by "being" may be unusual enough to avoid this apparent contradiction without, at the same time, lapsing into total eccentricity.

II

The first glimmer of an answer to the questions that have stopped us so far may appear through the final obstacle with which we have to contend. We have already seen that Nietzsche is convinced that the ego, construed as a metaphysical abiding subject, is a fiction. But also, as by now we might expect, he does not believe in the most elementary unity of the person as agent. Paradoxically, however, I think that his shocking and obscure breakdown of the assumed unity of the human personality may be the key to the solution of our problems. It may also be one of Nietzsche's great contributions to our understanding of the self and to our self-understanding.

Consider the breakdown first. As early as the second volume of *Human, All-Too-Human*, Nietzsche writes that the student of history is "happy, unlike the metaphysicians, to have in himself not one immortal soul but many mortal ones."[32] *The Gay Science* denies that consciousness constitutes "the unity of the organism."[33] The hypothesis that Nietzsche is merely denying the abiding of the self over time, as a number of modern philosophers have done, is disproved by the following radical and, for our purposes, crucial statement from *Beyond Good and Evil*:

> the belief that regards the soul as something indestructible, eternal, indivisible, as a monad, as an *atomon*: this belief ought to be expelled from science! Between ourselves, it is not at all necessary to get rid of "the soul" at the same time. . . . But the way is open for new versions and refinements of the soul-hypothesis; and such conceptions as "mortal soul", and "soul as subjective multiplicity", and "soul as social structure of the drives and affects" want henceforth to have citizens' rights in science.[34]

The idea of "the subject as multiplicity" is constantly discussed in *The Will to Power* where, among others, we find the following statement:

> The assumption of one single subject is perhaps unnecessary; perhaps it is just as permissible to assume a multiplicity of subjects, whose interaction and struggle is the basis of our thought and our consciousness in general? A kind of aristocracy of "cells" in which dominion resides? To be sure, an aristocracy of equals, used to ruling jointly and understanding how to command?[35]

This political metaphor for the self (which, despite Nietzsche's reputation, is at least more egalitarian than Plato's) can set us in the right direction for understanding the aphorism that concerns us. Nietzsche believes that we are not warranted in assuming *a priori* the unity of every thinking subject: unity in general is an idea of which he is deeply suspicious.[36] As Zarathustra says, "Evil I call it, and misanthropic—all this teaching of the One and the Plenum and the Unmoved and the Sated and the Permanent."[37] And yet (need we by now be surprised?) it is also Zarathustra who claims that "this is all my creating and striving, that I create and carry together into One what is fragment and riddle and dreadful accident" and that what he has taught his disciples is "my creating and striving, to create and carry together into One what in man is fragment and riddle and dreadful accident."[38]

Nietzsche's denial of the unity of the self follows, in my opinion, from his view that the acts of thinking and desiring (to take these as representative of the rest) are indissolubly connected with their contents, which are in turn essentially connected to other thoughts, desires and actions.[39] He holds, first, that the separation of the act from its content is illegitimate: "There is no such thing as 'willing'," he writes, "but only a willing *something*: one must not remove the aim from the total condition—as epistemologists do. 'Willing' as they understand it is as little a reality as 'thinking' is: it is pure ficiton."[40] It is this view, I think, which, in the face of his tremendous and ever-present emphasis on willing, also allows him to make the shockingly but only apparently incompatible statement that "there is no such thing as will."[41] His position on the nature of thinking is strictly parallel: "'Thinking', as epistemologists conceive it, simply does not occur; it is a quite arbitrary fiction, arrived at by selecting one element from the process and eliminating all the rest, an artificial arrangement for the purposes of intelligibilty."[42]

The considerations underlying Nietzsche's view must have been something like the following. We tend first to isolate the content of each thought and desire from that of all others; each mental act is supposed to intend a distinct mental content, whose nature is independent of the content of all another such acts. My thought that such-and-such is the case is *there* and remains what it is whatever I may come to think in the future: though it may turn out to be false, its significance is given and determined. Having isolated the contents of our mental acts from one another, we then separate the content of each act from the act that intends it. My thinking that such-and-such is the case is an episode which is taken to be distinct from what it is about. Having performed those two "abstractions," we are confronted with a set of similar entities, thoughts, that we then attribute to a subject which, since it performs all these qualitatively identical acts, we can safely assume to be unified.[43]

It seems to me that it is this view that underwrites Nietzsche's conviction that the deed is a fiction and the doer, "a second derivative." He appears to believe that we are tempted to take the self, without further thought, as one because we commonly fail to take the contents of our mental acts into account. But for him each "thing" is nothing more, and nothing less, than the sum of all its effects or features. Since it is nothing more than that sum, it is not clear that conflicting sets of features are capable of generating a single thing. But since it is nothing less, when we come to the case of the self, what we must attribute to each subject (what we must use to generate it) is not simply the sum of its mental acts considered in isolation.[44] Rather, we must attribute to it the sum of its acts along with their contents: each subject is constituted not simply by the fact *that* it thinks, wants and acts but also by *what* it thinks, wants and does. And once we admit contents, we also admit conflicts. What we think, want and do is seldom, if ever, a coherent set. Our thoughts contradict one another and contrast with our desires, which are themselves inconsistent and are belied, in turn, by our actions. Thus the unity of the self, which Nietzsche identifies with this set, is seriously undermined. Its unity, he seems to believe, is to be found (if it is to be found at all) in the unity and coherence of the contents of the acts performed by an organism. It is the unity of these effects that gives rise to the unity of the self, and not the other way around.

An immediate difficulty for this view seems to be caused by the fact that Nietzsche does not distinguish clearly between unity as coherence on the one hand and unity as numerical identity on the other. For it can be argued that even if the self is not coherent in an appropriate manner, it is still a single thing; in fact, it is only because the self is a single thing that it is at all sensible to be concerned with its unity. Even the idea that we are faced with conflicting, rather than merely with disparate, sets of thoughts and desires seems to depend on the assumption that these are the thoughts and desires of a single person.

We might think that we could avoid this difficulty if we argued that Nietzsche is in fact concerned with coherence and not with identity. But his identification of every thing with a set of effects results precisely in blurring this distinction, and prevents us from giving this answer. For since there is nothing above (or "behind") such sets of effects, it is not clear that Nietzsche can consistently hold that there is anything to the identity of each object above the unity of a set of effects. We have already seen him write that the subject is a multiplicity: but what is it that enables us to group some multiplicities together to form a subject and to distinguish them from others that constitute a different one?

At this point, the political metaphor for the self to which we have already appealed becomes important. On a very basic level, the identity that is necessary but not sufficient for the unity of the self is provided by the unity of the body. Nietzsche, we should notice, is consistent in holding that, like all unity, the unity of the body is not an absolute fact: "The evidence of the body reveals a tremendous multiplicity."[45] But this multiplicity is, in most circumstances, organized coherently; the needs and goals of the body are usually not in conflict with one another:

> The body and physiology the starting point: why?—we gain the correct idea of the nature of our subject-unity, namely as regents at the head of a communality (not as "souls" or "life forces"), also of the dependence of these regents upon the rule and of an order of rank and division of labor as the conditions that make possible the whole and its parts.[46]

Zarathustra, I think, makes the same point when he says of the body that it is "a plurality with one sense, a war and a peace, a herd and a shepherd."[47] Thus the coherence of the body's organization provides the common ground that allows conflicting mental states to be grouped together as belonging to a single subject. Particular thoughts, desires, actions, and their patterns, that is, character-traits, move the body in different directions, place it in different contexts, and can even be said to vie for its control. Dominant habits and character-traits, while they are dominant, assume the role of the subject; in terms of our metaphor, they assume the role of the leadership. It is such traits that speak with the voice of the self when they are manifested in action. Their own unity is what allows them to become the subject that, at least for a time, says "I." In the situation we are discussing, however, the leadership is not stable. Since different and often incompatible character-traits coexist in one body, different patterns assume the "regent's" role at different times. Thus we identify ourselves differently over time; and though the "I" always seems to refer to the same thing, the content of what it refers to does not remain the same, and may constantly be in the process of developing, sometimes toward greater unity.

Such unity, however, which is at best something to be hoped for, certainly cannot be presupposed; phenomena like *akrasia* and self-deception, not to mention everyday inconsistency, raise serious questions about it. In a recent discussion of these phenomena, Amélie Rorty, too, finds a political metaphor for the self illuminating. She urges that we think of the self as a medieval city, with many semi-independent neighborhoods and no strong central administration. She suggests that "we can regard the agent self as a loose configuration of habits, habits of thought and perception and motivation and action, acquired at different stages, in the service of different ends."[48] The unity of the self, which thus also constitutes its identity, is not something given, but something acquired; not a beginning, but a goal. And of such unity, which is essentially a matter of degree and which comes close to constituting a regulative principle, Nietzsche is not at all suspicious. It lies behind his earlier positive comments on "the One" and he actively wants to promote it. It is precisely its absence that he deplores when he writes of his contemporaries that "with the characters of the past written all over you, and these characters in turn painted over with new characters: thus have you concealed yourselves perfectly from all interpreters of characters."[49]

Nietzsche's view, after all, bears remarkable similarities to Plato's division of the soul in the *Republic*, which also faces difficulties in locating the agent. Nietzsche, of course, envisages a much more complicated division than Plato's and does not accept Plato's view that ultimately there are three (and only three) independent sources of human motivation. In addition, Nietzsche would deny Plato's preference of reason as the dominant source: what habits and character-traits are to rule is for him an open question, which does not necessarily receive an answer dictated by moral considerations.

Now the dominant traits can completely disregard their competitors and refuse even to acknowledge their existence: this constitutes a case of self-deception. Or they can acknowledge them, try to bring them in line with their own evaluations, and fail: this constitutes a case of *akrasia*. Or again they could try and manage in some way to incorporate them, changing both their opponents and themselves in the process and thus taking one step toward the integration of the personality which, in the ideal case, constitutes the unity we are pursuing:

> No subject "atoms." The sphere of a subject constantly growing or decreasing, the center of the system constantly shifting: in cases where it cannot organize the appropriate mass, it breaks into two parts. On the other hand, it can transform a weaker subject into its functionary without destroying it, and to a certain extent form a new unity with it. No "substance," rather something that in itself strives after greater strength, and that wants to "preserve" itself only indirectly (it wants to *surpass* itself—).[50]

This passage makes it clear that at least in some cases where Nietzsche speaks of mastery and power, he is concerned with mastery and power over oneself, with habits and character-traits competing for the domination of a single person. This is one of the reasons why I think that at least the primary (though not necessarily the only) object of the will to power is one's own self.[51] But more importantly, in this passage we find the suggestion that, as our metaphor has led us to expect, what says "I" is not the same at all times. We also see that the process of dominating (or, notice, of creating) the individual, the unity that concerns us, is a matter of incorporating more and more character-traits under a constantly expanding and, in the process, evolving rubric. It begins to appear that the distinction between being and becoming may be not quite as absolute as we originally feared.

Nietzsche often criticized the educational practices of his time. In his view, they encouraged people to want to develop in all directions instead of showing them how to fashion themselves, even by eliminating some beliefs and desires, into true individuals.[52] The project of becoming an individual with a unified set of features requires (a favorite term with him) hardness toward oneself: its contrary, "tolerance toward oneself, permits several convictions, and they get along with each other: they are careful, like all the rest of the world, not to compromise themselves."[53] But though Nietzsche envisages that certain character-traits may have to be eliminated if one is to achieve unity, he does not in any way consider that they are to be disowned. This is a crucial point, for it shows that the unity we are looking for is not a final stage which follows upon others, but the total organization of everything that one thinks, wants and does.

It is, in fact, one of Nietzsche's most strongly held views that everything one does is equally essential to who one is. This is another consequence of his re-duction of all objects to the sum-total of their effects on the world. He believes that everything that I have ever done has been instrumental to my being who I am today. And even if today there are actions I would not ever repeat, even if there are character-traits I am grateful to have left behind, I would not have my current preferences had I not had those other preferences at an earlier time: "The most recent history of an action relates to this action: but further back lies a pre-history which covers a wider field: the individual action is at the same time a part of a much more extensive, later fact. The briefer and the more extensive processes are not separated."[54]

It begins to seem, then, that Nietzsche has in mind not a final state of being which follows upon and replaces an earlier process of becoming. Rather, he is thinking of a continual process of greater integration of one's character-traits, habits and patterns of interaction with the world. This process can, in a sense, also reach backward and integrate into the personality even a discarded char-acteristic by showing its necessity for one's later development. The complex-ity of this process is exhibited in the following passage, which I will have to quote at length:

> *One thing is needful.*—To "give style" to one's character—a great and rare art! It is practiced by those who survey all the strengths and weaknesses of their nature and then fit them into an artistic plan until every one of them appears as art and reason and even weaknesses delight the eye. Here a large mass of second nature has been added; there a piece of original nature has been removed—both times through long practice and daily work at it. Here the ugly that could not be re-moved is concealed; there it has been reinterpreted and made sublime. Much that is vague and resisted shaping has been saved and exploited for distant views; it is meant to beckon toward the far and immeasurable. In the end, when the work is finished, it becomes evident how the constraint of a single taste governed and formed everything large and small. Whether this taste was good or bad is less important than one might suppose, if only it was a single taste![55]

Such a conception of personal unity faces a number of difficulties. Foremost among these, as we have already remarked, is the problem of self-deception. For one way to "give style" to one's character, to constrain it by a single taste, is sim-ply to deny the existence, force, or significance of antithetical tastes and traits, and to consider only part of oneself as the whole. Nietzsche seems to me to be aware of this problem, as is shown by his distinction between the two sorts of people who have faith in themselves. Some, he writes, have it precisely because they refuse to look: "What would they behold if they could see to the bottom of themselves!"; the others have to acquire it, and are faced with it as a problem: "Everything good, fine, or great they do is first of all an argument against the skeptic inside them."[56] The possibility of self-deception is always there; unity can always be achieved simply by refusing to acknowledge an existing multiplicity.

To be accurate, however, we should not say that unity can be achieved in this way: only the feeling of unity can be secured by this process. One can think that one has completed the arduous task described by the passage we are discussing without having actually succeeded. The distinction can be made because, after all, the notions of style and of character are essentially public. Nietzsche, of course, emphasizes the importance of each individual's evaluating itself by its own standards. Nevertheless, especially since he does not believe that self-knowledge is in any way privileged, such questions are finally decided from the outside. This outside may consist of a very select public (including oneself), of an audience which perhaps does not yet exist, but the distinction between the feeling and the fact of unity is to be pressed and maintained. Zarathustra taunts the sun when he asks what its happiness would be were it not for those for whom it shines.[57] Similarly, it takes observers for the unity to be manifest and therefore there. At the end of this essay we will see that these observers may have to be readers—and qualified readers at that.

A clear sign that unity is lacking is what has been called "weakness of will," akrasia, the inability to act on one's preferred judgment; this is an indication that competing habits, patterns of valuation and modes of perception are at work within the same individual, if one wants to use this term at all at such a stage. Nietzsche, of course, is notorious for his attacks on the notion of the freedom of the will; but he is no less opposed, naturally, to the notion of the compelled or unfree will, which he characterizes as "mythology." "In real life," he continues, "it is only a matter of strong and weak wills."[58] Yet at the same time, as we might also by now expect, Zarathustra can mention and praise occasions "where necessity was freedom itself."[59] And in *The Twilight of the Idols* we read that "peace of soul" can be either a mind becalmed, an empty self-satisfaction, or, on the contrary, "the expression of maturity and mastery in the midst of doing, creating, working, and willing—calm breathing, attained 'freedom of the will'."[60]

Freedom of the will so construed is the state in which there is no internal division in a person's preference-schemes, where desire follows thought and action follows desire with no effort and no struggle, where the distinction between constraint and choice might be thought to disappear. This state, which Nietzsche of course envisages as an almost impossible ideal, is remarkably similar to the condition in which Socrates, in Plato's early dialogues, thought every single agent actually to be and which thus led him to deny the very possibility of *akrasia*. Unfortunately, I cannot pursue here the connection between this suggestive analogy of attitude and Nietzsche's deeply ambivalent feelings toward Socrates. I must return instead to the subject at hand and point out that, again, the feeling that one is in this state can be produced by self-deception and that the problems this raises cannot be avoided. But Nietzsche is clear on the extraordinary difficulty with which such states can be reached. Success can again be described in the terms of our political metaphor: "*L'effet c'est moi*: what happens here is what happens in every well-constructed and happy commonwealth; namely, the governing class identifies itself with the success of the commonwealth."[61] What this involves is a maximization of diversity and a minimization of discord. The passage on character from *The Gay Science* suggests this point and so does the following note from *The Will to Power*: "The highest man would have the highest multiplicity of drives, in the relatively greater strength that can be endured. Indeed, where the plant 'man' shows himself strongest one finds instincts that conflict powerfully . . . but are controlled."[62] It is just because of this controlled multiplicity that Goethe, who according to Nietzsche bore all the conflicting tendencies of his century within him, became his great hero: "What he wanted was totality . . . he disciplined himself to wholeness, he *created* himself."[63]

This self-creation thus appears to be the creation, or imposition, of a higher-order accord among one's lower-order thoughts, desires and actions. It is the development of the ability or the willingness to accept responsibility for everything that one has done and to admit what is in fact the case, that everything that one has done actually constitutes who one is.

From one point of view, this willingness is a new character-trait, a new state of development that is reached at some time and that replaces a previous state, during which one would have been unwilling to acknowledge all one's doings as one's own. From another point of view, however, to reach such a state is not at all like what occurs when one specific character-trait replaces another, when courage replaces cowardice, or magnificence, miserliness. The self-creation Nietzsche has in mind involves the acceptance of everything one has done and, in the ideal case, its harmonization in a coherent whole. Becoming courageous involves avoiding all the cowardly sorts of actions in which one may have previously engaged and pursuing a new sort instead. Yet no specific pattern of behavior needs to be abandoned, or pursued, simply because one realizes that all one's actions are one's own. What, if anything, changes depends on what patterns or coherence already exist and what new ones one might want to establish. But because further change is always possible, Nietzsche's conception of self-creation must also be contrasted to the realization, or decision, of many of us that our character has actually developed enough and that it is neither necessary nor desirable to change in any further respects. As such, it shows itself not to constitute a static episode, a final goal which, once attained, forecloses the possibility of further change and development.

For one thing, it is not clear that such an "episode" can actually occur, that it does not represent, as we have said, a regulative principle. If there were a clear sense in which our thoughts, desires, actions and their patterns could be counted, then we might be able to succeed in fitting "all" of them together. Yet how our mental acts actually fit with one another clearly has a bearing on how they are counted. And this is also suggested by Nietzsche's own view that the contents of our mental acts are indissolubly connected together. For to reinterpret a thought or an action and thus to construe it, for example, as only part of a longer, "more extensive" process, as only part of a single mental act after all, has exactly the same consequence.

More importantly, however, the fact is that as long as one is alive one always encounters unforeseen situations and one keeps performing new actions and having new thoughts and desires. The occurrence of such mental acts can always impose the need to reinterpret, to reorganize, or even to abandon earlier ones in their light. Nevertheless, the exhortation of *The Will to Power* "to revolve about oneself; no desire to become 'better' or in any way other"[64] is, I think, quite compatible with the continuous development that we have been discussing. To desire to remain oneself in this context is not so much to want one's specific character-traits to remain constant: the same passage speaks of "multiplicity of character considered and exploited as an advantage." Rather, it is to desire to appropriate and to reorganize as one's own all that one has (or at least knows to have) done and to engage in organizing it into a single unified whole. It is to be able to accept all such things, good or evil, as things one has done. It is not to cultivate stable character-traits that may make one's range of reactions predictable and, in new situations, unsurprising. Rather, it is to develop the flexibility to be able to use whatever one has done, does, or will do as elements in a constantly changing, never-completed whole. Since such a whole is always in the process of incorporating new material and since the success of this incorporation may always involve the reinterpretation of older material, none of its elements need remain unchanged. Zarathustra's distrust of unity—his exhortations to avoid goals or stability—is his aversion to the stability of specific character-traits, parallel to the praise of "brief habits" we found in *The Gay Science*. By contrast, his proud description of his own teaching as carrying "into One what in man is fragment and riddle and dreadful accident" refers to the continual, never-ending integration, and reinterpretation, of such brief habits.

The final mark of this integration, its limiting case, is provided by the test involved in the thought of the eternal recurrence. This mark is the desire to do exactly what one has already done in this life if one were to live again: " 'Was *that* life?' I want to say to death," Zarathustra is made to exclaim " 'Well then! Once more!' "[65] Since Nietzsche considers the subject as the sum of its interrelated effects, the opportunity to live again would necessarily involve the exact repetition of the very same events; otherwise, there would be no reason to suppose that it was the same subject that was living again. Thus the question is not whether one would or would not do the same things again; in this matter, there is no room for choice. The question is only whether one would *want* to do the same things all over again and thus be willing to acknowledge all one's doings as one's own.[66]

III

It may finally begin to appear that becoming and being are related in a way that does not make nonsense of Nietzsche's imperative to "Become who you are." To be who one is, on the view we have been developing, is to be engaged in the constantly continuing and continually broadening process of appropriation we have been discussing, to enlarge one's capacity for responsibility for oneself which Nietzsche calls "freedom."[67] He describes as the greatest will to power the desire "to impose upon becoming the character of being" and considers the idea "that everything recurs [as] the closest approximation of a world of becoming to a world of being."[68] And the eternal recurrence, as we have taken it, is compatible with continued development. Its significance consists in one's ability to want at some point, and in the ideal case at every point, to go through once again and "innumerable times more" what one has gone through already. Such a desire presupposes, in the limiting case, that what one has done has been assembled into a whole so unified that nothing can be subtracted without that whole's coming down along with it. Being, for Nietzsche, is that which one does not *want* to be otherwise.

What one is then, is just what one becomes. Nietzsche's aphorism is an injunction to want to become what one becomes, not to want anything about it, about oneself, to be different. To become what one is, therefore, is not to reach a specific new state—it is not, as I have tried to argue, to reach a state at all. It is to identify oneself with all of one's actions, to see that everything one does (becomes) is what one is. In the ideal case, it is also to fit all this into a *coherent* whole, and to want to be everything that one is: it is to give style to one's character; to be, if you will allow me, becoming.

The idea of giving style to one's character brings us back to Nietzsche's view in section 290 of *The Gay Science* that to have a single character ("taste") may be more important than the question whether this character is good or bad. This idea, in turn, which is quite common in Nietzsche, raises the notorious problem of his "immoralism," his virulent contempt for traditional moral virtue and his alleged praise of cruelty and of the exploitation of the "weak" by the "strong." I can only make two brief sets of comments about this very complex issue on this occasion; the second set will bring me to the concluding part of this essay.

We should notice first that despite his glorification of selfishness, Nietzsche once again is equally serious in denying the very antithesis between egoism and altruism. He dreams, in a perhaps utopian manner, of "some future, when, owing to continual adaptation, egoism will at the same time be altruism," when love and respect for others may just be love and respect for oneself: "Finally, one grasps that altruistic actions are only a species of egoistic actions—and that the degree to which one loves, spends oneself, proves the degree of individual power and personality."[69] Furthermore, the crude idea that Nietzsche's immoralism and the doctrine of the will to power are simply licenses to mindless cruelty is undermined by his view that such cruelty, though it has certainly been practiced by people on one another and will continue to be practiced in the future, is only the coarsest expression of what he has in mind. In fact, he thinks that its net effect may be the opposite of its intent:

> Every living thing reaches out as far from itself with its force as it can, and overwhelms what is weaker: thus it takes pleasure in itself. The increasing "humanizing" of this tendency consists in this, that there is an ever subtler sense of how hard it is really to incorporate another: while a crude injury done him certainly demonstrates our power over him, it at the same time estranges his will from us even more—and thus makes him less easy to subjugate.[70]

We have already seen that such "subjugation" can result in a new alliance, a new unity, even a new self.[71] Since the self is not an abiding substance, its incorporating a new entity "without destroying it" can well result in a change of both the incorporated object and the incorporating subject. Nietzsche's ominous metaphors can, in the final analysis, be applied even to the behavior of a powerful and influential teacher.

I now want to suggest that what Nietzsche says about the importance of character in itself, independently of whether it is the character of a good or a bad person, should not be dismissed out of hand. I am not sure of the proper word in this context, and I use this one with some misgivings, but it seems to me that there is something admirable in the very fact that one has character, that one has style. This does not imply that merely having character overrides all other considerations and justifies any sort of behavior; this is neither true, nor is it asserted by the passage we are discussing. But the point does introduce into our evaluation of agents a more formal quality than simply the content of their actions. It introduces, as one consideration, the question whether their actions, whatever their content, make up a personality. This seems to me a sensible consideration and one, moreover, to which we often appeal in our everyday dealings with each other.

It is not clear to me that a consistently and irredeemably vicious person does in fact have a character; the sort of agent Aristotle calls "bestial" probably does not.[72] In some way there is something inherently praiseworthy in having character or style that does prevent extreme cases of vice from being praised even in the formal sense we have discussed. Perhaps this is simply due to the fact that the viciousness of such agents totally overwhelms whatever praise we might otherwise be disposed to give them. Probably, however, the matter is more complicated. The existence of character may not be quite as independent of the quality of the actions of which it constitutes the pattern: consistency may not in itself be a condition sufficient for its presence. Perhaps, to appeal to another Aristotelian idea, some sort of moderation in action (though not necessarily the exact mean necessary for virtue) may be in the long run necessary for the possession of character. Nietzsche, in any case, would attribute character to all sorts of agents and would praise them on its account even if their quality were seriously objectionable from a moral point of view.

If now we ask ourselves when it is that we feel absolutely free to admire characters who are (or who, in the nature of the case, would be if they existed) awful people, the answer is clear: we do so in the case of literature. Though we sometimes may find an actual immoral agent worthy of admiration on account of some other quality that may overshadow that agent's objectionable features, our admiration is bound to be most often mixed. The best argument for Nietzsche's view of the importance of character is provided by the great literary villains, characters like Richard III (in Shakespeare's version), Fagin, Fyodor Karamazov, Charlus. In their cases, we can place our moral scruples in the background. Our main object of concern with them becomes their overall manner of what they do, the very structure of their minds, and not primarily the contents of their actions. Here, we can admire without reservations.

Why did Nietzsche take this formalist approach to character? As a historical hypothesis, I offer the view that he developed his attitude toward character and the self in general, as he did in many other cases as well, by considering literature as his primary model and generalizing from it.[73] What is essential to literary characters is their organization; the quality of their actions is secondary. In the ideal case, absolutely everything a character does is equally essential to it; characters are supposed to be constructed so that their every feature supports and is supported by every other one. In the limiting case of the perfect character, no change is possible without corresponding changes, in order to preserve coherence, in every other features; and the net result is, necessarily, a different character. In connection with literary characters and with the works to which they belong, the more so the better they are; taking one part away may always result in the destruction of the whole. This, we have seen, is presupposed by the thought of the eternal recurrence as a test for the ideal life. My suggestion is that Nietzsche came to hold this view at least partly because his thinking so often concerned literary models.

It could be argued that our admiration of villainous or even inconsistent characters, who *can* be consistently depicted, is not directed at those characters themselves, but at the authors who have constructed them, and that the generalization from literature to life is quite illegitimate. But we should notice that when it comes to life, the "character" and the "author" are one and the same, and admiring the one cannot be distinguished from admiring the other. This is also the reason, I suspect, that though inconsistent characters *can* be admired in literature, they cannot be admired in life. In life, we want to say, there is no room for the distinction between the creator and the creature.[74] Though not perhaps in the manner this objection suggested, the parallel between literature and life is far from perfect.

Nietzsche, however, always depended on artistic and literary models for understanding the world and this accounts, in my opinion, for some of the most original and some of the most peculiar features of his thought. As early as *The Birth of Tragedy* he sees Dionysus reborn in the person of Wagner and in the new artwork by means of a process which is the exact opposite of what he took as the dissolution of classical antiquity.[75] But as Paul de Man has written, "Passages of this kind are valueless as arguments, since they assume that the actual events in history are founded in formal symmetries easy enough to achieve in pictorial, musical, or poetic fictions, but that can never predict the occurrence of a historical event."[76] Ronald Hayman has shown that Nietzsche, a compulsive letter-writer, preferred what in his time still was a literary genre in its own right to conversation and personal contact as a means of communication even with his close firends.[77] Often enough, we find Nietzsche urging that we fashion our lives in the way artists fashion their works: ". . . we should learn from artists while being wiser than they are in other matters. For with them this subtle power [of arranging things and of making them beautiful] usually comes to an end where art ends and life begins; but we want to be the poets of our life—first of all in the smallest, most everyday matters."[78] Similarly, he finds the peace of soul which we have seen him call "attained freedom of will" primarily in artists, who "seem to have more sensitive noses in these matters, knowing only too well that precisely when they no longer do something 'voluntarily' but do everything of necessity, their feeling of freedom, subtlety, full power, of creative placing, disposing and forming reaches its peak—in short, that necessity and 'freedom of will' then become one in them."[79]

How does then one achieve the perfect unity which we have seen Nietzsche urge throughout this essay, the unity which is primarily possessed by perfect literary character? How does one become both a literary character who, unlike either Charlus or Alyosha Karamazov, really exists, and also that character's very author?

One way of trying to achieve this perhaps impossible goal, I think, is to write a great number of good books that exhibit great apparent inconsistency but that also can be seen as deeply continuous with one another when they are studied carefully. At the end of this enterprise, one can even write a book about those books that shows how they fit together, how a single figure emerges out of them, how even the most damaging inconsistencies are finally necessary for that figure, or character or author or person (the word almost does not matter in this context) to emerge fully through them. Earlier, Zarathustra had claimed, "What returns, what finally comes home to me, is my own self and what of myself has long been in strange lands and scattered among all things and accidents."[80] Now Nietzsche writes of his *Untimely Meditations*, three of which concern important historical figures and one, history itself: ". . . at bottom they speak only of me. . . . *Wagner in Bayreuth* is a vision of my future, while in *Schopenhauer as Educator* my innermost history, my *becoming*, is inscribed."[81] In *The Gay Science* we had read that "now something that you formerly loved . . . strikes you as an error. . . . But perhaps this error was as necessary for you then, when you were still a different person—you are always a different person—as all your present 'truth'."[82] Now Nietzsche writes of *Schopenhauer as Educator*:

> Considering that in those days I practiced the scholar's craft, and perhaps knew something about this craft, the harsh psychology of the scholar that suddenly emerges in this essay is of some significance; it expresses the *feeling of distance*, the profound assurance about what could be my task and what could only be means, *entr'acte* and minor works. It shows my prudence that I was many things and in many places in order to be able to become one thing—to be able to attain one thing. I *had* to be a scholar, too, for some time.[83]

One way then to become one thing, one's own character, or what one is, is to write *Ecce Homo* and even to subtitle it "How One Becomes What One Is." It is to write this self-referential work, in which Nietzsche can be said to invent or perhaps to discover himself, and in which the character who speaks to us is the author who has created him and who is in turn a character created by or implicit in all the books written by the author who is writing this one.

Could this ever be a successful enterprise? No one has managed to bring literature closer to life than Nietzsche, yet the two refuse to become one, and thus his own ideal of unity may ultimately fail. Even if one insisted that more than any other philosopher Nietzsche can be identified with his texts, his texts may be all there is to him as a philosopher, but not as a person. To insist on that identification would be to do just what he so passionately argued against, to take part of him as essential and part of him as accidental. The unity he is after shows itself once more to be impossible to capture in reality. *Ecce Homo* leaves great parts of his life undiscussed and, unfortunately for him, his life did not end with it, but twelve miserable years later. To make a unified character out of all one has done, as Nietzsche wanted, would involve us in the vicious enterprise of writing our autobiographies as we lived our lives, and writing about that, and writing about writing about that. . . . And at some point, we would inevitably have to end. But, as he had written long before his own end, "Not every end is a goal. A melody's end is not its goal; nevertheless, so long as the melody has not reached its end, it also has not reached its goal. A parable."[84] This comes as close to explicating the aphorism which has occupied us and to expressing Nietzsche's attitude toward the relationship between art and the world as anything he ever wrote. But the doubt remains whether any melody, however complicated, could ever be a model a life (which is not to say a biography) can imitate.

Notes

An early version of this essay was prepared for the Chapel Hill Philosophy Colloquium in October, 1981. Richard Schacht's comments on that occasion, along with those of other friends and colleagues at other institutions, led to numerous improvements. The assistance of the readers of *The Philosophical Review* was also very valuable.

1. Friedrich Nietzsche, *Werke: Kritische Gesamtausgabe* (KGW), ed. by Giorgio Colli and Mazzino Montinari (Berlin: Walter de Gruyter, 1967 onward), VIII 2, p. 277. English translation in *The Will to Power* (WP), by Walter Kaufmann and R. J. Hollingdale (New York: Vintage Press, 1968), sec. 708.

2. KGW, VIII 2, p. 252; WP, sec. 570.

3. It does not, however, reach as far back as *The Birth of Tragedy* (BT), where Nietzsche writes that "the contrast between this real truth of nature and the lie of culture that poses as if it were the only reality is similar to that between the eternal core of things, the thing-in-itself, and the whole world of appearances" (sec. 19; KGW, III 1, pp. 54–55). English translation by Walter Kaufmann in *The Basic Writings of Nietzsche* (New York: Random House, 1968), p. 61. I am not yet convinced by the otherwise brilliant attempt of Paul de Man to show that the book's rhetoric undermines the distinction its content sets up; cf. *Allegories of Reading* (New Haven, Conn.: Yale University Press, 1980), pp. 79–102.

4. KGW, VI 3, p. 75. English translation, *The Twilight of the Idols* (TI) by Walter Kaufmann in *The Portable Nietzsche* (New York: Viking Press, 1954), p. 486.

5. KGW, VIII 3, p. 111; WP, sec. 461. Cf. KGW, VIII 3, p. 163; WP. sec., 567. Cp., "The antithesis of the apparent world and the true world is reduced to the antithesis 'world' and 'nothing'" (ibid.).

6. KGW, VI 3, p. 71; TI, "'Reason' in Philosophy," p. 483. Some relevant passages are KGW, VII 1, p. 193; VIII 2, p. 131; VIII 1, pp. 321–22; VIII 2, pp. 47–50; WP, secs. 473, 485, 519, 552.

7. KGW, V2, pp. 272–73. English translation by Walter Kaufmann in *The Gay Science* (New York: Vintage Press, 1974), sec. 374 (GS).

8. KGW, VIII 2, pp. 309–10; WP, sec. 524. It might be objected on Nietzsche's behalf that one should take into account his view that only a small part of our thinking is conscious; cf. GS, sec. 354, and KGW, VI 2, p. 11 (English translation by Walter Kaufmann, *Beyond Good and Evil* [BGE], sec. 3, collected in *The Basic Writings of Nietzsche*). Accordingly, the objection would continue, though *consciousness* develops along with our concepts of the external world, our belief in the ego as "substance" may already be part of our unconscious, "instinctive" thinking. But Nietzsche, it seems to me, thinks of instinctive thinking and acting (which he often considers to be goals to be achieved) as modes which specifically preclude our conscious differentiation between subject and object, doer and deed; cf., for example, KGW, VIII 3, p. 119; WP, sec. 423. Such instinctive action, with its attendant identification of agent and effect, is what Zarathustra has in mind when he urges his disciples to become such "that your self be in your deed as the mother is in her child" (KGW, VI 1, p. 119); English translation of *Thus Spoke Zarathustra* (Z) by Walter Kaufmann in *The Portable Nietzsche*, II 5. The same point is suggested by the important section 213 of BGE, KGW VI 2, pp. 151–52.

9. Nietzsche began writing *Ecce Homo* (EH) on his fourty-fourth birthday, October 15, 1888, and finished it on November 4 of that year. During that time, and before his collapse in January, 1889, he also managed to put together *Nietzsche Contra Wagner* and his *Dionysos-Dithyramben*, but both works consisted of pieces already published elsewhere and involved no new writing.

10. KGW, VI 3, pp. 291, 317–19. See Walter Kaufmann's translation in *Basic Writings of Nietzsche*, pp. 709–10, 737–39. R. J. Hollingdale gives some background material in his introduction to his own translation of the work (Harmondsworth, U.K.: Penguin Books, 1979), pp. 14–15.

11. KGW, III 1, p. 334. Quoted from Walter Kaufmann, *Nietzsche: Philosopher, Psychologist, Antichrist* (Princeton, N.J.: Princeton University Press, 4th., 1974), p. 158. Nietzsche had been fascinated by this idea since at least 1867, as a letter of his to Rohde indicates. He derived it from Pindar's Second Pythian Ode, line 73: *genoi'hoios essi mathōn*, having dropped, along with the last word, Pindar's reference to learning and knowledge, and his probable reference to the art of kingship. For a recent discussion of this crucial and difficult passage see Erich Thummer, "Die Zweite Pythische Ode Pindars," *Rheinisches Museum für Philologie* 115 (1972), pp. 293–307.

12. KGW, V 2, p. 197; GS, sec. 270. Kaufmann's translation, "You shall become the person you are," misses the imperative force of the German "*Du sollst der werden, der du bist.*" One might also try to use the biblical "Thou shalt," which is more appropriate in this context.

13. KGW, V 2, p. 243; GS, sec. 335.

14. KGW, VI 1, p. 293; Z, IV 1.

15. KGW, VI 2, p. 293. English translation by Walter Kaufmann in *The Basic Writings of Nietzsche*, I. 13. This idea informs *The Twilight of the Idols*, and appears in many of the notes collected in *The Will to Power*, where it is often discussed in connection with the image of the lightning; cf. secs. 481–92, 531, 548–49, 551–52, 631–34.

16. Cf., for example, WP, secs. 553–69, most notes dating between 1885 and 1888. I have discussed this issue (though much remains to be said about it still) in "The Eternal Recurrence," *Philosophical Review* 89 (1980), pp. 331–56.

17. KGW, VIII 2, p. 296; WP, sec. 477. A similar point is made in connection with willing in KGW, VIII 2, p. 296; WP, sec. 668. A further complication is introduced in KGW, VIII 3, pp. 286–87; WP, sec. 675.

18. KGW, V 2, p. 91; GS, sec. 54. The passage suggests that the distinction between appearance and reality often is motivated by an unwillingness to acknowledge the inconsistency of the object of one's inquiry.

19. KGW, V 2, p. 63; GS, sec. 17.

20. KGW, VIII 2, p. 49; WP, sec. 552. Nietzsche's approach also disposes of the following objection, raised by J. P. Stern, *A Study of Nietzsche* (Cambridge: Cambridge University Press, 1979), p. 116. Stern quotes the statement, "Your true self . . . lies immeasurably above that which you usually take to be your self" from the first paragraph of *Schopenhauer as Educator* (KGW, III 1, p. 334). He then identifies the "usual" self with "the social . . . and therefore inauthentic self" and asks: "But is it not equally possible that 'your true self' may lie immeasurably below 'your usual self', and that society, its conventions and laws, may mercifully prevent its realization?" But we have seen that Nietzsche does not believe that an asocial self or a self independent of relations to other selves exists and that therefore such a self (depending on one's sympathies) should or should not be repressed. For Nietzsche, there is nothing there to be either repressed or liberated. Cf. Richard Rorty, who (in "Beyond Nietzsche and Marx," *London Review of Books*, vol. 3, 19/2–4/3 1981, p. 6) writes of "the pre-Nietzschean assumption that man has a true self which ought *not* to be repressed, something which exists *prior* to being shaped by power."

Thus Spoke Zarathustra, I. 4, "On the Despisers of the Body" (KGW VI 1, pp. 35–37), needs to be discussed in this context. Zarathustra here distinguishes between the body, which he identifies with the self (*das Selbst*), and sense and spirit, which he identifies with consciousness (*das Ich*), that which says "I." He then argues that the body uses consciousness for its own purposes and that even those who turn against their bodies are really following the desires of their own (unconscious) selves. This appears at first sight to recall the Freudian model discussed above. But the similarity does not seem to me to go much further. For though Nietzsche, as he often does, envisages a distinction between consciousness and the unconscious, he associates a stable self precisely with these "despisers of the body": "Even in your folly and contempt . . . you serve your self . . . your self itself wants to die and turns away from life" exactly because it "is no longer capable of what it would do above all else: to *create beyond itself* . . . " (my italics). Thus the tendency of both the conscious and the unconscious self is, unless it is resisted for the many reasons that Nietzsche discusses in his later writings, to be in a continuous process of change and development.

21. KGW, VIII 1, p. 36; WP, sec. 593. I discuss some aspects of Nietzsche's view of truth in "Immanent and Transcendent Perspectivism in Nietzsche," *Nietzsche-Studien* 12 (1983), pp. 473–90.

22. KGW, VI 3, p. 145; TI, "Skirmishes of an Untimely Man," p. 554.

23. KGW, VI 1, p. 47; Z. I. 8.

24. KGW, VI 1, p. 106; Z. II. 2.

25. KGW, VIII 2, p. 53, VIII 1, p. 109; WP, secs. 516, 522.

26. This ambivalence if reflected in a number of passages of Harold Alderman's *Nietzsche's Gift* (Athens: Ohio University Press, 1977). For example, Alderman writes that "the Overman *is* the meaning of the earth . . . and yet we must also *will* that he shall be that meaning . . . [Zarathustra's 'Prologue'] says, in effect, both that something *is* the case and that we ought to *will* it to be so . . ." (p. 26). Elsewhere, he describes the section "On the Three Metamorphoses" as "Nietzsche's statement of the conditions under which we may create—which is to say encounter—ourselves . . ." (p. 35). Alderman does not discuss this problem explicitly, though at one point he writes that "to be oneself one must know one's limits; only thereby can one grow to meet—one's limits" (p. 126), which, in my opinion, places too much emphasis on the discovery-side of the distinction Nietzsche may be trying to undermine. Cf. KGW, VII 2, p. 134; WP, sec. 495; and EH, pp. 709–10.

27. Such an interpretation, along more individualistic lines, is implicitly accepted by Alderman in the last of the quotations in the preceding footnote.

28. KGW, VIII 2, p. 277; WP, sec. 708. This idea appears again and again in Nietzsche's notes: cf., among many others, KGW, VIII 2, p. 201; WP, sec. 639: "That the world is not striving toward a stable condition is the only thing that has been proved."

29. KGW, V 2, p. 215; GS, sec. 295.

30. KGW, V 2, p. 226; GS, sec. 310.

31. KGW, VI 1, pp. 106–7; Z. II. 2.

32. KGW, IV 3, p. 22; *Mixed Opinions and Maxims*, sec. 17; my translation.

33. KGW, V 2, p. 57; GS, sec. 11.

34. KGW, VI 2, p. 21; BGE, sec. 12. In connection with our earlier discussion, it is important to notice that Nietzsche goes on to say of "the new psychologist," who accepts such hypotheses, that "precisely thereby he . . . condemns himself to *invention*—and—who knows?—perhaps to discovery."

35. KGW, VII 3, p. 382; WP, sec. 490. The passage continues to list as one of Nietzsche's "hypotheses" a view of "The subject as multiplicity." In section 561 of *The Will to Power* (KGW, VIII 1, p. 102). Nietzsche writes that all "unity is unity only as organization and cooperation," and opposes this conception to belief in the "thing," which, he claims, "was only invented as a foundation for the various attributes." Unity thus is achieved when the elements of a system are directed toward a common goal, as the political metaphor we are discussing would lead us to expect.

36. Nietzsche's attack on the concept of unity, and on other traditional concepts in Western philosophy, is well documented by Eugen Fink, *Nietzsches Philosophie* (Stuttgart, Germany: Kohlhammer, 1960).

37. KGW, VI 1, p. 106; Z. II. 2.

38. KGW, VI 1, pp. 165, 244; Z. II. 21, III. 12.

39. Cf. "The Eternal Recurrence," pp. 345–48, for some comments relevant to this assertion. Cf. also KGW, VIII 3, pp. 128–30, VIII 1, p. 291; WP, secs. 584, 672.

40. KGW, VIII 2, p. 296; WP, sec. 668.

41. KGW, VIII 2, pp. 55–56; WP, sec. 488.

42. KGW, VIII 2, p. 296; WP, sec. 477; cf. KGW, VIII 3, pp. 252–54, VIII 2, p. 131; VIII 2, pp. 55–56; WP, secs. 479, 485, 488.

43. *Akrasia* or "weakness of will" may still be considered as a threat to this assumption even at this point, however.

44. Cf. KGW, VIII 2, p. 131; WP, sec. 485: " 'The subject' is the fiction that many similar states in us are the effect of one substratum: but it is we who first created the 'similarity' of these states; our adjusting them and making them similar is the fact, not their similarity (—which ought rather to be denied—)."

45. KGW, VIII 1, p. 104; WP, sec. 518.

46. KGW, VII 3, pp. 370–71; WP, sec. 492.

47. KGW, VI 1, pp. 35–37; Z. I. 4. A similar point may be made at KGW, VII 2, p. 280; WP, sec. 966: "In contrast to animals, man has cultivated an abundance of *contrary* drives and impulses within himself. . . ."

48. Amélie Rorty, "Self-Deception, *Akrasia* and Irrationality," *Social Science Information* 19 (1980), p. 920. On a more abstract basis, Robert Nozick tries to account for the self as a "self-synthesizing" entity in his *Philosophical Explanations* (Cambridge, Mass.: Harvard University Press, 1981), pp. 71–114.

49. KGW, VI 1, p. 149; Z. II. 15, a very important section in this connection. Cf. KGW, VI 2, p. 158; BGE, sec. 215, with its allusion to Kant: just as some planets are illuminated by many suns, and of different colors, "so we modern men are determined, thanks to the complicated mechanics of our 'starry sky', by different moralities; our actions shine alternately in different colors, they are rarely univocal—and there are cases enough in which we perform actions *of many colors.*"

The passage from *Thus Spoke Zarathustra*, with its painterly and literary vocabulary (*vollschreiben, überpinseln, Zeichendeuter*—the last word being more closely connected to the astronomical and astrological imagery of the sentence than Kaufmann's translation suggests), should be very congenial to deconstructive readers of Nietzsche, who find in his writings an insistence on the total absence of any "originary unity." A classic statement of the general position can be found in Jacques Derrida, "Structure, Sign, and Play in the Discourse of the Human Sciences," in *The Structuralist Controversy*, ed. by Richard Macksey and Eugenio Donato (Baltimore, Md.: Johns Hopkins University Press, 1970), pp. 247–64; but the view has now become very prevalent. It is clear that Nietzsche would agree that the unity in question is not given, and that it cannot be uncovered once all the "coats of paint" are removed: nothing would remain over if that were done. But this agreement need not, and does not, prevent him from wanting to *construct* a unity out of this "motley" (*bunt*) material. I discuss such issues in relation to literary criticism in "The Postulated Author: Critical Monism as a Regulative Ideal," *Critical Inquiry* 8 (1981), pp. 133–49.

50. KGW, VIII 2, pp. 55–56; WP, sec. 488. Cf. KGW, VIII 1, pp. 320–21; WP, sec. 617.

51. Cf. Stern, *A Study of Nietzsche*, ch. 7, esp. p. 122 with n. 1. We should remark that such a construal of the will to power, as well as the version of the eternal recurrence presented in this essay, may seem to imply that ultimately no clear distinction can be drawn between the experience of an individual (especially of a sufficiently powerful individual) and the outside world. For the world may appear to be the

product of such people's will to power. Such a solipsist view is also suggested by Nietzsche when he writes, as we have already seen, that Zarathustra's disciples "want to create the world before which [they] can kneel." However, as I shall try to show below, Nietzsche also holds that the process of "surpassing" involved here can have no end; there is no such thing as the total transformation of another subject, and there are always more subjects to be (at best partially) transformed. Thus the distinction between one's experience and the world can always be in principle maintained. In addition, it is not clear that Nietzsche's specific views on the unity of the self involve a commitment to such possible solipsist consequences of the will to power. They do, however, seem to me to depend on a refusal to identify the world with something like "unconceptualized reality." The world is given to us only under a description or, as Nietzsche would prefer, an interpretation. Recent expressions of such a view can be found in, among others, Nelson Goodman, "The Way the World Is," in his *Problems and Projects* (Indianapolis: Bobbs-Merrill, 1972), pp. 24–32, and Hilary Putnam, "Reflections on Goodman's *Ways of Worldmaking*," *Journal of Philosophy* 76 (1979), pp. 603–18, esp. 611–12.

52. KGW, VI 3, pp. 136–37; TI, "Skirmishes," pp. 545–46.

53. KGW, VI 3, p. 116; TI, "Skirmishes," p. 525. The passage continues: "How does one compromise oneself today? If one is consistent. If one proceeds in a straight line. If one is not ambiguous enough to permit five conflicting interpretations. If one is genuine." Cp. KGW, VI 3, p. 60; TI, "Maxims and Arrows," p. 473: "The formula of my happiness: a Yes, a No, a straight line, *a goal.*"

54. KGW, VIII 1, p. 285; WP, sec. 672. Cf. KGW, VIII 3, pp. 128–30; WP, sec. 584; and KGW, VI 3, p. 54; TI, "Maxims and Arrows," p. 467: "Not to perpetrate cowardice toward one's own acts! Not to leave them in the lurch afterward! The bite of conscience is indecent!" I discuss these issues in detail in "The Eternal Recurrence."

55. KGW, V 2, p. 210; GS, sec. 290.

56. KGW, V 2, p. 207; GS, sec. 284, cf. sec. 283; also KGW, VI 1, pp. 173–78; Z. II. 21.

57. KGW, VI 1, p. 5; Z. "Prologue," sec. 1.

58. KGW, VI 2, p. 30; BGE, sec. 21; cf. KGW, VI 2, pp. 25–28, 50–51; BGE, secs. 19, 36; KGW, VI 3, pp. 88–89; TI, "The Error of Free Will," pp. 499–500.

59. KGW, VI 1, p. 244; Z. III. 12.

60. KGW, VI 3, p. 79; TI, "Morality as Anti-Nature," p. 489.

61. KGW, VI 2, p. 27; BGE, sec. 19. Notice that nothing in the metaphor prevents the governing class from including all the members of the commonwealth.

62. KGW, VII 2, p. 289; WP, sec. 966; cf. KGW, VII 2, pp. 179–80, VIII 2, pp. 395–96; WP, secs. 259, 928.

63. KGW, VI 3, p. 145; TI, "Skirmishes," pp. 553–54. Nietzsche's remarks on persons as hierarchical structures of desires and character-traits interestingly prefigure the view discussed by Harry Frankfurt in "Freedom of the Will and the Concept of a Person," *Journal of Philosophy* 68 (1971), pp. 5–20. Where Nietzsche does not consider that every agent has a self, Frankfurt writes (p. 11) that not every human being need be a person: only agents who have certain desires about what their will is to be are persons for him. Further, just as Nietzsche considers that freedom of the will is not something presupposed by, but attained through, agency, Frankfurt writes: "The enjoyment

of freedom comes easily to some. Others must struggle to achieve it" (p. 17). Though in no way as fine-grained as his, the discussion that follows is indebted to Frankfurt.

64. KGW, VIII 2, p. 369; WP, sec. 425; cf. KGW, VI 1, pp. 391–400; Z. IV. 19.

65. KGW, 1, p. 392; Z. IV. 19. Cf. KGW, VII 3, pp. 171–72; WP, sec. 962. Gregory Vlastos has objected that, on such an interpretation of the eternal recurrence, Nietzsche is committed to the very strong view that if I were to desire my life again, I would have to want every totally insignificant thing to remain the same. But even if it is Nietzsche's theory, the objection continues, that everything I do is equally essential to who I am, surely, for example, the precise minute I happened to wake up on a particular morning could not possibly have an effect on my person. Nietzsche's point, I reply, is that one wants to repeat just those actions which *are* significant to one's being the person one is—those, in fact, are the very *actions* one wants to acknowledge as one's own. Insignificant details (unless one can interpret them so as to make them significant) make no significant difference to who one is. I discuss this point in detail in "The Eternal Recurrence," pp. 346–47.

66. This point is presented and discussed in detail in "The Eternal Recurrence."

67. KGW, VI 3, pp. 133–34; TI, "Skirmishes," p. 542. I shall try to suggest below how some of the excessive statements of this passage can be tempered in the light of other texts.

68. KGW, VIII 1, p. 320; WP, sec. 617. Nietzsche also writes here: "Becoming as invention, willing, self-denial, overcoming of oneself: no subject but an action, a positing, creative, no 'causes and effects.' . . . Instead of 'cause and effect' the mutual struggle of that which becomes, often with the absorption of one's opponent; the number of becoming elements not constant."

69. KGW, VIII 2, pp. 155–56; WP, sec. 786. Cf. KGW, VII 2, pp. 94–95; WP, sec. 964.

70. KGW, VII 1, pp. 533–34; WP, sec. 769, where its correct date should be Fall 1883.

71. KGW, VIII 2, p. 56; WP, sec. 488; cf. pp. 14–18 above, and KGW, VIII 3, pp. 165–66; WP, sec. 636.

72. *Nicomachean Ethics*, VI. 1, 6.

73. I have given arguments to that effect both in "The Eternal Recurrence," and in "Immanent and Transcendent Perspectivism in Nietzsche."

74. If this hypothesis is right, Nietzsche, in seeing life as work of art written by each individual as it goes along (an idea which can be found reflected in Sartre), can be considered as part of the great tradition working out of the metaphor of the *theatrum mundi*, and giving a secular turn to this view of the world as a stage on which a play observed by heaven is acted out. There is some irony in this, once again, for, as Ernest Curtius remarks, this tradition can also be traced originally to Plato (*Laws*, 644de, 804c). See Curtius's discussion of this metaphor in his *European Literature and the Latin Middle Ages* (Princeton, N.J.: Princeton University Press, 1953; first published, 1948), pp. 138–44.

75. KGW, III 1, pp. 116–25; BT, sec. 19.

76. Paul de Man, *Allegories of Reading*, p. 84.

77. Ronald Hayman, *Nietzsche: A Critical Life* (New York: Oxford University Press, 1980), p. 119 *et passion*.

78. KGW, V 2, p. 218; GS, sec. 299. The analogy is also made in section 301.

79. KGW, VI 2, p. 152; BGE, sec. 213.
80. KGW, VI 1, p. 189; Z. III. I.
81. KGW, VI 3, p. 319; EH, p. 737.
82. KGW, V 2, pp. 224–25; GS, sec. 307. Cp., among many other passages, KGW, VI 2, pp. 56–58; BGE, sec. 44.
83. KGW, VI 3, p. 319; EH, pp. 737–38.
84. KGW, IV 3, p. 290; *The Wanderer and His Shadow*, sec. 204; my translation.

III
HEIDEGGER

5

Intentionality and World: Division I of *Being and Time*

Harrison Hall

D IVISION I OF *BEING AND TIME* contains the complete account of early Heidegger's quarrel with and departure from the philosophical tradition. In
spite of the attempts by many, beginning with Husserl,[1] to incorporate Heidegger's insights into a more traditional framework, that departure was a radical one. For Heidegger the tradition that began in ancient Greece finds what
may be its ultimate expression in Husserl's phenomenology.

As Føllesdal and his successors have argued,[2] Husserl's phenomenology can
be understood as the joint product of two influences. From Brentano he took
the insight that the defining characteristic of consciousness is its intentionality—that is, its "of-ness" or directedness toward some object. But the model he
uses for understanding this intentionality or directedness is essentially the
same as Frege's model of linguistic reference, with the basic notion of meaning
or sense (*Sinn*) suitably generalized so as to apply to all acts of consciousness,
linguistic and nonlinguistic.[3] Just as Frege distinguishes the sense of a linguistic expression from its referent, so Husserl distinguishes the meaning of a conscious act from the object it is *about*. For both, the meaning is that in virtue of
which we can refer to or intend objects.

The result is a Fregean account of intentionality that avoids the obvious
problems facing Brentano's theory. If the directedness of consciousness is accounted for in terms of its relation to real objects, the perceptual equivalents
of failure of reference (hallucinations, illusions) defy explanation. But if this
directedness is explained in terms of perceived mental contents (images, per-
cepts), the distinction between veridical and nonveridical perception seems to
disappear. Husserl avoids this dilemma by accounting for the intentionality of

consciousness in terms of abstract intensional (with an "s") structures (analogous to linguistic meanings) through which consciousness is directed, rather than in terms of objects toward which it is directed or the actual mental contents that accompany its directed acts. Husserl uses the term *noema* to refer to these intensional structure or meanings. Thus, Brentano's thesis that every act has an object is transformed into the thesis that every act has a *noema*, or meaning. It is by virtue of such meanings that consciousness is directed toward or intends an object under a particular description and with an appropriate set of structured anticipations, past associations, and so on.

Since Heidegger places Husserl's theory of the intentionality of consciousness squarely within the philosophical tradition he seeks to criticize and correct, the notion of intentionality might seem a strange choice for explicating Heidegger's thought. And this would be reinforced by the virtual absence of the term in *Being and Time* and by Heidegger's refusal to characterize human experience in terms of the relation of consciousness to its objects. Nonetheless, Heidegger's lectures and notes from the period of *Being and Time* contain many references to and discussions of intentionality, and understanding the various senses of intentionality and the corresponding senses of the world for Heidegger is one way to make sense of Division I of *Being and Time*.

Before getting down to the important details of Heidegger's story, let me go straight to the bottom line and try to block the most common misunderstanding of *Being and Time*. There are at least three crucially important and crucially different notions of intentionality and world for Heidegger. There is (1) the intentionality and world of the theoretical subject (the passive observer or traditional knower and the objects observed or known), (2) the intentionality and world of the practical subject (the active, involved participant and the objects utilized), and (3) a more primordial intentionality and world (Heidegger would prefer "worldhood"), which precludes any use of the subject–object model and without which the understanding of the other two sorts of intentionality and world are necessarily misunderstandings. The most common misinterpretation of Heidegger's thinking here is to stop short of this more radical understanding of intentionality and world and to see him as simply drawing special attention to and asserting the special importance of the world of practical activity with its skillful subjects and useful objects. It is important to avoid this misunderstanding if we are to grasp Heidegger's departure from Husserl and the tradition.

I

Husserl shares with the tradition the desire to turn philosophy into a strict science. It is no accident that the most concise presentation of his philosophical method is titled *Cartesian Meditations*. And Husserl believed the key to the transformation of philosophy into such a science (phenomenology), and to its separation from the other sciences as well, was the exclusive focus of its attention toward the meanings (*noemata*) that mediate our experience of objects. Husserl's phenomenology sought to explain how consciousness was directed in various ways (e.g., perceiving or remembering) toward objects of various kinds (e.g., ordinary material objects or other people). Like Descartes's, Husserl's primary interest lay in what we would today refer to as the cognitive: acts of perception or observation and their relation to beliefs about the world.

On Husserl's account, even though not all of the aspects of a perceptual object are sensuously presented to the perceiver, such objects are completely intended in each conscious experience of them. He describes the meanings that mediate such experience as made up of both filled and unfilled components, corresponding respectively to the aspects of an object that are presented and appresented (Husserl's term for the co-intended but not sensuously presented aspects of an object from a particular perceptual point of view). Perceptual consciousness is of objects by virtue of systems of such meanings, and belief or knowledge is a matter of the consistency of our experience over time with such systems.

To this story about how meanings function to organize our experience of the world and provide us with the necessary epistemic credentials, Husserl added a story about the priority relations the various components of meanings have among themselves. This second story is a natural sequel to the first. The most basic or fundamental part of our sense of things consists of those characteristics needed in an account of perceptual objects. Value and relational predicates that go beyond the description of objects as simply perceived or observed are secondary, added to, and dependent upon the more fundamental components of perceptual meaning.

What Heidegger shares with Husserl's "philosophy as rigorous science" is the desire to get at things as they really are, free of any philosophical or other assumptions that could distort our point of view. And, like Husserl, he believes that such access is to be found by paying very careful attention to our actual experience of the world and of ourselves. He uses the term "phenomenology" to capture this getting things to reveal themselves to us in this way. But all the details of Heidegger's story differ markedly from Husserl's, and Husserl's priorities of meaning, which Heidegger identifies with the entire philosophical tradition, are simply reversed.

In Division I of *Being and Time* Heidegger discovers that our fundamental sense of things is not as objects of perception and knowledge, but rather as instrumental objects (equipment) that fit naturally into our ordinary practical activity:

> The kind of dealing which is closest to us is as we have shown, not a bare perceptual cognition, but rather that kind of concern which manipulates things and puts them to use. . . . (BT 95)

The less we just stare at the hammer-thing, and the more we seize hold of it
and use it, the more primordial does our relationship to it become, and the more
unveiledly is it encountered as that which it is—as equipment. (BT 98)

And our fundamental sense of our selves in the midst of such activity is not as
passive observers, but rather as purposively involved participants at home in
the practical world:

Dasein finds "itself" proximally in *what* it does, uses, expects, avoids—in those
things environmentally ready-to-hand with which it is proximally *concerned.* . . .
(BT 155)
    Proximally and for the most part, Dasein *is* in terms of *what* it is concerned
with. (BT 181)

Heidegger makes these discoveries by getting things to show themselves to
us as they really are in our ordinary dealings with them. And this turns out,
according to Heidegger, to be rather difficult, since in our ordinary dealings
with things they hardly show up at all in the traditional sense of being explicitly noticed or perceived. In ordinary practical activity we make use of things,
but we do not typically notice or attend to them. When we use the doorknob
to open the door and get into the next office, we do not attend to its perceptual characteristics. Our attention instead is directed toward where we are
going and what we are doing, and the doorknob is used so automatically in familiar surroundings like these that it withdraws from view and serves its instrumental function invisibly:

The peculiarity of what is proximally ready-to-hand is that, in its readiness-to-
hand, it must, as it were, withdraw in order to be ready-to-hand quite authentically. That with which our everyday dealings proximally dwell is not the tools
themselves. On the contrary, that with which we concern ourselves primarily is
the work. (BT 99)

Practical intentions seem to go through the things we use toward the goals
of purposes of our activity. The famous hammer of *Being and Time* has its
perceivable properties, of course, but for the most part they are not explicitly
noticed when the hammer is being skillfully employed. The skilled carpenter
uses the hammer to drive the nails to build the house to shelter a family,
thereby providing for her family either directly or indirectly. Explicit attention
is typically directed toward the work (nail driving and house building) rather
than the equipment used to accomplish it. It is this invisible functioning of
equipmental things that is definitive of their being in the world of practical activity according to Heidegger. His claim is that the hammer and doorknob really are what they are as practically employed. The trick is to see what they are

without changing them from instrumental to perceptual objects and breaking down the network of relations essential to their instrumental nature.

This trick can be accomplished when things go wrong in the right sort of way. When practical activity is interrupted by the failure of an instrumental thing, we suddenly see the network of relations in which that instrumental functioning was embedded. When the doorknob comes off in our hand or the head falls off the hammer, the transparent functioning ceases and the relation of that functioning to complexes of instruments (latches, doors, and hallways or nails, lunber, and the rest of the carpenter's tools and materials) and to our ongoing purposes and projects (getting into our office and finding a book to prepare a lecture or assembling boards and runners to repair some deteriorated stairs) comes suddenly into view.

Heidegger labels the ordinary way that objects are for us in the midst of practical activity "ready-to-hand." The way that such objects are for us during breakdowns in their normal functioning he calls "unready-to-hand." The complexes of instruments just referred to he calls "equipmental totalities." And the system of ongoing purposes and projects he refers to as hierarchical "toward-which," "in-order-to," and "for-the-sake-of" relations between our activities and our short- and long-term goals. What shows up when our normal activity is interrupted, when things we are using become unready-to-hand, is the world of practical activity (BT 105–6). This world *just is* the network of relations into which can be fitted the systems of equipmental totalities with their internal relations ("references") among the tools they contain and their external relations ("assignments") to the purposes of the humans who use them, and human beings with their practical ties to one another and to the objects they deal with. Ready-to-hand things *just are* their place in such a world. To be a hammer is to be related in the right way to nails and boards, to house repairing and parental caring or providing, and so on.

The intentionality of practical activity is typically directed through the objects we use toward the immediate purposes for which we use them. The space of practical experience is neither Euclidean nor perceptual in nature. Instead, it has dimensions of accessibility and interest. Things are "near" in the former dimension when they are accessible, in their assigned spots and available for use when needed; and they are "distant" when they are unavailable for use even if they are right under our noses. Things are "near" in the latter dimension when our interests make the activity of using them essential; and they are "distant" when they play no part in our current projects (BT 135–36, 140–42).

Heidegger is careful to avoid the term "perception" even when discussing the kind of looking around that is sometimes necessary in practical contexts. The term he prefers is "circumspection," a term referring to the kind of looking around that makes sense only against the practical background of world, and that is always guided by our practical interests and concerns (BT 98). The carpenter looks to see that the nail is going in straight when the confined space in which she works alters the skillful movements with which she would routinely drive the nail. Or she searches the parts of the workshop most likely to contain an object of the appropriate size and weight to substitute temporarily for the broken hammer. At no point in such circumspection is she just looking at the environment and noting disinterestedly the objective characteristics of the items perceived. Circumspection is itself a worldly activity, one that is purposive, skillful, and no less practical in its structural relations than the rest of the normal activity of daily life.

Heidegger argues that this practical world, the intentionality appropriate to it, and the sense things have for us within it are more fundamental than the traditional sense of the world as a collection of things in objective space, the intentionality of cognitive acts, and the sense things have for us within such acts. That priority or fundamentality comes to at least the following:

1. The practical world is the one we inhabit first, before philosophizing or engaging in scientific investigation—in Heidegger's words, it is where we find ourselves "proximally and for the most part."
2. The world in the traditional sense can be understood as derivative from the practical world, but not the other way around—that is, starting from Heidegger's account of the practical world we can make sense of how the traditional sense of the world arises, whereas any attempt to take objective perception and cognition as basic and construct the practical world out of the resources traditionally available is doomed to failure (BT 122, 146–47).

Heidegger's critique of the world as interpreted by the philosophical tradition occurs in the context of his discussion of the Cartesian picture of mental and material (or "corporeal") reality and their interrelationship. The ingredients of this world are a mind whose contents are mental representations (ideas) and an independent substantial reality (typically material) capable of being represented. The goal of philosophy and science within this tradition is to get at reality as it is in itself and then to find ways to guarantee that our mental representation of it is accurate. Getting at things as they are independent of our purposes and projects requires that we depart from the practical attitude and world and adopt the theoretical standpoint. Heidegger thinks of this standpoint as that of the disinterested spectator whose observation is motivated only by a kind of pure curiosity about the true nature of things. To adopt this standpoint is equivalent to just looking ("staring") at things and encountering those properties they present to us simply as perceivers. Heidegger calls things as they are encountered in this way "present-at-hand." Traditional ontology is thus the ontology of the present-at-hand, the theory that takes the things that figure in perception and traditional cognition rather than those that are the objects of circumspection and practical utilization as most basic (BT 127–30).

Heidegger offers a number of reasons to think that the traditional view is a mistake. I can only summarize them, since the arguments in each case would be too lengthy to reproduce here. First, he believes that the picture of subjects with their internal (private) representations confronting a world of independent (public) objects is the source of the traditional problem of knowledge (skepticism). We can avoid the problem only by avoiding the theoretical picture of reality that gives rise to it (BT 247–50). Second, the traditional account has no way to explain how things have value. Starting with present-at-hand objects that are independent of us, there seems to be no satisfactory account of the transition to objects with value predicates that seem to depend on the relations of the object to us. Heidegger attributes the traditional fact–value dichotomy and its associated problems to the traditional construal of the present-at-hand as most real or basic (BT 132).

At this point we have returned to the second and more important sense in which the practical world is primary or basic for Heidegger, the "you can't get there from here" challenge to traditional ontology. It is clear that we have access to both worlds, the theoretical and the practical, and that we encounter both present-at-hand and ready-to-hand objects. In Heidegger's view, Husserl's attempted explanation of how we add layers of meaning to our mental representations in order to get from bare things to the culturally useful and valuable objects of the world of everyday life is about the best that can be done given the traditional framework, and it is an obvious and complete failure. The practical (social, cultural) world is not the world of the present-at-hand plus some relations and relational predicates. We cannot get to the everyday world that Heidegger describes in that way.

But we *can* get from the ready-to-hand to the present-at-hand by something like subtraction of interest and involvement from ordinary practical activity. If the carpenter cannot find anything to substitute for the broken hammer and abandons her efforts to get on with the work, she may eventually reach the point of just looking at the things around her in the workshop, a condition that puts out of play the network of practical relations that make the ready-to-hand what it is. This breakdown of practical activity is not our only access to the present-at-hand. We are not always at work or in the midst of practical activity, not always characterizable in terms of making use of equipment in order to, and so on. And there are special kinds of practice, such as those involved in science, which seem to require a kind of just looking and seeing in order to achieve their own special purposes. The point is, however, that if we take the relational context of practical activity as basic, the modifications required to reach the theoretical point of view are intelligible in terms of a lessening of practical interest and concern or the substitution of special limited interests and concerns for the ordinary everyday ones, and the resulting decontextualization (or minimal contextualization) of the everyday world. Heidegger not only traces the route from the ready-to-hand to the present-at-hand in this way, he also shows how the space ("existential space") of practical activity can undergo a similar transformation and become objective space (BT 146–47). In Division II of *Being and Time* he attempts to tell the same story with respect to "existential" and objective time. If all of this is correct, the ready-to-hand and its practical world enjoy a priority over the present-at-hand and the theoretical world in terms of intelligibility or explanatory self-sufficiency, and Heidegger takes this to be equivalent to priority in the logical, ontological, and epistemological senses.

II

The third and most important sort of intentionality and world for Heidegger is much more difficult to get hold of then either the practical or the theoretical. The best way to do so is to return to the fundamental intentionality and world of practical activity and look for something even more fundamental that they presuppose—not in the direction of the present-at-hand, but in something like the opposite direction. The hammer "refers," according to Heidegger, to the nails and boards with which it is used. In fact, the "being" of equipment consists of such "reference" relations to other equipment in the same equipmental totality, as well as of "assignments" to the typical purposes for which it is used. But the hammer does not wear such relations "on its sleeve" or present them in the way that it seems to present its color or shape to any observer. To someone entirely unfamiliar with the tools and activity of the carpenter, the hammer is at best a present-at-hand object to be observed or thought about. The hammer is what it is as ready-to-hand—it is a piece of equipment with the appropriate practical relations—only for those familiar with the workshop and work of the carpenter. And it is fully ready-to-hand in the sense of functioning transparently and smoothly as equipment only for those skillfully coping with the carpenter's tools and tasks, those who are truly at home in the workshop.

Readiness-to-hand is tied in this way to specific familiarities and skills for coping in specific practical environments. And if we stopped with this insight, we could make sense of much of Heidegger's case against the philosophical tradition. This familiarity with specific practical environments certainly does not involve explicit mental contents or representations. There are no Husser-lian systems of meanings, or *noemata*, that mediate practical expertise. Nor is such expertise a matter of beliefs or cognitions.[4] The traditional emphasis on the cognitive, the attempt to explain all human behavior in terms of what we believe and how we consciously represent things to ourselves, cannot account for the implicit familiarity and competence that are the hallmarks of everyday practical activity. Explicit representations of things in the practical world and conscious beliefs we form within practical contexts always presuppose this nonrepresented and, for Heidegger, nonrepresentable background of familiar-ity and expertise.

There is, however, a background of familiarity and associated competence for dealing with things and with others that is even broader and more basic than those associated with specific practical activities and settings. Just as we have specific familiarity with the carpenter's workshop and specific skills for coping with things in the carpenter's environment enabling us to encounter the hammer as a hammer, so we have a general familiarity with things and others and a set of implicit skills for dealing with them that form the neces-sary background for our encountering anything at all. Heidegger's discussion of practical activity and the relations that constitute the practical world were meant to prepare us for grasping the more general "activity" of being human and the "worldly" structure it presupposes.

This sense of the world as the most general structure of involvements that enables and "calls forth" all human "comportment" is probably the central contribution of *Being and Time*, and it is the link between *Being and Time* and Heidegger's later writings. For Heidegger, specific ready-to-hand and present-at-hand environments are just particular cases of this general worldhood, and the skills and familiarity involved are just particular cases of the general fa-miliarity and ways of coping that constitute our human way of being in he broadest sense. Dealing with hammers is just a specific case of the more gen-eral skilled "comportment" of dealing with objects—identifying them, draw-ing near to them, picking them up, and so on—and our familiarity with the workshop is just a specific case of our more general being at home or "dwelling" in everyday environments—knowing (in the sense of possessing the skill or competence, not in the sense of having the right sort of beliefs) how to position and move ourselves, what to do and say, and so on.

These most general skills and familiarity are even more transparent and in-visible than specific practical ones. Not only do we not normally attend to them (because we attend to the activities in which we are involved through them), but the very notion of attending to them flies in the face of Heidegger's account of human being and world. The point of that account is that things show up for us or are encountered as what they are only against a background of familiarity, competence, and concern that carves out a system of related roles into which things fit. Equipmental things *are* the roles into which they are cast by skilled users of them, and skilled users *are* the practical roles into which they cast themselves. Breakdowns of practical activity can give us an opportunity to grasp the background of practical familiarity, competence, and concern associated with specific systems of practical relations and roles because the world of the carpenter, for example, is not the entire human world and being a carpenter is not the whole of being human. We have a broader and more basic background to fall back on. Attending to or grasping is a human activity. All human activity is worldly; that is, it requires a background of implicit familiarity, competence, and concern or involvement. But when it comes to our broadest and most basic sense of things, our sense of human being and world, there is no broader context from which we could attend to or grasp it. We cannot abandon our most general skills for dealing with things in order to make them reveal themselves as we can with the skills of the carpenter. Human being is skillful coping all the way down, and this broadest level of familiarity, competence, and involvement is rock bottom. We do not even consciously acquire such things. We grow up into them through socialization or enculturation. They are what we are, not what we are aware of.

It is this last point that Heidegger seeks to capture when he says that human being in its world ("existingly") and that the world has our ("Dasein's") way of being (BT 92, 416). We just *are* our most general and fundamental way of "comporting" ourselves toward things and human beings, and these same manners of "comportment" are the background without which things and others could not be encountered, namely, the world.

This third and most fundamental sense of intentionality and world provides another insight into the priority of practical intentionality and the practical world over theoretical intentionality and the world of the present-at-hand. The practical world adds some specialized ways of coping, together with their correlative familiarity relations, to the full-blown general background skills and familiar ways of dealing with things and others that make up *the* world. The theoretical world, however, is accessed by methodologically constraining our full range of general background skills and our range of specialized practical skills and purposes so that only those relevant to theoretical observation and cognition are "in play." The theoretical world has its own background skills and familiar ways of coping with things—it is still a "world" in Heidegger's language—and it uses the general competence and familiarity of *the* world as its background. Nevertheless, it is incomplete, deficient, or derived in relation to the practical world.

Values are built into both the world as the general background of all encountering and the world of practical activity. Values are implicit in the operation of our most general skills for dealing with things and others. The particular cultural form of this coping will tend to make certain kinds of things and relations stand out as important to the exclusion of others. One might think of the difference in the general ways of dealing with everyday things in Eastern and modern Western cultures as illustrative of this point. Until very recent Westernization, the Japanese and Chinese treated things like teacups and dishes with a reverence we in the West tend to reserve for works of art. These objects were crafted with great care, passed on through generations, and valued for their beauty and intricacy of design. Comparably useful Western items could be made of anything from mass-produced unbreakable ceramic material to Styrofoam or paper, and they are valued for the economy and speed of their manufacture and the ease and efficiency of obtaining, using, and reusing or disposing of them. The different background practices and perspectives lead to equally different styles of encountering and dealing with the things involved, and they make different features of the things relevant or irrelevant, important or unimportant. In addition, cultural background practices and perspectives embody tacit norms of appropriateness. Some of these may find expression as public norms of conduct, what one (*"das Man"*) does or does not do or say in certain situations (BT 164–68). But for the most part they remain unexpressed, as do the cultural norms that govern how close to people it is appropriate to stand to engage in casual conversation, the conduct of business, and so on. There is a felt correctness, of getting things "right," when our particular dealings with things and others are consistent with the implicit norms of our cultural background.

In the practical world there are obvious sources of value. Since the practical world includes human purpose and projects, things will take on value in relation to their potential positive or negative contributions to the achievement of those purposes and the success of those projects. The practical world consists primarily of practical activity in pursuit of such purposes, and the norms attached to specific activities will generate value judgments. There will be right and wrong ways to hammer, appropriate and inappropriate nails for a given purpose, and hammers that can be too light or too heavy for the task at hand.

III

In addition to covering intentionality and world in all its senses and parting ways with the philosophical tradition as indicated above, Division I of *Being and Time* lays the foundation for the discussion of authenticity and temporality in Division II. A sense of the overall project of *Being and Time* will help to make the connection between the previous discussion of human being and world and Heidegger's account of the various aspects of "inauthentic" human being toward the end of Division I. The overall project of *Being and Time* was to discover the meaning of being. The first half (the only part written) of the complete work as projected is an analysis of human being (or "Dasein"). The reason for starting with human being in the quest for being in general has already emerged (though not clearly) in our discussion of the world. Every human project is a taking up of a culturally available possibility and presupposes the culturally determined background of skills and familiarity that Heidegger calls the world. This world makes possible the encountering of specific entities ("beings"), and it embodies our implicit sense of what it is for them to be. So human being, by virtue of its inseparability from the world (human being is "being-in-the-world") necessarily includes a sense ("understanding") of what is to be, that is, of being. Division II argues that this understanding of being that we are is essentially temporal or historical ("temporality"), and the second (never written) half of *Being and Time* was to trace the historical development of our understanding of being in search of its transhistorical meaning, the meaning present but hidden in the history of Western metaphysics.

Getting back to Division I, it turns out that human beings can "understand" what it is to be in two different ways, authentically and inauthentically, and that the authentic way, not surprisingly, is the one that gives us the best access to the meaning of being. So Heidegger begins the analysis of inauthentic human being to prepare the way for the eventual understanding of authentic human temporality ("historicity") and the approach to the essential meaning of being through our historical (mis)understandings of it.

Practical projects or purposes are typically arranged in a hierarchical order. I hammer the nail to assemble the boards in order to build the house so that my family will have a suitable place in which to live. The hammering may be invisible to the skilled carpenter engaged in this hierarchy of purposes, but the other pieces of this purposive hierarchy are not. Awareness is directed toward the task at hand and its place in the larger project toward which it contributes. There are, however, invisible purposes ("for-the-sake-ofs") on the far end of this chain. I am concerned about housing my family "because" I strive to be a good spouse and parent "because" I strive to be a good human being. These most ultimate purposes are not typically things of which we are aware. They are bound up inextricably with the invisible general background of all our intentional relations, that is, with the world. It is the culturally determined background of experience that gives us our implicit sense of what it is like to get things like family relationships or being human "right."

In taking up particular practical projects and human purposes, we also take up or take over a variant of our cultural understanding of being. According to

Heidegger we typically do so either in an undifferentiated way or in the inauthentic manner. Here is what he has in mind. The current cultural understanding of being includes a sense of the appropriateness of human purposes and projects and of the manners in which we engage in them. This sense is mostly implicit, especially the deepest or most fundamental parts of it, but not entirely so. Much of it resides in public or social norms of comportment, at least some of which can be made explicit. These are the norms captured by such expressions as "One [*das Man*] just doesn't do that," "One doesn't do that here, in that manner . . .," or "One always . . .," and so on. These norms are the typical vehicles of peer control during adolescence. But Heidegger's point is that such norms are not limited to the world of adolescence but are everywhere, at least implicitly, as the potential expressions of the cultural sense of what it is appropriate to do when or where, and of the appropriate and inappropriate ways of doing it.

Heidegger identifies three aspects of our relation to being, to the cultural sense of appropriateness, the general skills for coping with entities, and the familiarity associated with them: mood, understanding, and discourse. In Division II these are associated with the three aspects of time—past, future, and present. By "mood" Heidegger means something like our sense of how we find ourselves to be. It is our implicit or felt sense of the brute facticity of the cultural sense of being that we inherit rather than choose, our "thrownness" into a world that was not of our making but with which we are nonetheless stuck (BT 174–76). By "understanding" Heidegger means literally taking a stand on. We take a stand on our own being whenever we choose a particular possibility or project. Every purposive, future-directed choice from among the culturally determined alternative possibilities expresses an understanding, in Heidegger's sense, of what it is to be a human being (BT 185–86). In addition, every circumspective encountering of the ready-to-hand in the course of our projects involves understanding in the full sense, the interpretation of something *as* what it is by virtue of its equipmental relations (BT 189–90). It is important to note that interpretation in Heidegger's sense need not be verbal at all. Finally, "discourse" for Heidegger is the articulation of the intelligibility (i.e., the being) of things (BT 204–5). Discourse involves communication and it makes use of language as its tool, but it is not necessarily a matter of speaking. We can sometimes communicate an understanding of something most effectively by keeping silent. And silence is essential to hearkening to and grasping the understandings communicated to us (BT 208–9).

For Heidegger, we are always choosing from among the cultural possibilities and against the cultural background of intelligibility into which we have been thrown. That is, we are always understanding ("taking a stand on") our being on the basis of our thrownness or facticity. Human being is essentially self-interpreting being ("-in-the-world"). But for the most part this self-interpreting is not only implicit—it is anonymous ("public" in Kierkegaard's sense). We choose, frequently without realizing we are choosing, to do "what one does." When these choices are virtually unconscious, we are existing in what Heidegger calls an undifferentiated mode vis-à-vis authenticity and inauthenticity. But when we *choose* to interpret our being in the public way—living in the world of the one (*das Man*), doing "what one does" because it is either the "right" or the comfortable thing to do—we "fall" into the inauthentic way of being (BT 221–24).

We have a tendency toward the inauthentic understanding of our being because of some facts of (human) life that are hard to take. These all have to do with the lack of ground, foundation, or objective justification for our being. The general background of intelligibility or world that gives us our most basic sense of things, others, and ourselves is itself without any ultimate source of intelligibility or ground. It is the deepest level for us or of us. It is that according to which we must interpret everything, but is itself nothing more than further interpretation. We are, and the world is, interpretation all the way down. What is rock bottom in terms of basic skills and felt familiarity is only contingently so—there is no further sense of correctness or final justification for the way we are. Even the choices we make from among the possible interpretations (purposes, projects) culturally available to us are utterly contingent—determined if at all by more fundamental implicit choices that are themselves contingent. In both directions our understanding of being is in this sense groundless. The sense of ourselves and our world that our cultural past sticks us with has no ultimate claim to validity, and the future-directed projects and practices that constitute our taking over of this cultural facticity and our interpretation of ourselves in terms of it are equally incapable of objective validation. Our practices, skills, and familiarity are grounded in nothing firmer than further practices, skills, and familiarity. And all of these facts of life can be brought vividly home to us by an attack of the mood Heidegger calls anxiety (BT 230–35).

Anxiety for human beings is analogous to breaking down for pieces of equipment. Just as the breaking down of equipment can show its worldly character by revealing its place in a network of relations in which it has become dysfunctional, so anxiety can show the groundless character of human being by revealing the contingency of the network of purposes and projects and their background of intelligibility in which we are no longer involved by virtue of our having become "dysfunctional." The details of exactly how that works and exactly what Heidegger thinks is revealed are best left to a discussion of Division II. What we have said in this section is sufficient to complete this brief sketch of inauthenticity: it is that into which we flee or fall to avoid anxiety and its unsettling revelations.

The inauthentic form of understanding is (idle) "curiosity" (BT 216–17). In order to avoid coming to grips with the unsettling deep truths about our being and world, we occupy ourselves with the kind of questioning of our being and world that can be satisfied by the superficial sense of things that (every) one has and by the kinds of irrelevant information that is the stuff of superficial conversation and gossip. And it is just such superficial conversation and gossip, "idle talk" for Heidegger, that makes up the inauthentic version of discourse (BT 213–14). Having no deep understanding of things to communicate authentically to others, and afraid of being silent for fear of "hearing" the deeper truth about our being (the "call of conscience"), we engage in the kind of noisy chatter that never questions or gets below the anonymous public understanding of things and, hence, never really says anything.

Heidegger believes that this inauthentic understanding of human being represents more than just an unfortunate failure of self-knowledge into which many of us fall. Toward the end of Division I of *Being and Time* he attempts to tie this misunderstanding to traditional metaphysics and its fundamental ontological mistake (BT 245–47). The claim is that inauthentic self-understanding is the first step toward the traditional misunderstanding of being. The story is as follows.

Falling into the inauthentic understanding of our being is equivalent to "absorption" in the public world (the world of *das Man*). This world is objective and is treated as such. It is essentially a world of objects. More important, the inauthentic understanding of this world seeks to ground or validate the norms that constitute it, and hence construes them as objective facts dictated by an underlying independent reality. It is but a short step from here to the (mis)understanding of ourselves as "real" objects of a special kind. This makes objectivity the fundamental category of being, our being as well as that of the rest of reality. At this point we arrive at the ontology of the present-at-hand and join Husserl and the rest of the philosophical tradition.

Notes

1. See, e.g., *The Crisis of European Sciences and Transcendental Phenomenology* (Evanston, Ill.: Northwestern University Press, 1970), pp. 123–48, 173–83.

2. See D. Føllesdal, "Husserl's Notion of *Noema*," *Journal of Philosophy* 66 (1969): 680–87; idem, "Husserl's Theory of Perception" in *Handbook of Perception*, vol. 1, ed. E. Carterette and M. Friedman (New York: Academic Press, 1974), pp. 377–85; and D. Smith and R. McIntyre, "Intentionality via Intensions," *Journal of Philosophy* 68 (1971): 541–61.

3. I should note at this point that although Brentano clearly influenced Husserl, it is quite likely that Frege was *not* instrumental in the actual development of either Husserl's

general theory of consciousness or his more specific account of linguistic experience. See J. Mohanty, "Husserl and Frege: A New Look at Their Relationship," *Research in Phenomenology* 4 (1974): 51–62. The reason for *understanding* Husserl's theory in terms of Frege's model is that Husserl explicitly acknowledges the parallel with his own theory, and it moves the point of possible confusion back one important step. There may still be very serious problems involved in making the Fregean distinctions across the entire range of conscious experience, but thinking in terms of Frege's model at least makes clear the kinds of distinctions Husserl is trying to make.

4. For an extended defense of this Heideggerian claim, see H. L. Dreyfus and S. Dreyfus, *Mind over Machine* (New York: Macmillan, 1986).

6

Becoming a Self: The Role of Authenticity in *Being and Time*

Charles Guignon

. . . we are collected and bound up into unity within ourself, whereas we
had been scattered abroad in multiplicity.

—St. Augustine, *Confessions* 10.29

1

IT WOULD BE HARD TO IMAGINE any twentieth-century philosopher who has
stirred up more interest in disciplines outside philosophy than Heidegger.
For the better part of a century, thinkers in various areas have turned to Heidegger's seminal work, *Being and Time* (1927), for new and more illuminating
ways of thinking about human existence. Part of the appeal of Heidegger's
conception of human existence lies in his powerful criticisms of some of the
basic assumptions of the Western philosophical tradition. Ever since the flow-
ering of philosophy in Greece, philosophers have tended to assume that anything that exists—whether it be a tool, a rock, a work of art, or a human
being—must be regarded as a *substance* of some sort, where substance is understood as that which underlies and remains constant through change. We
can see this traditional substance metaphysics in Descartes's conception of
humans as consisting of both mental and physical substances, and it is still evident in contemporary physicalist views, where humans are regarded as material organisms in a natural environment.

From his earliest writings to his last lectures and seminars, Heidegger chal-
lenged this traditional way of characterizing human existence. On his view,

the substantialist conception of humans is a product of the "metaphysics of presence," the tendency to think that the *being* of anything has to be conceived in terms of enduring presence. This objectifying outlook underlies our modern conception of ourselves as individuals with a unique subjective standpoint and an inbuilt "personal identity" enduring through time. And it explains why we are so comfortable thinking of ourselves as "subjects of inwardness," as individual centers of experience and action.

In the face of the seeming self-evidence of this substance ontology, Heidegger contends that the conception of the self that has come down to us from the tradition is a theoretical construct, the product of some fairly high-level theorizing that is, in fact, quite remote from our deepest, most fundamental sense of who we are. To show this, *Being and Time* sets out to describe human existence (or, as Heidegger calls it, *Dasein*) in a way that bypasses the assumptions of the tradition. In his attempt to identify the "essential structures" of human being (the "existentials"), Heidegger begins with a phenomenological characterization of our "average, everyday" lives as *agents* in familiar contexts of action, prior to reflection and theorizing. According to this description, to be a human is to be an unfolding *event* or *happening* that is so thoroughly enmeshed in a shared lifeworld that there is no way to draw a sharp line between either self and world or self and others. Given this conception of our existence as agency embedded in a field of relations, the substance ontology simply has no real role to play in grasping who we are.

Yet, as is well known, there is also another side of *Being and Time* that seems to point toward a quite different picture of our being as humans. This other perspective, which later became central to existentialism, focuses on Heidegger's concept of *authenticity* as a possible way of being for Dasein. Thanks to the writings of existentialists and pop psychologists during the last century, we have come to think of authenticity as a matter of getting in touch with and expressing our unique being as individual selves, and this conception suggests that each of us has a substantial self we can access and express. Such a conception of humans as individual selves *seems* to draw support from *Being and Time*. We are told, for instance, that Dasein has to be addressed with a personal pronoun (e.g., " 'I am,' 'you are' "), because Dasein's being is characterized by *in each case mineness* (*Jemeinigkeit*).[1] And we find frequent references to an *authentic Self* that is said to underlie and make possible all the various ways of being that are possible for Dasein. Heidegger even goes so far as to say that being a "They-self" in our everyday practical lives is only an "existentiell [that is, particular, specialized] modification of the authentic Self" (317), where the authentic Self is regarded as an essential structure or existentiale.

But it would be wrong to assume from claims of this sort that Dasein is, at the most basic level, an individual subject in the traditional sense. On the contrary, the characterization of Dasein as "in each case mine," Heidegger says, is only a *formal indication* that needs phenomenological clarification before its full meaning can be understood (150, 361). As the description of everyday agency unfolds, we find that "*proximally*, it is not 'I,' in the sense of my own Self, that 'am,' but rather the Others, whose way is that of the They" (167). Seen from this standpoint, Heidegger can conclude that "authentic being-one's-Self [is] an existentiell modification of the They—of the They as an essential existentiale" (168).[2]

These quotes suggest that *Being and Time* puts forward two views of the self, views that stand in a tension with one another. On the one hand, a human being is conceived as a happening that is inextricably bound up in a web of relationships and lacking any substantial identity independent of these relationships. On the other hand, Heidegger speaks of the "authentic Self" and suggests (primarily in the second division of *Being and Time*) that it is only by realizing our "ownmost ability to be" an authentic Self that we can become fully human. In what follows, I want to try to work out this complex account of human existence and the conception of the self underlying it.

2

To fully understand how Heidegger develops his conception of human existence, we need to get clear about the method employed in *Being and Time*. The phenomenology of Dasein is carried out in two stages.[3] In the first stage, Heidegger identifies certain "formal" structures of Dasein that are supposed to provide initial clues as to what might be disclosed in the course of the investigation. These formal characterizations, he says, provide a "prior sketch" (*Vorzeichnung*) or "fore-having" (*Vorhabe*), a set of anticipations that will guide our attempt to work out the being of Dasein. Formal indicators are, in the terminology of traditional phenomenology, "empty intentions," for they anticipate concrete forms of experience but do not yet contain that experience.

In the second stage, Heidegger presents a phenomenological description of everyday life in order to show the concrete content such formal structures may have in actual modes of existing. This second stage provides a phenomenological demonstration for what is only formally indicated in the initial stage. Where the formal characterizations only indicate what Dasein is *in potentia*, as an "*ability*-to-be" (*Seinkönnen*), the description of concrete, existentiell ways of being shows how these potentialities can and do take an actual shape in our lives. It is a fundamental assumption of Heidegger's phenomenological method that no ontological claims can be accepted unless they are supported by concrete experience. What is proposed in the "formal indications" of the first stage therefore requires concrete "attestation" as the analysis proceeds—as Heidegger says, his existential analytic first "presupposes" formal structures that are put into words *"so that [Dasein] may decide for itself whether, as the entity which it is, it has the composition of being which has been disclosed in the projection of its formal aspects"* (362).[4]

The initial formal characterization of Dasein (sections 4 and 12) suggests that Dasein is not a thing or object, but rather is an *event*—the unfolding realization of a life as a whole. Heidegger captures this way of thinking of human existence by saying that what is distinctive about Dasein is that its *being*—that is, its life as a whole—is *at issue* for it (32). In other words, we are beings who *care* about what we are: we care about where our lives are going and what we are becoming in our actions. Because our being is at issue for us in this way, we are always taking a *stand* on our lives in what we do. To say that I take a stand on my life means that I do not always act on my immediate desires and basic needs, for I have second-order motivations and commitments that range over and affect the sorts of first-order desires I have. For example, given my concern to be a person who is capable of self-control, I make an effort to moderate my cravings for chocolate, and this second-order commitment keeps those first-order cravings in check (at least sometimes).[5] My second-order commitments make up the motivational set that underlies my *identity* as an agent in the world. I can be a moderate, stable person—or, for that matter, a slacker or a loser—only because there are overarching motivations that shape my life and give me an orientation in the world. Heidegger points to this notion of taking a stand when he says that Dasein always has some *understanding* of being: "It is peculiar to this entity that with and through its being [i.e., the stand it takes], this being [i.e., its life in the world] is disclosed to it. *Understanding of being is itself a definite characteristic of Dasein's being"* (32).[6]

What must humans be like for there to be an understanding of this sort? To make sense of our capacities, Heidegger proposes that we think of human existence as a happening with specific structural components or dimensions. The first structural component of human existence is called *thrownness*. We are always thrown into a world, already under way in realizing specific possibilities (roles, self-interpretations, etc.) that define our place in the surrounding social world. Heidegger holds that our thrownness or situatedness at any time is made manifest through the moods in which we find ourselves (where even the pallid grayness of everyday life counts as a mood).

A second structural component of our lives is called *projection*. To be human is to be constantly projected into the future in accomplishing things through our actions. We are always "ahead of ourselves" to the extent that, in each of our actions, we are moving toward the realization of possibilities that define us as agents of a particular sort. Heidegger says that the concept of projecting is familiar to us through such everyday activities as "planning in the sense of the anticipatory regulating of human comportment."[7] But the concept of projection refers to something more basic than conscious goal-setting and planning. As a fundamental structure of human existence, projection refers to the fact that we are "outside ourselves" (*ex-sistere*), beyond immediate givenness, in taking a stand on our lives as a totality. As goal-directed and under way in the world, we are always moving toward the realization of our lives as a whole. Heidegger calls this futural projection "being-toward-the-end" or "being-toward-death."

Note that what defines our being, on this account, is not our condition in the present, not the sum of all that has happened up to this moment, and not the enduring presence of some thing. What defines our being are the specific ways we are pressing forward into the possibilities of acting and being that are opened up by the cultural context into which we are thrown. When Dasein is seen as an event, it is possible to see that we just *are* what we *make of ourselves* in living out our lives. It follows that my identity (that is, my *being*) as a person of a particular sort is defined by the way my actions are contributing to composing my life story as a whole.

Heidegger makes it clear that the ongoing happening of our lives never exists in isolation from the wider context of the world. According to the description of everyday activities, our lives are always enmeshed in concrete situations in such a way that there is no way to draw a sharp distinction between a "self" component and a "world" component. On the contrary, in our pretheoretical lives, there is usually such a tight reciprocal interaction between self and situation that what is normally *given* is a tightly interwoven whole. This fundamental self–world unity Heidegger calls *being-in-the-world*. His claim is that, when everything is running its course in ordinary life, the distinction between self and world presupposed by the tradition simply does not show up.

The everyday practical lifeworld is also always a shared, social world. As we are engaged in our ordinary involvements, we act according to the norms and conventions of the common world in such a way that there is no sharp distinction to be made between ourselves and others. The public world is the medium through which we first find ourselves and become agents. Heidegger says that "this common world, which is there primarily and into which every maturing Dasein first grows, . . . governs every interpretation of the world and of Dasein."[8] Even working alone in a cubicle involves being attuned to the patterns and regularities that make possible the coordination of public life.

It follows that in our day-to-day lives we are not so much "centers of experience and action" as we are the "They" or the "one" (*das Man*) as this is defined by our culture. We find ourselves first and foremost as crossing-points or placeholders in familiar public contexts. This social mode of being is itself a product of history. As Heidegger says,

> Whatever the way of being it may have at the time, and thus with whatever un-
> derstanding of being it might possess, Dasein has grown up both into and in a
> traditional way of interpreting itself: in terms of this it understands itself proxi-
> mally and, within a certain range, constantly. By this understanding, the possi-
> bilities of its being are disclosed and regulated. (41)

Since our possibilities of understanding and self-evaluation are all drawn from the ongoing flow of our shared historical context, our own identity as agents is something that arises from, and only makes sense in relation to, our culture's history. In this sense we are all, at the most basic level, placeholders in the ways of understanding and acting opened up and sustained by the They.

3

Early in *Being and Time*, Heidegger identifies what he calls Dasein's "authentic Self" or "authentic ability-to-be a Self" as an essential structure that is definitive of all instances of Dasein, regardless of the particular existentiell possibilities they might be enacting at the time. It is because being an authentic
Self is an essential structure in this sense that Heidegger can say that being a
They-self in everyday social existence must be understood as "an existentiell
modification of the authentic Self" (365). The conception of Dasein as an authentic Self is distinguished from the concrete mode of existence Dasein
achieves when it actually *realizes* this potentiality and becomes authentic, an
existentiell mode Heidegger calls "authentic being-one's-Self." The *authentic
Self* is said to be a potentiality or "ability-to-be," whereas *authentic being-one's-
Self* is a possibility, a specific and personal way of giving shape to one's authentic Self.

It is important to see here that the vocabulary of "potentiality" does not
imply that Dasein can ever exist simply as raw potentiality that has not yet
been realized. As Heidegger says, "being-a-self *is* in every case only in its
process of realization [*Vollzug*]."[9] Dasein exists only in specific, concrete
forms: This is what is meant by saying that "only the particular Dasein decides
its existence. . . . The question of existence never gets straightened out except
through existing itself" (33). On this view, even inauthentic existence is a way
of taking over the authentic Self, though its way of living deforms or falls short
of what is possible for our being as authentic Selves. It is precisely because
there can be a gap between our *ability-to-be* and our *concrete ways of realizing
it* that Heidegger invokes the ancient injunction, given its modern meaning by

Nietzsche: "Become what you are" (186). In Heidegger's view, being a Self is an accomplishment rather than a given. Selfhood is something we have to do rather than something we find.

We can get clearer about the concept of the authentic Self by focusing on the account of Dasein's most basic essential structure, understanding. Heidegger defines Dasein's understanding as a "self-projective being toward its ownmost ability-to-be" (236). This definition brings together some of the key notions built into Heidegger's conception of human existence. It suggests, first of all, that each of us has a life lying before us as something we can and will be. Second, the definition of understanding tells us that, in each of our actions, we are taking some stand on the life we have to live. Even a seemingly trivial action can be a self-definition to the extent that it undertakes a commitment concerning the sort of person I am becoming in my life as a whole— for example, being a punctual person, being a lifelong bachelor, or being a careless driver. In projecting ourselves into the future in our involvements, our existence is essentially *futural*. It is because Dasein exists as a "bringing itself to fruition" (*sich zeitigen*) that temporality (*Zeitlichkeit*) characterizes its being. Finally, to say that we exist as "*self*-projections" is to say that our own choices at any moment are defining us as beings of a certain sort. We are, for this reason, self-making or self-constituting beings; we just *are* what we make of ourselves in the course of living out our lives. This is what Heidegger means when he says that "the essence of [Dasein] is existence" (171).

Heidegger distinguishes two basic orientations a self-projection can have. Dasein can understand itself primarily in terms of the *world* and others, a form of projection in which one is dispersed and "lost" in the whirlwind of daily involvements. Or Dasein can "disclose itself to itself in and as its ownmost ability-to-be" (264). This second form of projection is called "*authentic disclosedness*," and it is described as a form of projection that "shows the phenomenon of the most primordial truth." In Heidegger's words, "The most primordial, and indeed the most authentic disclosedness in which Dasein, as an ability-to-be can be, is the *truth of existence*" (264). As this description makes clear, authentic and primordial truth, the truth of existence, just *is* what is disclosed in Dasein's disclosive projection when it is projected toward its ownmost ability-to-be.

4

Our account so far has shown that the "authentic Self," understood as Dasein's ownmost ability-to-be, only gains its specific content or "filling" as being-in-the-world by taking up and incorporating concrete possibilities of self-interpretation.

But, as we have seen, the concrete possibilities of self-understanding we can take over in being-in-the-world all come from the They. For the most part in our everyday lives, we are dispersed into They-possibilities, doing what "one" does as *anyone* might do such things. Being a "They-self" in this way promotes a mode of existence Heidegger calls "inauthentic." The German word for "authentic," *eigentlich*, comes from the stem *eigen* which means "own," so an inauthentic life would be one that is unowned or disowned. As inauthentic, my life is not my own but rather that of the They. Such a life is characterized by falling, fleeing, and forgetting; it is a life in which one is blind to one's ownmost ability-to-be and to the possibility of realizing what, as an authentic Self, one truly is. Drifting with the flow of the latest fads and preoccupations, an inauthentic life is fragmented and disjointed, lacking any cohesiveness or focus.

It is against the backdrop of this picture of average, everyday, inauthentic existence that Heidegger introduces his account of authenticity. The notion of authentic existence is first introduced in the context of some methodological remarks Heidegger makes at the outset of Division II of *Being and Time*. The proximal goal of *Being and Time*, he says, is to grasp the meaning of Dasein's being—that is, to make sense of what it is for Dasein to be. As a concrete, phenomenological inquiry, we start by looking at a particular instance of Dasein, ourselves. Heidegger now points out that this project of grasping the meaning of Dasein's being requires that we understand this entity as a *unity* and as a *whole*.

The point of this claim becomes clear if we reflect on what is involved in trying to make sense of a text. It is a fundamental principle of hermeneutics that "only that which really constitutes a unity of meaning is intelligible."[10] In literary interpretation, this principle tells us that, in interpreting a text, we must project a coherent, overall meaning for the text as a whole before we can begin to make sense of its parts. The same principle seems to be at work in trying to grasp the meaning of Dasein's being: One must have a conception of Dasein as unified and as a whole before one can begin to inquire into the meaning of its being. This wholeness cannot be seen as something pieced together from parts, for, as Heidegger says, one would need to have an architect's plan in advance to see how the pieces should hang together before one could attempt such an assembling operation (226). But neither can we arbitrarily impose a unifying principle from outside. If one is to remain faithful to the idea of phenomenology, this unity and wholeness must actually *present itself* in a concrete way of being of Dasein itself. Insofar as phenomenology must ground "the ontological 'truth' of the existential analysis" on "primordial existentiell truth" (364), the primordial existentiell truth must be discernible in a way that shows the fundamental unity and totality of Dasein's being.

If Dasein's ordinary ways of being are generally dispersed and distracted, however, how are we to encounter Dasein as a unified whole? The answer follows quite naturally from the conception of Dasein as an event. The *being* of an event (i.e., *what happened*) is determined by the culmination or outcome of the event—by the unfolding of the event "from start to finish." In the same way, Heidegger says that we can get the *whole* of Dasein into our phenomenological view only if we grasp it as it is "from its 'beginning' to its 'end.'" That is, we must be able to understand Dasein as it is " 'between' birth and death" (276). But this formulation seems to suggest that we can grasp Dasein's being only when it has actually *become* a whole—that is, when its life has run its course and it has reached death. And this surely would be absurd, for it would mean that Dasein's being is intelligible only when it is *no longer*, that is, when its being has terminated and Dasein no longer *is*. To avoid this absurdity, Heidegger suggests that we think of death not as an impending event, but as *a way of being* of Dasein. What is at issue in the notion of death is not the idea of Dasein's being at its end, but rather Dasein's being "*toward*-its-end" in a way that imparts continuity and wholeness to its being.[11]

Identifying such a mode of existence requires that we presuppose and interpret a particular "way of taking existence," a specific existentiell way of being that is possible for Dasein. In lectures delivered shortly after *Being and Time*, Heidegger said that grounding the account of Dasein's being involves "the construction [*Konstruktion*] of one of the most *extreme* possibilities of Dasein's authentic and whole ability-to-be," its way of existing in an "extreme existentiell commitment" which first "reveals the essential finitude of Dasein's existence" (MFL 139–40, my emphasis). The "extreme model" he is referring to is *authentic being-one's-Self*. In other words, the claim is that we can begin to work out an account of the meaning of Dasein's being only if we look at the form it takes when Dasein is authentic.

In *Being and Time*, authentic existence is described in terms of the idea of "anticipatory resoluteness." Each of the two components of this conception of authenticity, anticipation and resoluteness, contributes to making visible the wholeness and unity of Dasein's being. The first, *anticipation*, makes manifest the wholeness of Dasein in the specific way of "anticipating" or, more literally, "running forward toward" death. In Heidegger's use, the term "death" refers to the fact that, as finite beings, our lives are going somewhere or are adding up to something as a whole. Dasein's being is fundamentally *futural* to the extent that it is always already under way toward making something of its life as a totality. Whether we realize it or not, each of us exists as a movement directed toward the fulfillment of an entire life. The conception of life as *being-toward-the-end* means that our lives are moving toward achieving some configuration of meaning as a whole—some *Gestalt* or, as Heidegger calls it later, some *morphê*—and that the overall shape our lives take is *at issue* for us. Authentic running-forward toward this totality consists in projecting oneself toward one's being-a-whole in a way that imparts coherence, continuity, and cohesiveness to one's life. Such a life has what Heidegger calls *constancy* and *steadiness*. Only in a focused, clear-sighted pressing forward into the whole of its life can Dasein fully *realize* its being "toward-the-end" and so show up as a whole.

The second component of authentic existence, *resoluteness*, brings to light both the wholeness and the unity of Dasein's being. The concept of resoluteness presupposes the notion of being "simplified." Since Dasein's lack of unity and wholeness in everydayness results from its being dispersed and strewn out over an "endless multiplicity of possibilities which offer themselves as closest to one" (453), Heidegger says that "the mode of disclosure in which Dasein brings itself before itself must be such that in it Dasein becomes accessible as *simplified* in a certain manner" (226). This simplifying is achieved when Dasein pulls itself back from its forgetful dispersal in the world and makes a resolute *commitment* to something that gives its life a defining content. As resolute, Heidegger says, Dasein "*gives* itself the current factical Situation" (355) with a degree of clarity and focus that is lacking in average everydayness. In such a resolute commitment, Dasein overcomes its uprootedness and groundlessness by becoming its own ground, and it thereby achieves the constancy (*Ständigkeit*) of "having taken a stand" (369). Taking an authentic stand on one's Situation makes it possible to fully realize what one is as an ability-to-be—as Heidegger says, "Dasein becomes 'essentially' Dasein [only] in . . . authentic existence" (370). Or, as he puts it later, resolute commitment is an "explicit self-choice" (*ausdrücklichen Sichselbstwählen*) which involves a constantly *repeated* and "complete self-commitment" to what Dasein "already always is" (MFL 190). Through resoluteness and repetition, Dasein devotes itself in a coherent, simplified way to "what is world-historical in its current Situation" (442).

Anticipatory resoluteness pulls Dasein away from its entanglement in beings and "brings Dasein back to its ownmost ability-to-be-a-Self" (354). Indeed, it is only in resoluteness that one *becomes a Self*—that is, has an *identity*—in the fullest sense of that word.[12] It is in this sense that resoluteness constitutes "the primordial *truth* of existence" (355). What this means is that, when one is resolute, one no longer simply intends Dasein's basic structures in an empty, "formal" way. Instead, in actually *living out* what is projected in the "fore-having" of one's structures of being, what is projected in the "formal indication" is now given content and fulfilled. Resoluteness realizes Dasein's being as a unified temporal unfolding and so brings its being-a-whole into a concrete form for the first time. Resolute disclosure is "the primordial truth of existence," because *what* is to be discovered in such a disclosure is nothing other than *the disclosure itself*. This seems to be what Heidegger means when he says that, in resoluteness, "Dasein is revealed . . . in such a way that Dasein *is* this revealing and being-revealed" (355). One has *become* the very thing one hoped to find in this search for the truth about the being of Dasein. Since there is, in this case, a perfect coincidence of "knowing" and what is to be "known," Heidegger says that in resoluteness, "one's ability-to-be becomes authentic and wholly transparent" (354).

5

It should be clear from this account of authentic existence that the primary role played by the notion of authenticity in Division II is to provide phenomenological content for what was initially projected only in "formal indications" earlier in *Being and Time.* On this view of Heidegger's method, the only way to ground the insights put forward by fundamental ontology is to actually become a *Self,* where this is understood as a way of being focused, coherent, temporally unified, and "transparent" about *"all* the constitutive items which are essential to" Dasein (187).

It seems, then, that the primary role of the concept of authenticity in *Being and Time* is epistemological: It provides concrete evidence for what was initially intended only in a formal indication. It follows that the only way to fully grasp the account of human existence presented in *Being and Time* is to actually *become* authentic. Phenomenology is possible only for authentic individuals.

But the hortatory tone of Division II of Heidegger's greatest work makes it clear that Heidegger also regards an authentic existence as one that is higher and more fulfilling than inauthentic everydayness. As we saw, the German word for authenticity comes from the stem meaning "own," and it suggests that an authentic existence is one that is "owned up to" in a unique way. Instead of drifting aimlessly into various "They" roles and doing "what one does," authentic Dasein seizes on its "mineness" and lives in a way that takes over the decisions it is already making as a participant in the They. Heidegger says that authenticity is a matter of "choosing to choose," that is, of making one's choices one's own and so being "answerable" or "responsible" (*verantwortlich*) for one's life (313, 334).

What makes it possible for us to take ownership of our own lives is the experience of *anxiety.* In anxiety, according to Heidegger, we are faced with the ultimate contingency of the They-possibilities we pick up from the public world. Anxiety brings us face-to-face with our "being-toward-death," with the fact that we exist as a task of making something of our lives as a whole. Facing up to our existence as finite projections, we see that each of our actions contributes to composing our life stories as a whole.

Confronting death can lead you to see the weightiness of your own existence. Recognizing that not everything is possible, you see that it is up to you to decide what form your life is taking and will take overall. To take a stand on your own death, then, is to live in such a way that, in each of your actions, you express a lucid understanding of where your life is going—of how things are adding up as a whole. A life lived in this way becomes simplified, focused, and coherent in its future-directedness: As Heidegger says, "one is liberated from one's lostness in those possibilities which may accidentally thrust themselves upon one; and one is liberated in such a way that for the first time one can authentically understand and choose among those factical possibilities lying before" one's death (308). Facing death, and recognizing the ultimate contingency of the ways of living made accessible by the They, we are able to see possibilities "*as* possibilities," something we *choose*, and we see our lives as something we are defining through our choices.

It should be obvious that this conception of authenticity has nothing to do with getting in touch with some "inner" reality. Instead, authenticity is a matter of living in such a way that your life has cumulativeness, purposiveness, and wholeheartedness. By achieving "a sober understanding of what are factically the basic possibilities for Dasein" (358), you can focus on what is truly worth pursuing in your life. Only through such a decisive appropriation of possibilities does Dasein first become "individuated" and so a true "Self."

Heidegger emphasizes the fact that authenticity does not detach us from everyday social existence. The authentic individual is deeply implicated in and obligated to the historical context in which he or she lives. But becoming authentic does transform the *way* we live in the world. In our ordinary lives, our actions generally have an instrumentalist "means/ends" structure. We do things in order to win the rewards that come from having performed in a socially acceptable way. These rewards are thought of as something external to the action itself, for example, the cocktail at the end of the day, the two-week vacation each year, a comfortable retirement in later years. Given such a means/ends orientation to life, we tend to live as strategic calculators, trying to figure out the most cost-efficient means to obtaining the ends we desire.

In contrast, the authentic individual experiences actions as contributing to the formation of a life as a whole. Life then has a "constituent/whole" structure: I act *for the sake of being* a person of a particular sort, and I experience my actions as constituents of a life that I am realizing in all I do. In this sort of life, the ends of acting are not external rewards that might be obtained in some way other than by performing this action. They are instead *internal* to the action and hence define the meaning of that action. Thus, although both the "means/ends" and "constituent/whole" styles of life may consist in the same actions, there is an important qualitative difference in the actions themselves. There is an obvious difference between helping others *in order to* feel good and helping others *for the sake of being* a caring, decent person. And there is an important difference between telling someone the truth in order to gain her trust and telling the truth as part of being a truthful person. In each example, the action is the same, but the quality of life expressed in the action is different. In the authentic way of living, I take responsibility for the character I am forming through my actions, and I assume my identity by being answerable for the kind of person I am.

The concept of authenticity therefore provides the basis for making sense of the connectedness, continuity, and coherence of life. The integrity of a life history—its *selfsameness*—is grounded not in some enduring substance, but in what we *do* in the world. Acting is a matter of resolutely drawing on the pool of possibilities opened by one's culture and remaining firm and wholehearted in one's commitments. Such a life has a narrative structure. Just as a narrative gains its meaning from the direction the course of events is taking "as a whole," so an authentic life gains its meaning from the way the events and actions are focused on realizing something as a totality. In Heidegger's view, it is only by living in this way that one can *be* an individual or a Self.

Notes

1. Heidegger, *Being and Time*, trans. J. Macquarrie and E. Robinson (New York: Harper & Row, 1962), 68. (Hereafter cited in text by page numbers in parentheses.)

2. Heidegger is exceptionally precise in his use of these technical terms. Throughout *Being and Time*, the "They" and the "authentic Self" are always "existentials," that is, essential structures, whereas "They-self" and "authentic-being-one's-Self" are "existentiell modifications."

3. These stages do not correspond to the two "divisions" of *Being and Time*. Both stages appear at various times in the development of both divisions.

4. In earlier lectures, this project of finding concrete fillings had been described as the "primordial *evidence situation*" in which we decide whether "the object authentically gives itself as that which it is and as it is" (*Gesamtausgabe* 61: 35).

5. This way of putting the idea is drawn from Harry Frankfurt's "Freedom of the Will and the Concept of a Person," *Journal of Philosophy* 67 (January 1971): 5–20. Heidegger's own formulation of the idea traces back to Hegel's "Introduction" to the *Phenomenology of Spirit*. In Heidegger's view, even the person Frankfurt calls "wanton" must have second-order commitments (to being wanton) if he or she is to count as an instance of Dasein.

6. Gadamer points out that the original meaning of the German word for understanding, *Verstehen*, was the legal sense of asserting one's own standpoint, a root meaning that supports Heidegger's conception of understanding as "standing up for"

or "taking a stand" (*stehen für . . .*). Hans-Georg Gadamer, *Truth and Method*, trans. J. Weinsheimer and D. G. Marshall (New York: Crossroad, 1989), 260–61, n. 173.

7. Heidegger, *The Fundamental Concepts of Metaphysics: World, Finitude, Solitude* (orig. 1929/30), trans. W. McNeill and N. Walker (Bloomington: Indiana University Press 1995), 362. (Hereafter cited as FCM.)

8. Heidegger, *History of the Concept of Time* (orig. 1925), trans. T. Kisiel (Bloomington: Indiana University Press, 1985), 249.

9. Heidegger, *The Metaphysical Foundations of Logic* (orig. 1928), trans. M. Heim (Bloomington: Indiana University Press, 1984), 139 (my emphasis). (Hereafter MFL.)

10. Gadamer, *Truth and Method*, 294; translation modified slightly.

11. To be "toward the end" is not to be concerned about the possibility of one's "demise," where demise is regarded as a sort of "perishing." Heidegger takes great pains to say that the existential concept of death should be distinguished from the notions of demise and perishing (see Being and Time, sec. 49). Rather, it is truer to Heidegger's thought to think of the "end" as a project of self-fulfillment, as the task of realizing one's own (*eigen*) human potential. And, of course, such an "end" is one we may never be able to attain—as Heidegger says, "Authenticity is only a modification but not a total obliteration of inauthenticity" (*The Basic Problems of Phenomenology* [orig. 1927], trans. A. Hofstadter [Bloomington: Indiana University Press, 1982], 171; hereafter BPP). As inescapably tied to the They, authentic being-one's-Self is always shadowed by inauthenticity.

12. Heidegger draws a distinction between the formal logical concept of *identity,* which asserts that each thing is identical to itself, and the existential idea of *selfsameness,* where this is understood as *ipseity,* as knitting together an interconnected and unified whole through time. To say that "Dasein has a peculiar selfsameness with itself in the sense of *selfhood*" (BPP 170), then, is to say that the self has a narrative unity by virtue of the fact that a stand on the future provides the orientation in terms of which the past is drawn forward as a resource for action in the present. See Paul Ricoeur, "Narrative Time," *Critical Inquiry* 7 (Autumn 1980): 169–90.

IV
SARTRE

7

Sartre's Early Ethics and the Ontology of *Being and Nothingness*

Thomas C. Anderson

FOR DECADES THERE HAS BEEN controversy over whether the ontology Sartre sets forth in *Being and Nothingness* is compatible with an ethical theory. Some have claimed that its pessimistic portrayal of human existence—as a useless passion doomed to failure, an unhappy consciousness which cannot escape its unhappy state[1]—and its negative account of human relations—as inevitably conflictive[2]—rendered ethics meaningless or impossible. Others have maintained that Sartre's denial of all objective moral values inevitably resulted in complete moral relativism.[3] Still others, myself included, have contended that such conclusions involve serious misinterpretations of Sartre's early phenomenological ontology, and that the latter in fact provides the foundation for a coherent (though not flawless) ethics whose general outline is suggested by Sartre himself in some early published works.[4]

All interpreters agree that Sartre frequently took public moral stands and that he employed notions having a moral character, notions such as bad faith, authenticity, radical conversion, the city of ends, and so on. But disagreement remains about both the meaning of these concepts and their compatibility with his early ontology. Of course, these controversies would presumably have been resolved long ago if Sartre had finished the work on ethics that he promised at the end of *Being and Nothingness*.

Fortunately, three years after his death Sartre's adoptive daughter published two of his notebooks, entitled *Cahiers pour une morale* and written in 1947–48, which are part of the ethics he was then working on as the sequel to his ontology. While these six hundred pages of notes do not constitute a completed text and comprise only about one-fifth of a larger collection which was lost, they still furnish a great deal of insight into the ethics Sartre was developing complementary to, and grounded in, his early ontology. My purpose is to show how the *Cahiers* (in spite of its inevitable ambiguities and inconsistencies) can help resolve many of the contentious issues surrounding that Sartrean ethics.

Of course, this article concentrates on two early works in Sartre's career, and he later modified some, though certainly not all, of the positions he adopted in this period. However, in order to assess the extent of any such modification it is necessary to determine exactly Sartre's early position. It will be my contention in what follows that the *Cahiers* shows that many standard interpretations of the ontology of *Being and Nothingness* are erroneous and, as a result, that they see the later Sartre shifting more radically than he did in fact. On the other hand, insofar as Sartre does significantly modify his early positions in some areas, especially his understanding of interpersonal relations, it is important to recognize that the changes actually begin very early, in the *Cahiers* (as well as in other published works of this period).

Speaking of the latter, I should note that the notebooks we have were written at the same time as *What Is Literature?* and shortly after the publication of *Existentialism and Humanism* and "Materialism and Revolution." In my analysis I will briefly refer to these works where appropriate and point out some of the interesting parallels between positions taken in them and in the *Cahiers*.[5] Let me add that even though these early published works contain some of the same positions that are found in the *Cahiers*, the latter offers far more explanation of, and justification for, these positions.

Actually, the *Cahiers* was the first of three ethics Sartre worked on in his lifetime. While I believe that a number of the basic positions Sartre adopts in it (for example, the primary moral ideal and goal he proposes) are maintained throughout is career, I will not pursue this point here except to note that in interviews toward the end of his life Sartre stated he was "returning" to this first morality "enriching" it and not rejecting it.[6] In this article, I intend rather to focus on three important issues of interpretation of *Being and Nothingness*, issues about which commentators have been in sharp disagreement. These issues are central to understanding *Being and Nothingness* and, therefore, must be resolved if one is to determine the extent to which Sartre's later positions constitute a shift from his earlier ones. Specifically I will seek to answer the following questions: (1) Does the ontology of *Being and Nothingness* doom human existence to inevitable failure and meaninglessness, thus rendering ethics pointless? (2) Since Sartre rejects all objective values in *Being and Nothingness*, can he offer any coherent reason for preferring one value or set of values over another in his ethics? (3) If conflict is the very "essence" of human relations, as *Being and Nothingness* claims, what is the significance of ethical norms?

My procedure in treating each question will be first to present the often conflicting positions of Sartre's commentators, then to use the *Cahiers* in an attempt to resolve their disputes, and finally to offer some evaluation of Sartre's position and that of his commentators.

Does the ontology of *Being and Nothingness* doom human existence to inevitable failure and meaninglessness, thus rendering ethics pointless? Those who answer affirmatively point to the extremely pessimistic statements Sartre utters in his conclusion to *Being and Nothingness*: "all human activities are equivalent . . . all are on principle doomed to failure. Thus it amounts to the same thing whether one gets drunk alone or is a leader of nations."[7] A basic ontological reason for his nihilism is, of course, that Sartre believes that every human being's fundamental urge is for the impossible, namely, to be God. We desire to be a being that would be necessary, that is, exist by right rather than by contingency, but one that would preserve its freedom and consciousness by being itself the cause or foundation of its own necessity. Putting it in terms of freedom and choice, Sartre writes, "my freedom is a choice of being God and all my acts and all my projects translate this choice and reflect it in a thousand and one ways."[8] Again, referring to man's fundamental project, he says, "he can choose only to be God."[9] Since we can never achieve the status of an *ens causa sui*, no matter how much money, power, or virtue we attain, this fundamental desire or choice renders our existence a "useless passion," and the for-itself is "by nature an unhappy consciousness with no possibility of surpassing its unhappy state."[10] What sense, then, does ethics make in the face of this inevitable failure?

In reply, defenders of Sartre point to other early published works that indicate that he did not think that human existence was inevitably a useless failure. *What Is Literature?* proposes that in the creation of the aesthetic object man's existence is not in vain but meaningful, even joyful. And neither it nor "Materialism and Revolution" is pessimistic in tone, for in both Sartre suggests that it is eminently worthwhile to strive to achieve the city of ends, the classless society of democratic socialism.[11] Equally important is the general position he asserts in *Existentialism and Humanism*, namely, that our existence will possess as much meaning and significance as we ourselves give it[12]—a position certainly compatible with the ontology of *Being and Nothingness* which insists that human beings are the sole creators of meaning and value in a universe that itself possesses no objective or transcendent values.

Furthermore, on the last few pages of *Being and Nothingness* Sartre seems to hold out the possibility that human beings do not have to choose the project of being God as the primary value and goal of their lives. (And the statements he makes there about the failure of all human pursuits, as well as his

remark about the unhappy state of the for-itself, refer precisely to the vain desire and futile search for that impossible goal.) Of equal importance, and overlooked by most critics, is a crucial distinction Sartre makes early in that same
work between goals that one seeks as values on the prereflective level and
goals-values that one reflectively chooses.[13] Being God is a goal-value in the
first sense for Sartre, for contingent human beings inevitably, structurally, desire to be *ens causa sui*. But goals-values in the second sense are those one
freely chooses, and at the end of *Being and Nothingness* Sartre seems to allow
for the possibility that being God need not be reflectively chosen as the primary goal-value one actively pursues. However, since he suggests this possibility only briefly in a couple of pages, and only through a series of questions,
and since, as we saw, he also claims that man "can choose only to be God," his
position is not altogether clear.

By comparison the *Cahiers* is quite clear. Though in it Sartre reasserts his
view that human beings on the unreflective level inevitably aspire to be God,
he leaves no doubt that they need not *reflectively* choose this as their supreme
goal, nor should they if they wish to avoid failure (or "Hell," as he now calls
it). The following selection, written in 1945 and published as an appendix to
the *Cahiers*, makes this plain. Sartre writes: "the first project or original choice
that man makes of himself . . . is to join an *en-soi-pour-soi* [in-itself-for-itself]
and to identify himself with it, briefly to be God and his own foundation."[14]
This project, or choice, he goes on, is made unreflectively, and to live according to it is Hell (inevitable failure), and so the question becomes "will one exit
from Hell" and attain "salvation"? This question can be posed "only at the reflexive level." The question is, he continues, "whether reflection will accept responsibility for the first project of freedom or not accept it, and will be purifying reflection refusing to have anything to do with it."[15] And, he concludes,
"accomplice reflection is only the prolongation of the bad faith which is found
at the heart of the primitive nonthetic project [to be God], whereas pure reflection is a rupture with this projection and the constitution of a freedom
which takes itself for an end."[16] This distinction between a pure reflection,
which breaks with the God project, and an accomplice (or impure), which
simply goes along with it, is not new but was present in *Being and Nothingness*
and earlier in *The Transcendence of the Ego*, although both places treated in detail only impure reflection.[17] In fact, in *Being and Nothingness* Sartre stated explicitly that he was not going to discuss pure reflection and the conversion
that attains it. The study of "the nature and role of purifying reflection," he
said there, "cannot be made here [in a work of ontology]; it belongs rather to
an *Ethics*."[18] Of course, the *Cahiers* is, or was to be, that ethics, and it does indeed contain an extensive treatment of pure reflection, its rejection of the God
project, and its grasp of human freedom.

The *Cahiers* also unequivocally identifies pure reflection with the radical conversion from bad faith that Sartre occasionally refers to in *Being and Nothingness*, and like *Existentialism and Humanism*, it states that it is up to human beings, the only sources of meaning and value in the universe, to provide meaning (salvation) for their lives. Even though there are no transcendent or objective values that confer meaning on our existence, it is not a failure (Hell) if *we* choose to value it. In itself our existence is neither meaningful nor meaningless, neither justified nor unjustified, Sartre says. It is up to us, and to us alone, to justify it: "Man, the unjustifiable foundation of every justification"; and, again, "It is me, who nothing justifies, who justifies myself."[19] Thus, according to the *Cahiers*, a meaningless existence can be avoided by human beings if they choose something other than being God as their primary goal and value. (We have yet to see what this something should be.)

Unfortunately, what complicates the issue is that the *Cahiers* also repeats the assertion made in *Being and Nothingness* that men can *choose* only being God as their ultimate value. In the same appendix quoted from above, Sartre also says the following about the project to be God:" "This project is first in the sense that it is the very structure of my existence. I exist as choice, but this choice [of God] ... is made on an unreflective plane."[20] Though he insists that this unreflective choice is "freely made," he also maintains that "it can do nothing but posit the in-itself-for-itself."[21] It is true that Sartre immediately goes on to indicate, in passages cited earlier, that on the *reflective* level human beings need not choose the God project; nevertheless, such a reflective choice cannot erase my unreflective choice since it is "the very structure of my existence."[22] In other words, Sartre's position in the *Cahiers* (as in *Being and Nothingness*) is that the project to be God both must be (nonreflectively) freely chosen and need not be (reflectively) freely chosen as man's primary goal-value. But I would argue that to speak of a free choice (whether unreflective or not makes no difference) when no other fundamental options are possible than the project to be God is simply to misuse the term. A free choice with no options is self-contradictory. It makes better sense to speak of man's basic unreflective structural desire, passion, or project (all Sartre's words) to be God as just that, a desire, passion, or project, but not as a free choice. If one limits this latter term to its ordinary sense (which, Sartre admits, means an ability to select among at least two possibilities),[23] we find, as we saw above, that in the *Cahiers* he clearly holds that it is possible, and even necessary if one is to avoid failure, to choose some other fundamental goal than the unattainable one of being God.

I suspect that it was Sartre's overwhelming desire in his early ontology to protect human freedom against all comers that explains his overextended use of terms such as *choice* and *freedom*. Recall, for instance, that at this stage he insisted that *every* conscious act was a free choice, as were such "states" as emotions and desires. In fact, consciousness was *identified* with freedom and choice, and its free projects were often said to be *totally* responsible for the world and its structures.[24] Though the Sartre of *Being and Nothingness* admitted that human freedom was immersed in facticity, he tended to minimize the power of facticity to restrict and curtail freedom. The later Sartre made no such mistake, for he emphasized the power of social and political structures created by others to constrain one's freedom.

I have argued that in the *Cahiers* Sartre advises human beings to cease choosing God as their primary goal and value. However, some commentators claim that Sartre's position is that human beings should pursue this unattainable goal even though they realize that it is unattainable. We should become an *ens causa sui* in an analogous or "symbolic" way, István Mészáros says, and Linda Bell asserts that Sartre wants men to keep this impossible goal as a "regulating ideal" to guide their behavior.[25]

The problem with this interpretation of Sartre's position is that it seems to ignore his own wish at the close of *Being and Nothingness* that we "put an end to the reign of this value [the project to be God]," not to mention his advice in the *Cahiers* that we "renounce" the God project and "refuse to have anything to do with it." Furthermore, Sartre himself indicates in *Being and Nothingness* that his lengthy descriptions of symbolic ways of becoming an *in-itself-for-itself*, through doing and appropriation (having), are descriptions of activities of those who have not undergone the "purifying reflection" necessary for ethics.[26] And the *Cahiers* goes even farther and explicitly labels as "inauthentic" the attempt to symbolically become *causa sui*.[27]

The response of the *Cahiers* to our first issue, then, is that human existence is not inevitably a failure or a useless passion, since human beings can reflectively choose freely to renounce (though not eradicate) their fundamental passion to be God. They can choose as their primary end and value something other than the *ens causa sui*, even though they can never cease structurally to desire that impossible goal. But what should be chosen in its place according to Sartre? This brings us to our second issue: Since Sartre rejects all objective values in *Being and Nothingness*, can he offer any coherent reason for preferring one value or set of values over another?

Critics of Sartre claim that since for him all values are created by human freedom, all are equally arbitrary or subjective. For example, Sartre himself may prefer human freedom and the classless society, but since the value of these objects comes only from his free choice, anyone can freely choose to value the exact opposite. Because he denies objective values, Sartre has no basis for claiming that one person's moral values, including his, should be preferred to any others.[28]

On the other hand, many have noted that on the last two pages of *Being and Nothingness* Sartre appears to suggest that human freedom is the goal one should choose in place of being God. Certainly it is generally recognized by defenders and critics alike that in *Existentialism and Humanism*, "Materialism and Revolution," *What Is Literature?* and elsewhere (including some very late interviews) Sartre does propose human well-being and, more specifically, human freedom as his primary goal.[29] Many have also observed that *Existentialism and Humanism* appears to offer a very concise argument in support of such a choice, an argument that, his critics notwithstanding, is rooted in Sartre's ontological denial of objective values. This cryptic argument has been analyzed elsewhere in some detail, and so I will only repeat it briefly here. *Existentialism and Humanism* suggests that since human freedom is in fact the source of all value, "strict consistency" requires that that freedom be chosen by the individual as his or her primary value.[30] Sartre's point appears to be that if any other object is chosen as one's value, such a choice and value would have little worth if the freedom from which it issued is not itself valued more basically. Needless to say, there is controversy about the validity of this argument, which I will address below.

As for the *Cahiers*, freedom is clearly proposed as an alternative goal to God. Thus, in a text cited above (note 16), Sartre states that pure reflection refuses to have anything to do with the project to be God and, instead, is "the constitution of a freedom which takes itself for an end." Actually, Sartre refers to the goal or end of his morality in various ways in his notebooks, but all are intimately connected to freedom and most are practically equivalent to it. Thus, while he speaks of the final goal of humanity as the freedom of all, the whole or totality of freedom, and of men's ultimate end as "establishing a reign of concrete freedom," "the human reign,"[31] he also calls this reign and goal the city or realm of ends, where each treats the other as an end and all live in intersubjective unity.[32] This city is in turn identified with socialist society in which there is no ruling class. And the classless society in its turn is designated as the place where "freedom is valued and willed as such."[33] In one passage he goes so far as to say that the ultimate goal of man is not mutual love or respect, nor even a classless society or city of ends. Rather, "the person is his goal under the form of *ek-stase* [i.e., freedom] and gift."[34]

However, this reference to the human person as gift confuses matters by suggesting another ultimate goal than freedom. And indeed the *Cahiers* does say that the human being's "absolute end" after pure reflection or conversion is the creation of the world, and even the "salvation" of the world by making freedom its origin. It states that the "task" and "destiny" of man is generosity, that is, to give oneself to Being so as to make it appear as a world.[35] It is true that to choose as one's absolute end the creation of the world means to choose man as free (for it is precisely because man is free that he is the creator of the world); nevertheless, to make one's goal the free revelation of Being as world is not identical to making human freedom one's goals. For the latter makes *man's* being its goal; the former makes *being's* appearance and foundation primary. Unfortunately, in different places the *Cahiers* affirms each one as the converted person's primary goal.

In fact, this second goal, the free creation of the world, remains extremely formal in the notebooks and sounds much like the goal of all artistic creation for Sartre, namely, the presentation of an object as totally founded by freedom. Just as freedom is always the foundation of every human work of art, so the converted person wills freedom to be the foundation of the real world.[36] The problem with this is that freedom always is just such a foundation no matter what world it makes appear—one of peace, justice, and beauty or one of war, brutality, and ugliness. Unlike the goal of freedom for all in a classless society, which has content to it, the goal of creativity offers no guidance about what kind of world human beings should create. I suspect this is one reason Sartre later labeled the ethics of the *Cahiers* pejoratively a "writer's ethic" and criticized it for being too abstract.[37]

Fortunately, there are rather clear indications that freedom for all is really the primary goal of the notebooks. In some passages Sartre suggests that the reason human beings freely create a world, and thereby give meaning and justification to being, is to attain meaning and justification for their own free existence.[38] Since human reality is fundamentally a being-in-the-world ontologically grounded in being, it can have meaning ultimately only if the world and being have meaning. Thus, though the *Cahiers* proposes two somewhat different primary goals for the ethics it sets forth, creativity seems to be basically a means, while human reality, or human reality as free, is its ultimate end. It is worth mentioning that *What Is Literature?* also discusses the relation between creativity and the classless society or city of ends. However, it mainly considers the creation of works of art; the *Cahiers* is mainly concerned with the creation of the world. *What Is Literature?* argues that since literature is an appeal of freedom to freedom it can "only realize its full essence in a classless society" which will be "the reign of human freedom."[39]

But why should a free human reality be the ultimate end of Sartre's ethics? Certainly not because it possesses some objective or intrinsic value, for Sartre's ontology denies this. The argument of the *Cahiers*, the most elaborate ever offered by Sartre, is put in terms of meaning and justification. As we have already noted, in his universe only human beings, or, more precisely, human beings as free, create all meaning and value. But if any human creations, of self or world, are to possess an *ultimate* (or absolute) value or significance, their source or ground itself must especially be of value. After all, how significant would be a meaning that came from and rested on a valueless source and foundation? As the *Cahiers* often puts it, creation must be justified, given an *absolute* foundation. But man is precisely such a foundation, for he is the absolute—that is to say, irreducible and only—source of all justification in the universe. Man alone can supply a meaningful foundation or justification for his own existence, by accepting in pure reflection his ontological freedom and conferring value on it. If he does so it will thereby possess value and justification, and whatever it creates will in turn be grounded in meaning and so also justified. Thus Sartre argues that freedom should be valued above all else, for only then will it and its creations receive an ultimate (absolute) meaning and justification.[40] (Note that his extended argument of the *Cahiers* is quite similar to the one briefly indicated in *Existentialism and Humanism*.)

A number of critics, while admitting that Sartre does propose freedom as his primary moral value, complain that he remains extremely vague in these early years about the concrete content to be included in such a goal. And Sartre himself later voiced this criticism of his early work. As we noted, the *Cahiers* does identify the reign of freedom with the classless society and socialism, but neither is discussed in any detail. Similarly, when he speaks of creativity as man's goal, Sartre asserts that our task is to reveal the maximum amount of being, for doing so will give maximum meaning to the world and to human existence. Yet, since he admits that all human attitudes create meaning, and that whatever happens to a human being allows him to create more, it is unclear just what creating the maximum amount of being actually entails.[41]

The most powerful suggestion the notebooks offer is their insistence that freedom must be willed concretely, and this means willing human reality not as pure freedom but as freedom immersed in facticity. It is precisely my facticity that makes my freedom and its projects concrete, that gives shape and direction to the goals I seek and the values I create. It is also my facticity that expands or contracts my freedom. It follows that if the social conditions in which I live are oppressive and restrict my freedom, a choice of freedom entails the change or removal of these oppressive structures.[42] To will freedom concretely means to structure the personal and social facticity or situation of human beings so that they have more freedom. The most freedom for all will be available in a classless society where each treats the other as an end. Thus, Sartre's goal here, while lacking in specific details, is not totally contentless.[43] Some years later Sartre's insistence that human freedom is always enveloped in facticity will lead to emphasizing human needs and their role in specifying our goals. This will give even more content to freedom as a goal, for choosing freedom will then mean making attainable those many and various goals that can fulfill human needs. But that is later; needs have only minor significance in the *Cahiers* and in other works of this early period.[44]

It remains to evaluate Sartre's argument that human beings should choose freedom as their primary value. A number of authors have observed that this is persuasive only if one first values logical consistency, rationality, or consistency with reality.[45] Recall that Sartre's argument, developed at some length in the *Cahiers*, maintains that freedom should be valued because it is in fact the source of all values and meaning in the world, including that of my own life. He suggests that it would not be rationally consistent or consistent with the facts of the matter ("consistent" is Sartre's very word in *Existentialism and Humanism*) to value some goal and not value that freedom through which that goal is valued in the first place. But, of course, in Sartre's universe one may freely choose to value irrationality or inconsistency instead of their opposites, for neither possesses any intrinsic or objective value. Is Sartre, in spite of his ontology, presupposing in his argument that rational consistency and consistency with reality have objective value? Some critics have made this charge. I believe rather that Sartre fully recognizes that in the final analysis consistency has value because one freely gives it value. As he says in *Being and Nothingness*, the choice to be rational is "beyond all reasons" and "prior to all logic" because it is precisely by that choice that one confers value on logic and rational argumentation.[46] Indeed it is impossible to give reasons in support of valuing logical consistency or rationality without begging the question!

On the other hand, Linda Bell has claimed that Sartre's argument for freedom rests on the fact that in order to freely value anything whatsoever one must first value freedom: "the choice of anything as a value entails the more fundamental choice of freedom as a value." This is true, she assets, because "he who wills the end wills the means" and because in Sartre's world freedom "bears a unique position of means to every other value."[47]

But what does it mean to say that "he who wills the end wills the means"? If Bell is claiming that one cannot *in fact* will an end without also willing the means to it—in other words, that willing the end must actually "entail" willing the means—I believe she is incorrect. Surely I can will a goal, such as a healthy body, and yet not will the means to it, such as daily exercise or a low-cholesterol diet. People do this all the time. It may be illogical or stupid to will ends without willing the means to them, but we can in fact do so. To say that "he who wills the end wills the means" can only mean that it is irrational, logically inconsistent, to will an end and not also will the means, because one logically (though not factually) "entails" the other. I agree that he who wills the end (a meaningful life) should, to be reasonable, will the means to it (freedom). However, I repeat, for Sartre human beings have no absolute obligation to be reasonable or logically consistent, for being or doing so has no objective value. To claim, as Bell does, that "one who allegedly wills the end without at the same time willing the means is not in earnest about willing the end" may also be true. But this does not mean that one cannot really will one without willing the other; moreover, "earnestness" has no more objective value for Sartre than does consistency.

A somewhat similar argument is offered by Thomas Flynn.[48] Admitting that Sartre's own defense of the need to be rationally consistent is "weak," Flynn suggests that Sartre should have referred to "existential" rather than "logical" consistency. Thus, Flynn says, for a person to freely choose "unfreedom" is not logically inconsistent but "a futile and empty gesture; in fact a nonact." To freely choose unfreedom is "impossible in practice"; it is like choosing not to choose. I think Flynn is correct; it is existentially, or practically, inconsistent to freely choose unfreedom (though it is too strong to claim it is "impossible in practice," for it is evident that people often do freely choose unfreedom, for example freely choosing to enslave themselves to drugs). However, the notion of existential inconsistency does not addresses the main conclusion Sartre wishes to defend, namely, that freedom should be the *primary* value one chooses in place of being God. Granted, it is existentially inconsistent to freely choose *un*freedom; but it is not existentially inconsistent to freely choose power or pleasure or God (rather than freedom) as one's *fundamental* value, so long as one still awards some lesser value to freedom. Thus I do not think that Sartre can appeal to existential consistency in order to demonstrate that freedom should be one's primary value. Instead, he seems to be correct in suggesting that it would be logically inconsistent, and inconsistent with reality, including human reality, to desire a meaningful existence and not first and foremost value human freedom.[49]

In the *Cahiers* Sartre argues for human freedom as the primary value one should choose in place of being God. The person who undergoes a pure reflection, a conversion, and chooses freedom as his end is called the "authentic" individual.[50] And the authentic individual, Sartre says, does not choose just his own personal freedom as his goal; he chooses to recognize and support as well other freedoms in the city of ends. This brings us to the third and last issue to be discussed: Sartre's view of human relations. If conflict is the essence of human relations (as *Being and Nothingness* apparently maintains), what is the point of ethical norms, especially any that would oblige me to respect and promote the freedom of others?

Countless critics have maintained that Sartre in *Being and Nothingness* holds that all human relations are essentially conflictual.[51] They point out that he describes in great detail a panorama of relations, including love, and shows that ultimately all involved conflict inasmuch as they are attempts at domination and subjugation of oneself by others and/or of others by oneself. Does not Sartre himself state, "Conflict is the original meaning of being-for-others," at the very beginning of his discussion of concrete human relations? Likewise, at the end of this same discussion, even after admitting that human beings do occasionally cooperate and work together, he insists that this does not "modify the results of our prior investigation," namely, that "the essence of the relations between consciousnesses is not the *Mitsein*, it is conflict."[52]

Of course, other early works such as "Materialism and Revolution" and *What Is Literature?* speak of mutual recognition and even collaboration of freedoms,[53] but does this more positive view indicate a radical shift from *Being and Nothingness*, or is Sartre's position there not as negative as it appears? Some commentators have singled out the extremely intriguing footnote he places at the end of *Being and Nothingness*. "These considerations," he writes, "do not exclude the possibility of an ethics of deliverance and salvation. But this can be achieved only after a radical conversion which we cannot discuss here."[54] These commentators claim that this footnote indicates that the human relations Sartre describes there in detail are intended to be relationships only among individuals who have not undergone a conversion, in other words, individuals who attempt to be *ens causa sui* and so react negatively to others who confer on them an object status they cannot control. Of course, it is tenuous to base such a claim on a footnote. Let us turn to the *Cahiers* to see if it throws any light on how we should interpret Sartre's early view of human relations.

The *Cahiers* reveals the second group of commentators to be correct, for Sartre tells us that *Being and Nothingness* was attempting to set forth not the essential nature or necessary structure of all human relations but only the relationships among unconverted individuals, among inauthentic persons, those who have not undertaken a pure reflection. Early in his notebooks Sartre writes that "the struggle of consciousnesses [only] has meaning before conversion." "After conversion there is no longer an ontological reason for remaining in struggle." Elsewhere he asserts that conversion means "morality without oppression," and in an explicit reference to *Being and Nothingness* he states that conversion can transform the "Hell" of human passions described there.[55] Likewise he stresses repeatedly that oppression or domination is not an inevitable ontological condition, nor a necessary result of history, but a free human decision.

Conversion removes domination and conflict because a converted individual renounces the God project. He no longer attempts to be in total control of his own being like an *ens causa sui*. Thus Sartre states that he is not "troubled" by the fact that others objectify him and give him a dimension of being, his being-object, which he cannot control. By conversion or pure reflection I not only accept my freedom, "I accept my being-object" as an inevitable part of my human condition. As a result my objectivity need not be a cause of alienation and conflict: "It only becomes so if the Other refuses to see in me also a freedom. If, on the contrary, he makes me exist as existing freedom as well as being-object . . . he enriches the world and myself."[56] If both the others and I undergo conversion, reject the God project, and choose our mutual freedoms as our goal, our objectification of each other is not oppressive, nor a source of conflict, but a positive enhancement of our existence. We can cooperatively work together, adopting each other's free projects in intersubjective relationships, which Sartre here calls "authentic love." Relationships of this kind constitute the city of ends or reign of freedom which is the ultimate goal of his morality. Indeed, not only is conflict not a necessary component of human relations according to the *Cahiers*; it can in principle be totally overcome, Sartre says, by a "conversion of all," "an absolute conversion to intersubjectivity," which would involve the transformation of present society into a classless one where each individual would recognize and will the freedom of all.[57]

The problem with the more benign view of human relationships in the *Cahiers*, in which each one wills the freedom of all, is that it appears to be radically incompatible with fundamental epistemological positions of *Being and Nothingness*. For Sartre speaks there as if knowledge of others inevitably involves objectifying them, necessarily entailing an alienation of their free subjectivity. To objectivity a subject is to reify it, that is, to "degrade" it to the status of a thinglike object; "objectification is a radical metamorphosis."[58] This is the reason Sartre states that even if I should want to take the other's freedom as my end, the fact that I do so turns it into an object and thus "violates" it. *Being and Nothingness* goes even farther and denies the possibility "of the simultaneous apprehension of [the other's] freedom and of his objectivity." It limits human relations to those of subject to object or object to subject. Sartre writes that we can never achieve "the plane where the recognition of the Other's freedom would involve the Other's recognition of our freedom."[59]

Though the *Cahiers*, as I noted earlier, does stress the possibility of overcoming conflict and oppression, it also repeats many of these themes. It, too, speaks of objectification by others as the "negation of my subjectivity" and thus as a "sin against freedom" because objectification involves freedom's alienation, an alienation "from which man cannot exit." In the same vein the *Cahiers* states that "reification [is] the first ontological phenomenon" between human beings and asserts that to take freedom as an end is to "substantialize" it.[60] However, unlike *Being and Nothingness*, Sartre does not say in his notebooks that a human being can be grasped only as an object or as a free subject. Rather, he asserts that these narrow alternatives of his earlier work "can be transformed by conversion," which enables us to apprehend each other as both freedom and object, and even primarily as freedom. Because it described human relations before conversion, *Being and Nothingness* lacked, Sartre says, an understanding of the "reciprocal recognition" or "reciprocal comprehension" of freedoms.[61]

The *Cahiers* does indeed contain a rather lengthy discussion of comprehension (or recognition). This explains that unlike knowledge or the look, which simply objectify the other subject, comprehension grasps the other as freedom by sympathetically involving itself in his pursuit of his goals. Comprehension is not merely a passive contemplation or viewing of the other's freedom and its projects, but rather "anticipating" in myself the operation of the other toward his ends. I "outline," Sartre says, "the adoption of the other's goal by myself." I freely "engage myself" in the other's free projection toward his ends and in so doing "preontologically" (i.e., prior to knowledge) grasps his freedom without objectifying it.[62]

For Sartre this sympathetic engagement in the freedom of the other suggests a unity between persons that was totally misising in *Being and Nothingness*. Though he insists that such unity is not an ontological fusion of individuals into some superindividual reality, he does describe it as a "certain interpenetration of freedoms" where "each freedom is totally in the other." Relations of this kind are also present in the authentic love and friendship, he says. They involve a "unity of diversity" or a "sameness" that respects the other free individual and overcomes radical separation and otherness; in them, "otherness is recaptured by unity, even though it always remains ontically."[63] This unity enables me to apprehend and will the other's freedom as such, without degrading or reifying it. The inevitable objectification of the other that still occurs is, then, not primarily a debasement or a source of conflict, since it is objectification by one who is "the same," one who comprehends the other person primarily as a free subject.

The *Cahiers* constitutes a significant advance beyond the narrow subject–object human relations described in *Being and Nothingness*. It allows for and explains the possibility of comprehending and willing others, as both freedoms and objects. It also significantly supplements other early published works which, although they assert the possibility of subject-to-subject relations, contain no discussion of conversion or comprehension which make such relations possible. Still, Sartre leaves unanswered a question crucial for ethics. Even if one can eliminate human conflict and oppression, and the degrading forms of objectivity, even if one can unite with other subjects and will their freedom, why, according to Sartre, should he do so? What, if any, moral obligation requires me to respect and will the freedom of others rather than seek to dominate and destroy it? Why not choose just my own freedom and ignore that of others? Sartre's answer in his notebooks is anything but clear, but to pursue these issues will require another article.[64]

I have shown here that the *Cahiers* provides invaluable assistance in interpreting Sartre's early ontology and its relationship to morality. It unquestionably supports the view that he did not intend in *Being and Nothingness* to portray the definitive human condition as one of failure, meaninglessness, or conflict. Rather, as he says on the third page of the notebooks, "*Being and Nothingness* is an ontology before conversion." I might add that with its treatment of pure reflection, conversion, comprehension, and justification, and its argument for valuing freedom, the *Cahiers* also contains far more explanation of the bases for positions taken in other early works that do these works themselves. Thus the *Cahiers* shows that even in these early years Sartre believed that if persons renounced the God project and instead willed concretely their mutual freedoms, they could create a life that overcomes despair and conflict. This would be a life in which human beings unite in comprehension and authentic love, act to give meaning and justification to their existence, and strive to realize the human reign, the city of ends.

Notes

1. The following have advanced such criticisms: R. Bernstein, *Praxis and Action* (Philadelphia, 1971); R. Jolivet, *Sartre: The Theology of the Absurd*, trans. by W. Piersol (New York, 1967); I. Mészàros, *The Work of Sartre* (Atlantic Highlands, N.J., 1979); A. Philonenko, "Liberté et mauvaise foi chez Sartre," *Revue de Métaphysique et de Morale* 86 (1981); R. Williams, "The Problem of God in Sartre's *Being and Nothingness*," in *Phenomenology in a Pluralistic Context*, ed. by C. Schrag and W. McBride (Albany, N.Y., 1983).

2. Recent authors who have maintained that the early Sartre held that human beings are inevitably in conflict are: P. Caws, *Sartre* (Boston, 1979); R. Aronson, *Jean-Paul Sartre—Philosophy in the World* (London, 1980); C. Brosman, *Jean-Paul Sartre* (Boston, 1983); T. Flynn, *Sartre and Marxist Existentialism* (Chicago, 1984); W. Schroeder, *Sartre and His Predecessors* (Boston, 1984); J.-L. Chrétien, "Une Morale en suspens," *Critique* 39 (November 1983); F. Elliston, "Sartre and Husserl on Interpersonal Relations," in *Jean-Paul Sartre, Contemporary Approaches to His Philosophy*, ed. by H. Silverman and F. Elliston (Pittsburgh, 1980); R. Good, "A Third Attitude toward Others: Jean-Paul Sartre," *Man and World* 15 (1982).

3. Caws, *Sartre*; M. Warnock, *Existentialist Ethics* (London, 1967); H. Veatch, *For an Ontology of Morals* (Evanston, Ill., 1981); R. Frondizi, "Sartre's Early Ethics: A Critique," in *The Philosophy of Jean-Paul Sartre*, ed. by P. Schilpp (LaSalle, Ill., 1981); Chrétien, "Une Morale en suspens"; H. Spiegelberg, "Sartre's Last Word on Ethics in Phenomenological Perspective," *Research in Phenomenology* 11 (1981).

4. T. Anderson, *The Foundation and Structure of Sartrean Ethics* (Lawrence, Kan., 1979); H. Barnes, *An Existentialist Ethics* (Chicago, 1978); F. Jeanson, *Sartre and the Problem of Morality*, trans. by R. Stone (Bloomington, Ind., 1980). Others who have defended Sartre from one or more of these criticisms are: L. Bell, "Sartre, Dialectic, and the Problem of Overcoming Bad Faith," *Man and World* 10 (1977); T. Busch, "Sartre's Use of the Reduction; *Being and Nothingness* Reconsidered," in Silverman and Elliston, eds., *Jean-Paul Sartre, Contemporary Approaches*; Flynn, *Sartre and Marxist*

Existentialism; P. Knee, "Le Problème moral comme totalisation chez Sartre," *Dialogue* 23 (1984); A. Manser, *Sartre, A Philosophic Study* (New York, 1967); Spiegelberg, "Sartre's Last Word."

5. *What Is Literature?* trans. by B. Frechtman (New York, 1966) (hereafter *WIL*); "Materialism and Revolution," in *Literary and Philosophical Essays*, trans. by A. Michelson (New York, 1962) (hereafter *MR*); *Existentialism and Humanism*, trans. by P. Mairet (London, 1973) (hereafter *EH*). An extensive comparison of these works with the *Cahiers* would, of course, be most valuable, but that is not the purpose of this essay.

6. *Sartre by Himself*, film script trans. by R. Seaver (New York, 1978), 42–43; "The Last Words of Jean-Paul Sartre," trans. by A. Foulke, *Dissent* (Fall 1980), 398–400.

7. *Being and Nothingness*, trans. by H. Barnes (New York, 1956), 627 (hereafter *BN*). See note 1 above.

8. Ibid., 599.

9. Ibid., 566. See also 93–94. We might point out that Sartre apparently held the view throughout his life that human beings naturally desire to be God, for he asserts it in some very late interviews, such as "Self-Portrait at Seventy," in *Life/Situations*, trans. by P. Auster and L. Davis (New York, 1977), 61.

10. *BN*, 90.

11. *WIL*, 24, 25, 37, 187, 191, 192; *MR*, 250, 253–55.

12. *EH*, 54.

13. *BN*, 93-95.

14. *Cahiers pour une morale* (Paris, 1983), 577 (hereafter *CM*). I take responsibility for all translations, but I must acknowledge the valuable assistance of Patricia Radzin and Ann Owens. Also see 491, 492, 495, 498–502.

15. Ibid., 578.

16. Ibid.

17. *BN*, 159 ff. *The Transcendence of the Ego*, trans. by F. Williams and R. Kirkpatrick (New York, 1957), 99.

18. *BN*, 581. The same statement is made on 628.

19. *CM*, 22–23, 498. See also 455, 463–64.

20. Ibid., 577.

21. Ibid., 578.

22. Ibid., 577.

23. Ibid., 339.

24. *BN*, 462, 553–56, 599. A good recent article on this topic is by D. Føllesdal, "Sartre on Freedom," in Schilpp, ed., *The Philosophy of Jean-Paul Sartre*. In my opinion, a similar overemphasis on freedom is present in *WIL*; see, for example, 23, 28, 33. *MR*, on the other hand, gives significant weight to materiality as limiting freedom, 245 ff.

25. Meszeros, *The Work of Sartre*, 242; L. Bell in her review of my *The Foundation and Structure of Sartrean Ethics* in *Man and World* 14 (1981), 223–24.

26. *BN*, 581. His whole discussion in part IV, chap. 2, sec. 2, is said to be "aimed only at accessory reflection."

27. *CM*, 536. Page 495 advocates "renouncing" the God project; 578 refers to a "rupture" with it and "refusing" it. Actually, when Bell speaks of guiding our behavior

by the regulative idea of God, she is not, in my opinion, using the term God in the strict Sartrean sense, namely, as an e*ns causa sui,* a conscious being that is the foundation of its own necessity. Her main point seems to be that Sartre believes that a harmony, a unity, both within the various aspects of the self and in the self's relation to its being for others, is achievable and desirable. I have no quarrel with this; Sartre does advocate such harmonies (see *CM*, 467, 484; *WIL*, 37–38); but I do not see how they involve his notion of God in any strong sense.

28. Some of these critics are listed above in note 3.

29. *EH*, 51; *WIL*, 108, 192; *MR*, 245, 253; *Critique of Dialectical Reason,* trans. by A. Sheridan-Smith (London, 1976), 673: "Self-Portrait at Seventy," 84; *On a raison de se revolter* (Paris, 1974), 347; *BN*, 581, 627. Given such texts, I am amazed that Joseph McMahon would write that "Sartre never believed that men should seek to be free," *French Review* 54, no. 6 (May 1981), 879.

30. *EH*, 51. Thomas Flynn has analyzed this argument in detail in chap. 3 of *Sartre and Marxist Existentialism,* as have I in chap. 3 of *The Foundation and Structure of Sartrean Ethics.*

31. *CM*, 483, 406, 302, respectively.

32. Ibid., 17, 95, 174, 177, 302, 416–17.

33. Ibid., 434. See also 19, 169–70, 302, 421. *WIL*, 105, 108, 187, 191, 192; and *MR*, 253, also identify the reign of freedom with democratic socialism. Even in very late interviews Sartre continued to make this identification. See *On a raison,* 347; "Self-Portrait at Seventy," 84.

34. *CM*, 177. *WIL* also states that socialism is not the end but the (last) means before the end that is to place the human person in possession of his freedom, 192.

35. *CM*, 137, 463–64, 490, 499–502.

36. Ibid., 461. Compare with *WIL*, 23, 24, 36, 37, 107.

37. M. Contat and M. Rybalka, *The Writings of Jean-Paul Sartre, A Bibliographical Life,* trans. by R. McCleary, (Evanston, Ill., 1974), I, 228, 295; interview with C. A. Van Peursen, "In gesprek met Jean-Paul Sartre," in *Wending* (The Hague) 9 (March 1954), 18–20, 22–24; *On a raison,* 77–78.

38. *CM*, 135–37, 455, 463–64, 499–504, 512–13, 549–52.

39. *WIL*, 105, 108. Aronson discusses this in chaps. 2 and 3 of his *Jean-Paul Sartre–Philosophy in the World.*

40. *CM*, 465, 498, 502, 514, 543.

41. Ibid., 500–507, 513, 522.

42. Ibid., 148–49, 346–52, 487, 522. *WIL*, 43–45, and *MR*, 252, make the same point.

43. Flynn, *Sartre and Marxist Existentialism,* 38, while admitting that Sartre argues for "choosing freedom," claims that this freedom "is neither the object nor the specific content of our choice. Rather it is what Sartre terms the form of our choice, the ultimate meaning of our actions." This statement is perplexing, for how can one choose freedom as the ultimate meaning of action and not make it the object or content of his choice? Granted, in *EH* Sartre does refer to freedom as the form of his morality and state that it is a form that admits of a variety of concrete contents. Nevertheless, this form cannot be totally contentless, else one could never determine what matter (specific content) is or is not compatible with it. I do agree, however, that in *EH* (and *CM*) Sartre gives little detail about what concrete contents are compatible with freedom.

44. In a lengthy collection of unpublished notes used for a lecture he gave in 1964 at the Gramsci Institute in Rome, Sartre claims that human need is the root of morality and of moral norms. This manuscript is now at the Bibliothèque Nationale, Paris. I thank Robert Stone, Elizabeth Bowman, Michel Rybalka, and Madame Mauricette Berne of the BN, for their assistance in making it available to me.

45. Anderson, *The Foundation and Structure of Sartrean Ethics*, 50–65; Bell, "Sartre, Dialectic, and the Problem of Overcoming Bad Faith," 298; Bernstein, *Praxis and Action*, 154–55; Jolivet, *Sartre: The Theology of the Absurd*, 66; Veatch, *For an Ontology of Morals*, 76–77; S. Lee, "The Central Role of Universalization in Sartrean Ethics," *Philosophy and Phenomenological Research* 46 (1985–86), 63–64.

46. *BN*, 479, 570.

47. Bell, review, 225–26.

48. *Sartre and Marxist Existentialism*, 37–39.

49. Let me add that I do think Sartre's argument here is sound but, to repeat myself, only if human beings first value rationality and consistency. And Sartre himself concedes that we have no absolute obligation to do so.

50. *CM*, 488–92, 497, 577–78.

51. See above, note 2.

52. *BN*, 364, 429.

53. *MR*, 250, 254; *WIL*, 29, 30, 32, 35.

54. *BN*, 412. In the pages that precede his treatment of human relations (361–64), Sartre also states that the relations to be discussed are those that occur in the context of the God Project.

55. *CM*, 16, 26, 515. Places where he states that oppression is a human choice are 13, 353, 395–96.

56. Ibid., 515. See also 17–18, 26, 91, 113–14, 293–94, 433–34.

57. Ibid., 17–18, 54–55, 95, 421, 430, 487, 522–24.

58. *BN*, 273.

59. Ibid., 408–10.

60. *CM*, 18, 136, 177, 398, 429, 484.

61. Ibid., 515, 430. In my opinion Chrétien's review of *Cahiers*, "Une Morale en suspens," gives far too little weight to the role of conversion and comprehension in overcoming human conflict. Of course, conversion does not eradicate our desire to be God; it simply refuses to value that impossible goal. Thus there will always be a tendency for the converted individual to "fall" by going along with his fundamental desire and so again enter into conflict with others.

62. The *Cahiers* discusses comprehension at 285–303. *BN* mentions comprehension (lxiii, 251, 289, 291, 439) but does not use the term primarily to refer to the apprehension of others but of oneself.

63. *CM*, 16–17, 300, 303, 417, 430.

64. I discuss Sartre's arguments for choosing the freedom of others in "The Obligation to Will the Freedom of Others According to Jean-Paul Sartre," *The Question of the Other*, ed. by A. Dallery and C. Scott, (Albany, N.Y., 1989).

8

The Sartrean *Cogito*: A Journey between Versions

Dorothy Leland

THE SARTREAN *COGITO*, SENSIBLE TO MANY of Sartre's commentators, has from our first meeting refused to present a constant face. And it seems intellectually dangerous to force on the Sartrean *cogito* a banal consistency lacking in Sartre's own description, particularly given the pivotal role which the *cogito* plays in Sartre's ontology. Thus, rather than attempting to determine which of Sartre's versions of the *cogito* is the "real" version—the most consistent, the most frequently invoked, or whatever—I have tried there to capture the Sartrean *cogito* in its changes of face in order to determine their source and reason. This is a risky business—tracing the configuration of an uncertain physiognomy—but perhaps less risky than questioning Sartre's words for what he "would" say or collapsing an aberrant formulation into a preferred version for the sake of preserving internal coherence.

I

Critics of Sartre claim that he has smuggled Cartesianism in the back door of his ontology. In *Being and Nothingness* we have a philosophy which begins with the consciousness of being consciousness, and though Sartre explicitly rejects the Cartesian *cogito*, his own ontological argument begins with the consciousness he calls the pre-reflective *cogito*. In *The Transcendence of the Ego, The Emotions,* and again in *Being and Nothingness,* Sartre argue that the reflective character of the Cartesian *cogito*, with its attachment to an ego, is an operation in the second degree. Yet, as Marjorie Grene has thoughtfully shown, Sartre "has assimilated to his very bones" as the fulcrum of philosophy "the self-contained now of self-consciousness."[1] Sartre's criticism of Descartes is that he turned the *cogito* into a "thinking substance," something which need not have happened had Descartes not chosen as his starting point the reflective instead of the pre-reflective *cogito*. Sartre's pre-reflective *cogito* proposes to strip the Cartesian *cogito* of its substantial being, leaving us instead with a pure translucidity which slithers inexorably out of the reach of those of us who wish to critically examine this new starting point of philosophy.

However paradoxial it might seem to attempt to penetrate what by definition is "radically impenetrable," the notion of consciousness as a pure translucidity which can never be an object of intuition or thought does need examining. And this is not because I am opposed to a good mystery but because the Sartrean *cogito* is essentially a mystification: It fails both on the level of phenomenological description and as the necessary condition rendering reflection possible. In examining what Sartre has to say about consciousness in *The Transcendence of the Ego* and in *Being and Nothingness*, we will find that Sartre repeatedly offers us conflicting versions of the being of the pre-reflective *cogito*. And we will find that the reasons for these conflicting descriptions seem to lie in Sartre's unwillingness, finally, to reject his Cartesian heritage.

Although the view of the *cogito* offered to us in *The Transcendence of the Ego* is modified somewhat in *Being and Nothingness*, we find in this early work the germination of the dualism which later plagues Sartre's ontology. Sartre, of course, denies that consciousness is dual; yet the unity which he gives to consciousness is threatened by his insistence that consciousness possesses an "immanent" consciousness of itself. While rejecting a dualism of substance, Sartre seems to posit a duality of object and act within consciousness. In *The Transcendence of the Ego*, Sartre accepts Husserl's notion of intentionality, which redefine the Cartesian *cogito* as *cogitatio*; yet in rejecting Husserl's explanation of self-consciousness, Sartre reintroduces Descartes' immanent consciousness (of) self in the modified form of the pre-reflective *cogito*. Sartre finds that Husserl's transcendental "I" would tear consciousness from itself since consciousness is an absolute limited only by itself. Consciousness as absolute means for Sartre that consciousness is present to itself as the pre-cognitive foundation of all that is known to the reflecting *cogito*. This leads us directly to Sartre's notion of non-positional consciousness— consciousness of consciousness, or consciousness which is not for itself its own object.

In defining the non-positional consciousness, Sartre gives the following formulations: (1) The type of existence of consciousness is to be consciousness of itself (consciousness as consciousness of consciousness); (2) Consciousness is aware of itself in so far as it is consciousness of a transcendent object; and (3) Consciousness is not for itself its own object.[2] Non-positional consciousness of consciousness thus appears as an accompanying "aspect" of positional consciousness. Pre-reflectively, consciousness as intention is "plunged" into the world of objects and is a positional positing *of*, which, however, knows itself non-positionally as this positing. By intentionality consciousness transcends itself, and non-positional self-awareness, in refusing to posit itself as an object, would seem to "point" to what it is positionally consciousness *of* as an identity which is simultaneously an otherness. Consciousness, Sartre tells us, knows itself as intention, as positional of objects, yet this knowing of itself is not a structure of intentionality. It is instead the "law of existence" of intentional consciousness.

Sartre's pre-reflective consciousness thus appears as a "thetic" knowing of its objects and as a non-positional knowing of itself as a knowing of its objects. That Sartre's pre-reflective consciousness as a unity of intention and self-consciousness has this dualistic character is revealed in his references to the "non-reflecting apprehension of one consciousness by another consciousness" and in his discussion of "thinking consciousness" on the one hand and consciousness as it is absorbed in its object on the other hand (TE: 46–49). Yet Sartre also clearly insists that pre-reflective consciousness is not a synthesis of two consciousnesses: This synthesis is effected by the reflecting consciousness which is consciousness of itself and consciousness of reflected consciousness. In contrast, a consciousness "in the first degree" knows itself as intention non-positionally and hence does not posit itself as an object. And because this "original" consciousness of consciousness does not posit itself as an object, it is non-divisional—apparently an intuitive apprehension of its own positionality *of*.

Sartre invokes his description of the pre-reflective *cogito* to show that the "I think" is not the primary structure of consciousness. And in purging the ego from the primary structure of consciousness, Sartre offers us descriptions of the pre-reflective *cogito* as consciousness engaged in the world prior to subject–object distinctions. Only in reflection does this dualism emerge as reflecting consciousness addresses itself to a reflected consciousness. However, Sartre's descriptions of pre-reflective consciousness as engaged consciousness, in which no presence of consciousness to itself is experientially indicated, are continually qualified by his insistence that there is an "accompanying" self-referential consciousness in every conscious act. And while Sartre insists that pre-reflective consciousness is not dual, this claim remains problematic. That the expression "consciousness of consciousness" implies at least a spatial distance may merely be a difficulty inherent in the necessary spatiality of linguistic expression; however, to speak of one consciousness apprehending *another* consciousness implies a distance of non-identity that is not the mere function of linear expression.

That the Sartrean *cogito* "contains" a subject-object distinction is revealed in the identification of non-positional, non-thetic consciousness with reflecting consciousness. In speaking of non-thetic reflecting consciousness, Sartre claims that this involves "consciousness of the object and non-positional consciousness of itself" (TE: 47). Here we seem to have awareness of the object of awareness plus awareness of the awareness of the object of awareness. Reflecting consciousness, Sartre insists, "becomes positional only by directing itself upon the reflected consciousness which itself was not a positional consciousness of itself before being reflected" (TE: 45). Thus non-positional reflecting consciousness appears as a quasi-reflective structure which, while being aware of itself as consciousness of an object, does not posit itself as an object. The immanence of non-positional consciousness precludes such an objectification. Yet the nature of this awareness of self remains unspecified in *The Transcendence of the Ego*. In addition, because non-positional consciousness involves an awareness of the awareness of an object of awareness, this self-awareness becomes a second "object" (or the quasi-object of a quasi-reflection) of consciousness, distinguishable from the transcendent object of our intention. Pre-reflective consciousness, it seems, is at once "absorbed" in its transcendent object yet aware of itself as awareness *of*—an immanence which, in thrusting all content outside of itself, cannot be identical with the object it posits. Thus when consciousness posits itself as an object, it apprehends itself always inadequately as a reflected consciousness—as an object distinct from the act of awareness itself: The consciousness which grasps its transcendent object always escapes itself while it is at the same time aware of itself non-positionally.

Obviously what needs to be understood is the nature of this quasi-reflective structure. And to do this, we need to turn to *Being and Nothingness* where Sartre attempts such a clarification. However, the paradoxes which emerge, if only sketchily, in *The Transcendence of the Ego*, do not escape Sartre in his ambitious ontology. Sartre wishes to have at once a consciousness which is indistinguishable from its knowing-of-objects and a consciousness which is radically severed from its objects. Consciousness is at once defined by a relation of transcendence which it is (consciousness as concretely engaged in the world) while at the same time not having to be itself this transcendence. Non-positional consciousness is to be prior to subject–object distinctions, yet paradoxically contains these distinctions within the dualistic aspects of itself. In fact, three versions of consciousness emerge tentatively in *The Transcendence of the Ego* and will again be found with their sometimes competing claims in *Being and Nothingness*: (1) The pre-reflective *cogito* as engaged or absorbed in its object with no presence of consciousness of itself indicated; (2) The pre-reflective *cogito* as a unity of intention and self-consciousness; and (3) The pre-reflective

cogito as self-consciousness and as a limiting condition of intentional or positional consciousness.

II

In *Being and Nothingness*, Sartre begins by defining consciousness as a "knowing being" in its capacity as being, not as being known. Hence we find, as was
indicated in *The Transcendence of the Ego*, that knowing being is something
other than knowledge turned back upon itself: Knowing being is not first being
known. This proposition leads Sartre to an examination of the "first" consciousness of consciousness—non-positional consciousness. Sartre argues that
while all consciousness is positional—knowledge only of its objects—the necessary and sufficient condition for a knowing (positional) consciousness to be
knowledge of its objects is "that it be consciousness of itself as being that
knowledge."[3] This is a sufficient condition, "for my being conscious of being
conscious of that table suffices in fact for me to be conscious of it" (BN: 11).
And this is a necessary condition, "for if my consciousness were not consciousness of being consciousness of the table, it would then be consciousness
of that table without being so" (BN: 11). Consciousness cannot be ignorant of
itself, Sartre claims, or else it would be unconscious—which is absurd. Yet how
can consciousness be consciousness of being consciousness of a transcendent
object without positing itself as an object, without being known? Sartre an-
swers this question by again invoking non-positional consciousness as a quasi-
reflective structure which unlike reflection proper grasps without objectifying.

Positional consciousness of consciousness is knowledge of consciousness,
which means that it is directed toward something which is not it, toward consciousness as an object of reflection. Since positional consciousness is always
"exhausted" in aiming at its object, it must transcend itself. Hence what is
known by the positional consciousness is only its object—the revealed rather
than the revealing. However, Sartre argues, every positional consciousness of
an object is at the same time a non-positional consciousness of itself. Here
there is no positing of consciousness as known. Instead, consciousness is present to itself not as a thing but as an "operative intention" which can only exist
as a "revealing-revealed." Thus non-positional consciousness is one with the
consciousness of which it is consciousness: "At one stroke it determines itself
as consciousness of perception and as perception" (BN: 14).

Sartre blames the syntax of language for the difficulties in expressing the
notion of non-positional consciousness (of) self without evoking the idea of
knowledge. In describing the non-positional consciousness, he wishes to
avoid the knower-known dyad and the necessity of grounding ontology in

epistemology. Hence he argues that consciousness (of) self is not dual. For example, pleasure is neither "before" nor "after" consciousness of pleasure. Instead, pleasure is the "being of self-consciousness and this self-consciousness is the law of being of pleasure" (BN: 15). Furthermore, Sartre argues, self-consciousness is the "*only mode of existence which is possible for a consciousness of something*" (BN: 24). Consciousness is first a "plenum of existence" and the positional consciousness is essentially a witnessing consciousness which poses the nothingness of the first consciousness (that is, consciousness as reflected-on which is pure appearance and total emptiness) for a synthesis of recognition.

Sartre's discussion of non-positional consciousness (of) self leads him to conclude that nothing is the cause of consciousness and that consciousness is the cause of its own way of being. Knowledge, Sartre argues, has been given its ontological foundation in the immanence of self to self. However, Sartre also wishes to argue that consciousness is not the foundation of its being; and he does this by claiming that consciousness "in its inmost nature is a relation to a transcendent being" (BN: 22). Sartre's "ontological proof" rests on the assertion that transcendence is the constitutive structure of consciousness; and immanence is confined within the apprehension of a transcendent. Self-consciousness becomes the "other" of this "otherness," of this transcendence which it is in the form of negation. And in so becoming consciousness also becomes inescapably dual.

Hence in elaborated form we find in *Being and Nothingness* the same paradoxical tendencies which we noticed in Sartre's discussion of the *cogito* in *The Transcendence of the Ego*. Non-positional consciousness is first defined as an "operative intention" prior to subject-object, knower-known distinctions. Then this engaged unity is qualified, and at the "heart" of non-positional consciousness a duality is revealed. In redefining consciousness (of) consciousness as subjectivity and as a revealing intuition implying something revealed, Sartre gives to his consciousness as "immanence" a duality by reintroducing the dyad knowing-known. Furthermore, the relation of transcendence characteristic of positional consciousness has now come to qualify the immanence of non-positional consciousness. Sartre's argument is as follows: The object (e.g., table) of knowledge cannot be identified with knowledge, or it would be consciousness and disappear as table. And since the known cannot be reabsorbed into knowledge, we must discover for it a being which is not the being of knowledge. In fact, Sartre maintains, the transphenomenality of the being of consciousness requires that of the being of the phenomenon, and the "ontological proof" of this can be derived not from the reflective *cogito* but from the pre-reflective being of the *percipiens*. However, the pre-reflective *cogito* Sartre invokes here is not the non-positional consciousness as operative intention; for Sartre's ontological proof is established by reference to positional consciousness—consciousness as consciousness of something. Consciousness (of) self is redefined as an absolute subjectivity, as a revealing intuition implying something revealed. And reflecting and the reflected emerge as ontologically distinct regions of being.

Thus, even in the early chapters of *Being and Nothingness*, non-positional consciousness emerges—paradoxically—as a positional consciousness, as a relation to a transcendent being. For example, in his chapter on the "Immediate Structure of the For-itself," Sartre makes the following claim: To say "belief is consciousness (of) belief" is never to make a statement of identity, for the subject and the attribute are radically different even though within the "indissoluble" unity of one and the same being. Here non-positional consciousness is described as a reflection which is its own reflecting. And this "double game of reference" is such that each term "refers to the other and passes into the other, and yet each term is different from the other" (BN: 122). Hence we have a duality which is a unity—or so Sartre would have us believe. Yet, as Sartre goes on to say, "at the limit of coincidence with itself, in fact, the self vanishes to give place to identical being" (BN: 123). Thus the "self" of consciousness (of) self is by nature reflexive. What does the self refer to? A relation between the subject and himself, Sartre now tells us, a relation which is a duality and which represents an "ideal distance within the immanence of the subject in relation to himself, a way of *not being his own coincidence . . .*" (BN: 124).

Non-positional consciousness cannot admit to Sartre's conflicting definitions. Either it is first a way of existing the world prior to subject-object distinctions, or it is a relation between subject and object. In giving being known its ontological foundation, Sartre defines non-positional consciousness (of) consciousness as a plenum of existence which admits to no duality. The knower-known dyad is posited as a structure of positional consciousness and is discussed as a secondary, emergent structure. Having thus rescued the ontological question from the murky waters of epistemology, Sartre next proceeds to redefine non-positional consciousness as an implicit duality—the duality reflecting-reflection which leads him to posit two distinct ontological dimensions (his "ontological proof"). The duality reflecting-reflection is further specified when Sartre connects consciousness with a subject which is non-substantial and points to what it lacks (himself or being-in-itself). Non-positional consciousness becomes the consciousness existing the distance between reflecting-reflection—the structure of distance previously granted only to positional consciousness. Hence the dyad knowing-known is reintroduced into non-positional consciousness, the consciousness (of) consciousness originally posited to escape this problem. And non-positional consciousness now appears as "haunted" by the presence of that with which it should coincide to be itself.

This raises a crucial question: How does the scissiparity of reflection which gives rise to reflecting consciousness and a reflected consciousness differ from the quasi-reflective structure of self-consciousness? Sartre never clarifies this distinction, though he continually asserts its validity. Sartre does, however, talk about reflection and even distinguishes two types of reflection. And it becomes clear in reading these discussions that reflection involves an internal negation by which I separate myself from myself in an attempt to recover what I lack. What links a reflecting consciousness and a reflected consciousness is "nothing": The reflecting consciousness is present to reflected consciousness as knowledge, which is an internal negation. But if reflection is essentially an internal negation, what is the quasi-reflective structure of non-positional consciousness? What distinguishes the separation of self from self in reflection from the disengagement of the subject from itself in non-positional consciousness? This "immanent" disengagement also seems to be in essence an internal negation; for consciousness (of) self is seen by Sartre as a pure negativity and nothingness, as a separation of the subject from itself.

Perhaps we can find our answer by looking at Sartre's identification of non-positional consciousness (of) self with "original" consciousness as ontological act. The presence of consciousness to itself, when interpreted as the origin of negativity, is referred to by Sartre as a "fissure" within consciousness and as a "phantom dyad" which can exist only as a unity. Here pre-reflective consciousness appears not to be synonymous with non-positional consciousness; instead, it is a "fissured" unity of positional and non-positional consciousness, of consciousness as act and consciousness as absorbed in its object. The latter "aspect" of pre-reflective consciousness is a relation of consciousness to being, while the former "aspect" is a relation of consciousness to the "first" relation of consciousness to being. This "doubling" relationship is referred to variously by Sartre as a questioning of being by being, as consciousness knowing it is not what it is and is what it is not, as consciousness existing as transcendence (for the object) yet positing itself as not being its transcendence and thus as a lack of being.

If we interpret pre-reflective consciousness as a unity of non-positional consciousness [consciousness (of) self] and positional consciousness (consciousness of a transcendent object), then the difference between the structure of reflection and that of "quasi-reflection" becomes synonymous with the difference between "origin" or ground and the derivative structures of consciousness. The one is abstract, ideal—a logical condition—while the other is concrete and real (a difference, for example, between the abstract "origin" of negation and knowledge as a concrete negation). However, this explanation also seems far from satisfactory precisely because of Sartre's insistence that "original" consciousness is an *event* not a mere logical condition. Consciousness is always

concrete consciousness in situation. Yet Sartre also insists that the distance sep-
arating consciousness from itself in consciousness (of) self is "ideal." It is ideal,
Sartre tells us, because it is the distance of nothingness or that of internal negation, which means that subject and predicate can only exist as a unity (i.e., the
being of both is effected by the negation). Thus, consciousness (of) belief is the
unity of one being as nothingness, as "fissured." Such an explanation, however,
remains an abstraction unless connected with a concrete consciousness where
distance is never "ideal," where space—though a function of internal negation—is objectively organized and known. If consciousness (of) self is an internal negation and concrete, how can it not result in the objectivity of "thises,"
how can it not be the structure of reflection?

There is a third possible answer to our question, which involves seeing reflection only as that consciousness which gives rise to an ego by disengaging
itself from the "world" and objectifying reflecting consciousness as reflected
consciousness. However, if we consider pre-reflective consciousness merely as
engaged consciousness with no experience of consciousness (of) self, then the
problem of the quasi-reflective structure of self-consciousness simply disap-
pears. It is not solved by referring back to another of Sartre's versions of the
pre-reflective *cogito*. In fact, it is precisely because engaged consciousness is
qualified as a self-reflection that the problem arises of "immanent" reflection
versus reflection "proper" or emergent reflection. Though Sartre does speak of
the pre-reflective *cogito* as a "plenum of existence," this *cogito* is gradually ef-
faced as Sartre moves to his discussion of ontological structures and determinations. Man's nothingness in the form of the "reflecting-reflection" or presence to self becomes the ground upon which Sartre's discussions of the
structure of the for-itself, time, freedom, original project, etc., are generated.
Thus it is crucial to ask now why Sartre has admitted such confusions into his
philosophy: Why has Sartre given us such seemingly contradictory versions of
the *cogito*?

III

The problem of "sorting" through Sartre's various versions of the *cogito* is
largely a problem of tracing Sartre's transition from phenomenological description to ontological analysis. Early in *Being and Nothingness*, consciousness as a particular experience, as a "plenum of existence" is referred for its
possibilities to ontological determination. The phenomenological notion of
consciousness as a relation of intentionality is modified by Sartre when he begins to question the being of consciousness, a modification which involves
introducing the unity of intention and self-consciousness as the structural

foundation of an existing consciousness of something. And it is here that Sartre insists that the self-givenness of a consciousness is the necessary condition for being conscious of a transcendent object—a self-givenness which is itself not a reflection, an objectification. Thus it is Sartre's movement from viewing pre-reflective consciousness as an "operative intention" to seeing it as a non-positional reference to itself that needs to be examined.

Consciousness as intentionality, Sartre argues, has as its necessary condition for being consciousness of a particular object consciousness of knowing. Epistemologically, then, non-positional consciousness is to explain how consciousness of the intentional object of consciousness is possible. This pre-cognitive foundation which Sartre would give to knowledge is one which purports to escape the infinite regress of knowing our knowing by giving knowing itself an ontological foundation, an irreducible being. Hence, Sartre argues, existing consciousness exists a dual condition: It is consciousness of its object and consciousness of itself as being consciousness of its object. This must be, Sartre insists, since there can be no unconscious consciousness.

This ontological grounding of existing consciousness of something represents Sartre's initial "departure" from phenomenological description to ontological determination. Phenomenologically, consciousness as an operative intention or as a "plenum of existence" is not relational. Consciousness as a "revealing-revelation" knows no duality, no subject-object or subject-predicate distinction. But in questioning the being on the basis of which revelation or the phenomenon of being is revealed, Sartre posits consciousness as a relation; and in doing so, phenomenological description is surpassed by ontological interpretation. This is a surpassing only because Sartre's ontological framework seems to be in conflict with this phenomenology as he strives to explain how an intention can be consciousness. For engaged consciousness is given a necessary condition which is only necessary given a pre-conceived ontology.

There is no problem with seeing the non-thetic consciousness which is existing consciousness as the limiting case for other forms of consciousness. Here, for example, my awareness-of-reading-the-book would be a limiting condition for my being aware of my awareness-of-reading-the-book. This latter consciousness is a reflecting consciousness which posits engaged consciousness as an object; hence, the awareness which is aware of the awareness-of-reading-the-book is separated from the original awareness-of-reading-the-book by a reflective distance which transforms and modifies by objectifying the engaged consciousness on which it reflects. This is essentially congruent with Sartre's explanation of reflection. However, rather than seeing engaged consciousness as a limiting condition of reflecting consciousness, Sartre maintains that non-positional consciousness (of) self is the limiting condition. And in so arguing, Sartre fallaciously claims that intentional consciousness would be unconscious if it were not consciousness (of) self. This is not a phenomenological necessity: Sartre has already argued that engaged consciousness—consciousness as a "plenum of existence"—is awareness-of-an-object, and it would be contradictory to suggest that awareness-of-reading-the-book is not really what we have described it to be. Sartre does not reject his description. Instead, he qualifies it. And when he speaks of non-thetic consciousness (of) self he has moved from the realm of the phenomenon to the realm of ontological determination.

If the unity which Sartre has described as a "plenum of existence" is not a qualified unity which is the limiting condition of all reflective qualifications, then the notion of a non-thetic consciousness-of-self is a contradiction. And Sartre, in attempting to give reflection pre-reflective conditions, paradoxically "inserts" a reflective dualism into pre-reflective consciousness. More precisely, he sees consciousness as a unity with two "movements" or "aspects" (intention and self-consciousness, transcendence and immanence) which exist as a circle. Thus, while Sartre is aware of the dissociation into a duality of engaged consciousness in the "hands" of reflection, he nonetheless wishes to argue that this engaged unity is inherently "fissured" without having to exist the spatial distance of a reflection. To do this, he argues that the distance of self-consciousness is an ideal distance, and in so arguing an abstract *cogito* has come to qualify existing consciousness.

Sartre's ontology seems to rest on an epistemological imperative, borrowed from Descartes and stripped of the ego: Instead of Descartes' "I think that I think" Sartre gives us "thinking thinking its thinking of objects" as an indubitable starting point for philosophy. Knowledge for Sartre is intuitive, grounded in the "immanence" of self-consciousness which is essentially a "detachment" from the "world" in the form of negativity. Yet as much as Sartre wishes to ground knowledge ontologically in the immanence of self to self, his attempt is essentially a failure. It is a failure precisely because the quasi-reflective structure of self-consciousness is indistinguishable from the structure of reflection, except if posited as a logical condition. And if posited as a logical condition, then we find that a pre-conceived ontology has been imposed upon phenomenological description.

When Sartre claims that consciousness unaware of itself would be unconscious consciousness—an absurdity—he has assumed that consciousness as intentionality is, without consciousness (of) self, unconsciousness. It is for this reason that Sartre is, at most, a reluctant phenomenologist, finding it necessary to qualify ontologically even the most basic of phenomenological notions. For Sartre, consciousness is not primarily and fundamentally a unified engagement of "world" but a relation, the terms of which cannot be collapsed one into the other. Thus, Sartre maintains that if intentional consciousness were not also self-consciousness, the "subject" pole of the relation would be absorbed into its "object" pole and consciousness as such would disappear. From the beginning, then, Sartre interprets consciousness of _____ as a consciousness which is *not* "world" and as a consciousness which in tearing itself from being is the determination of "world," of intention.

Of course, whether or not Sartre is a phenomenologist is a question of classification and influence and is not as important as recognizing the different sort of ontology that would have been written if consciousness for Sartre was fundamentally outward directed rather than self-referential. If consciousness, as Merleau-Ponty was to insist, is always engaged in a total, historical situation, and if reflection is rooted in this engagement, then consciousness can never be a naked consciousness, an immanence of self to self. "Rootedness" in the world versus "negation" of world, "attachment" versus "detachment": These are fundamentally different metaphors depicting man's "existential" situation based on fundamentally different ways of interpreting the being of consciousness. Sartre's own choice should be obvious: Consciousness as intentionality, as appearance, as rooted in the world, is subjected to ontological determination which transforms a relation of rootedness into one of negation and which collapses the attachment of consciousness to world into the immanence of consciousness (of) self.

Notes

1. Marjorie Grene, *Sartre* (New York, 1973), p. 38.
2. Jean-Paul Sartre, *The Transcendence of the Ego*, trans., F. Williams and R. Kirkpatrick (New York, 1957). References to this edition are identified in text as TE.
3. Jean-Paul Sartre, *Being and Nothingness*, trans., Hazel E. Barnes (New York, 1966), p. 11. References to this edition will hereafter be identified in text as BN.

Bibliography

Works on Existentialism

Barnes, Hazel Estella. *Existentialist Ethics.* Chicago: University of Chicago Press, 1978.

Barrett, William. *Irrational Man: A Study in Existentialist Philosophy.* Garden City, N.Y.: Doubleday, 1958.

Blackham, Harold J. *Six Existentialist Thinkers.* New York: Harper Torchbooks, 1952.

Busch, Thomas W. *Circulating Being: From Embodiment to Incorporation: Essays on Late Existentialism.* New York: Fordham University Press, 1999.

Cochrane, Arthur C. *The Existentialists and God; Being and the Being of God in the Thought of Søren Kierkegaard, Karl Jaspers, Martin Heidegger, Jean-Paul Sartre, Paul Tillich, Etienne Gilson and Karl Barth.* Philadelphia: Westminster Press, 1956.

Cooper, David E. *Existentialism: A Reconstruction.* 2d ed. Malden, Mass.: Blackwell, 1999.

Critchley, Simon, and William R. Schroeder, eds., *A Companion to Continental Philosophy.* Malden, Mass.: Blackwell, 1998.

D'Amico, Robert. *Contemporary Continental Philosophy.* Boulder, Colo.: Westview Press, 1999.

Giles, James., ed. *French Existentialism: Consciousness, Ethics, and Relations with Others.* Amsterdam: Rodopi, 1999.

Gordon, Lewis R., ed. *Existence in Black: An Anthology of Black Existential Philosophy.* New York: Routledge, 1997.

——— . *Existentia Africana: Understanding African Existential Thought.* New York: Routledge, 2000.

Grene, Marjorie Glicksman. *Dreadful Freedom: A Critique of Existentialism.* Chicago: University of Chicago Press, 1948.

——— . *Introduction to Existentialism.* Chicago: University of Chicago Press, 1976.

Grossman, Reinhardt. *Phenomenology and Existentialism: An Introduction.* Boston: Routledge & Kegan Paul, 1984.

Kruks, Sonia. *Situation and Human Existence: Freedom, Subjectivity, and Society.* Boston: Unwin Hyman, 1990.

Macquarrie, John. *Existentialism.* Philadelphia: Westminister Press, 1972.

———. *An Existentialist Theology: A Comparison of Heidegger and Bultmann.* New York: Harper & Row, 1965.

Mahon, Joseph. *Existentialism, Feminism, and Simone de Beauvoir.* New York: St. Martin's Press, 1997.

McBride, William L., ed. *Sartre and Existentialism: Philosophy, Politics, Ethics, the Psyche, Literature, and Aesthetics.* 6 vols. New York: Garland, 1996.

Miller, James. *History and Human Existence: From Marx to Merleau-Ponty.* Berkeley: University of California Press, 1979.

Murdoch, Iris. *Existentialists and Mystics: Writings on Philosophy and Literature.* Baltimore: Penguin Books, 1994.

Olafson, Frederick A. *Principles and Persons: An Ethical Interpretation of Existentialism.* Baltimore: Johns Hopkins University Press, 1967.

Reinhardt, Kurt Frank. *The Existentialist Revolt; The Main Themes and Phases of Existentialism: Kierkegaard, Nietzsche, Heidegger, Jaspers, Sartre, Marcel.* Milwaukee, Wisc.: Bruce, 1952.

Sanborn, Patricia F. *Existentialism.* New York: Pegasus, 1968.

Schrag, Calvin O. *Existence and Freedom: Towards an Ontology of Human Finitude.* Evanston, Ill.: Northwestern University Press, 1961.

Solomon, Robert C. *From Hegel to Existentialism.* Oxford: Oxford University Press, 1987.

———. *From Rationalism to Existentialism: The Existentialists and Their Nineteenth-Century Backgrounds.* New York: Harper & Row, 1972.

Tuttle, Howard N. *The Crowd Is Untruth: The Existential Critique of Mass Society in the Thought of Kierkegaard, Nietzsche, Heidegger, and Ortega y Gasset.* New York: P. Lang, 1996.

Wahl, Jean André. *Philosophies of Existence: An Introduction to the Basic Thought of Kierkegaard, Heidegger, Jaspers, Marcel, Sartre.* Translated from the French by F. M. Lory. London: Routledge & Kegan Paul, 1969.

Warnock, Mary. *Existentialism.* London: Oxford University Press, 1970.

———. *Existentialist Ethics.* London: Macmillan, 1967.

Westphal, Merold. *God, Guilt, and Death: An Existential Phenomenology of Religion.* Bloomington: Indiana University Press, 1984.

Wilson, Colin. *The New Existentialism.* London: Wildwood House, 1966.

Wolin, Richard. *The Terms of Cultural Criticism: The Frankfurt School, Existentialism, Poststructuralism.* New York: Columbia University Press, 1992.

Works by Kierkegaard

Princeton University Press is publishing Kierkegaard's works in multiple volumes, translated by Howard. V. Hong and Edna H. Hong. Additional works in translation are listed below.

Attack upon "Christendom," 1854–1855. Translated by Walter Lowrie. Princeton, N.J.: Princeton University Press, 1968.

The Concept of Dread. Translated by Walter Lowrie. Princeton, N.J.: Princeton University Press, 1957.

Concluding Unscientific Postscript. Translated by David F. Swenson and Walter Lowrie. Princeton, N.J.: Princeton University Press, 1968.

Either/Or: A Fragment of Life. Translated by Alastair Hannay. Harmondsworth, U.K.: Penguin Press, 1992.

Fear and Trembling. Translated by Alastair Hannay. Harmondsworth, U.K.: Penguin Press, 1985.

Papers and Journals: A Selection. Translated by Alastair Hannay. Harmondsworth, U.K.: Penguin Press, 1996.

Philosophical Fragments. Translated by David F. Swenson and Howard V. Hong. Princeton, N.J.: Princeton University Press, 1962.

The Present Age. Translated by Alexander Dru. London: Collins, 1962.

The Sickness unto Death. Translated by Alastair Hannay. Harmondsworth, U.K.: Penguin Press, 1989.

Works on Kierkegaard

Collins, James Daniel. *The Mind of Kierkegaard.* Princeton, N.J.: Princeton University Press, 1983.

Connell, George B. *To Be One Thing: Personal Unity in Kierkegaard's Thought.* Macon, Ga.: Mercer University Press, 1985.

Crites, Stephen. *In the Twilight of Christendom: Hegel versus Kierkegaard on Faith and History.* Camersbury, Pa.: American Academy of Religion, 1972.

Daise, Benjamin. *Kierkegaard's Socratic Art.* Macon, Ga.: Mercer University Press, 1999.

Davenport, John J., and Anthony Rudd, eds. *Kierkegaard after MacIntyre: Essays on Freedom, Narrative, and Virtue.* Chicago: Open Court, 2001.

Dunning, Stephen N. *Kierkegaard's Dialectic of Inwardness: A Structural Analysis of the Theory of Stages.* Princeton, N.J.: Princeton University Press, 1985.

Dupré, Louis. *Kierkegaard as Theologian; The Dialectic of Christian Existence.* New York: Sheed and Ward, 1963.

Elrod, John W. *Kierkegaard and Christendom.* Princeton, N.J.: Princeton University Press, 1981.

Evans, C. Stephen. *Passionate Reason: Making Sense of Kierkegaard's* Philosophical Fragments. Bloomington: Indiana University Press, 1992.

Ferguson, Harvie. *Melancholy and the Critique of Modernity: Søren Kierkegaard's Religious Philosophy.* London: Routledge, 1995.

Ferreira, M. Jamie. *Transforming Vision: Imagination and Will in Kierkegaardian Faith.* Oxford: Clarendon Press, 1991.

Gardiner, Patrick. *Kierkegaard: A Very Short Introduction.* Oxford: Oxford University Press, 2002.

Gouwens, David J. *Kierkegaard as Religious Thinker.* Cambridge: Cambridge University Press, 1996.

Hall, Ronald L. *Word and Spirit: A Kierkegaardian Critique of the Modern Age.* Bloomington: Indiana University Press, 1993.

Hannay, Alastair. *Kierkegaard: The Arguments of the Philosophers.* Edited by Ted Honderich. London: Routledge & Kegan Paul, 1991.

——. *Kierkegaard: A Biography.* Cambridge: Cambridge University Press, 2001.

Hannay, Alastair, and Gordon D. Marino, eds. *The Cambridge Companion to Kierkegaard.* Cambridge: Cambridge University Press, 1998.

Kellenberger, James. *Kierkegaard and Nietzsche: Faith and Eternal Acceptance.* New York: Macmillan, 1997.

Kirmmse, Bruce H. *Kierkegaard in Golden Age Denmark.* Bloomington: Indiana University Press, 1990.

León, Céline, and Sylvia Walsh, eds. *Feminist Interpretations of Søren Kierkegaard.* University Park: Pennsylvania State University Press, 1997.

Lippitt, John. *Humour and Irony in Kierkegaard's Thought.* New York: St. Martin's Press, 2000.

Lorentzen, Jamie. *Kierkegaard's Metaphors.* Macon, Ga.: Mercer University Press, 2001.

Mackey, Louis. *Kierkegaard: A Kind of Poet.* Philadelphia: University of Pennsylvania Press, 1971.

——. *Points of View: Readings of Kierkegaard.* Tallahassee: Florida State University Press, 1986.

Malantschuk, Gregor. *Kierkegaard's Thought.* Translated by Howard V. Hong and Edna H. Hong. Princeton, N.J.: Princeton University Press, 1971.

Marino, Gordon D. *Kierkegaard in the Present Age.* Milwaukee, Wisc.: Marquette University Press, 2001.

Matutík, Martin J., and Merold Westphal, eds. *Kierkegaard in Post/Modernity.* Bloomington: Indiana University Press, 1995.

Mooney, Edward F. *Knights of Faith and Resignation: Reading Kierkegaard's Fear and Trembling.* Albany: State University of New York Press, 1991.

——. *Selves in Discord and Resolve: Kierkegaard's Moral-Religious Psychology from Either/Or to Sickness unto Death.* New York: Routledge, 1996.

Pattison, George, and Steven Shakespeare, eds. *Kierkegaard: The Self in Society.* Basingstoke, U.K.: Macmillan, 1998.

Perkins, Robert L., ed. *International Kierkegaard Commentary.* Macon, Ga.: Mercer University Press, 1984–.

——, ed. *Kierkegaard's Fear and Trembling.* Tuscaloosa: University of Alabama Press, 1981.

Phillips, D. Z., and Timothy Tessin, eds. *Kant and Kierkegaard on Religion.* New York: St. Martin's Press, 2000.

Pojman, Louis. *The Logic of Subjectivity: Kierkegaard's Philosophy of Religion.* Tuscaloosa: University of Alabama Press, 1984.

Smith, Joseph H., ed. *Kierkegaard's Truth: The Disclosure of the Self.* New Haven, Conn.: Yale University Press, 1981.

Stack, George J. *Kierkegaard's Existential Ethics.* Tuscaloosa: University of Alabama Press, 1977.

Taylor, Mark C. *Journeys to Selfhood: Hegel and Kierkegaard.* Berkeley: University of California Press, 1980.

———. *Kierkegaard's Pseudonymous Authorship: A Study of Time and the Self.* Princeton, N.J.: Princeton University Press, 1975.

Watkin, Julia. *Historical Dictionary of Kierkegaard's Philosophy.* Lanham, Md.: Scarecrow Press, 2001.

Weston, Michael. *Kierkegaard and Modern Continental Philosophy: An Introduction.* London: Routledge, 1994.

Westphal, Merold. *Becoming a Self: A Reading of Kierkegaard's* Concluding Unscientific Postscript. West Lafayette, Ind.: Purdue University Press, 1996.

———. *Kierkegaard's Critique of Reason and Society.* Macon, Ga.: Mercer University Press, 1987.

Works by Nietzsche

An edition of the works of Nietzsche in English is currently being edited by Bernd Magnus. Additional translations are listed below.

Basic Writings of Nietzsche. Edited by Walter Kaufmann. New York: Modern Library, 2000.

Beyond Good and Evil. Translated by Walter Kaufmann. New York: Vintage Books, 1967.

The Birth of Tragedy Out of the Spirit of Music and *The Case of Wagner.* Translated by Walter Kaufmann. New York: Vintage Books, 1967.

The Dawn. Translated by R. J. Hollingdale. Cambridge: Cambridge University Press, 1982.

Ecce Homo: How One Becomes What One Is. Translated by Walter Kaufmann. New York: Vintage Books, 1967.

The Gay Science. Translated by Walter Kaufmann. New York: Vintage Books, 1974.

Human, All Too Human. Translated by Marion Faber and Stephen Lehman. Lincoln: University of Nebraska Press, 1984.

On the Genealogy of Morals. Translated by Walter Kaufmann. New York: Vintage Books, 1967.

Thus Spoke Zarathustra. Translated by Walter Kaufmann. New York: Penguin Books, 1981.

Twilight of the Idols and *The Antichrist.* Translated by R. J. Hollingdale. London: Penguin Books, 1968.

Untimely Meditations. Translated by R. J. Hollingdale. Cambridge: Cambridge University Press, 1983.

The Will to Power. Translated by Walter Kaufmann and R. J. Hollingdale. New York: Vintage, 1967.

Works on Nietzsche

Abbey, Ruth. *Nietzsche's Middle Period.* New York: Oxford University Press, 2000.

Ackerman, Robert John. *Nietzsche: A Frenzied Look.* Amherst: University of Massachusetts Press, 1990.

Ahern, Daniel R. *Nietzsche as Cultural Physician.* University Park: Pennsylvania State University Press, 1995.

Alderman, Harold. *Nietzsche's Gift.* Athens: Ohio University Press, 1977.

Allison, David B. *Reading the New Nietzsche:* The Birth Of Tragedy, The Gay Science, Thus Spoke Zarathustra, *and* On the Genealogy of Morals. Lanham, Md.: Rowman & Littlefield, 2001.

———, ed. *The New Nietzsche.* New York: Dell Publishing Company, 1977.

Ansell-Pearson, Keith. *An Introduction to Nietzsche as Political Thinker: The Perfect Nihilist.* Cambridge: Cambridge University Press, 1994.

Ansell-Pearson, Keith, and Howard Caygill, eds. *The Fate of the New Nietzsche.* Aldershot, U.K.: Avebury, 1993.

Babich, Babette E. *Nietzsche's Philosophy of Science: Reflecting on the Ground of Art and Life.* Albany: State University of New York Press, 1994.

Barker, Stephen. *Autoaesthetics: Strategies of the Self after Nietzsche.* Atlantic Highlands, N.J.: Humanities Press, 1992.

Bataille, Georges. *On Nietzsche.* Translated by Bruce Boone. New York: Paragon House, 1992.

Clark, Maudemarie. *Nietzsche: On Truth and Philosophy.* Cambridge: Cambridge University Press, 1990.

Conway, Daniel W. *Nietzsche's Dangerous Game: Philosophy in* The Twilight of the Idols. New York: Cambridge University Press, 1997.

Cooper, David E. *Authenticity and Learning: Nietzsche's Educational Philosophy.* London: Routledge & Kegan Paul, 1983.

Danto, Arthur. *Nietzsche as Philosopher.* New York: Macmillan, 1965.

Del Caro, Adrian. *Nietzsche contra Nietzsche: Creativity and the Anti-Romantic.* Baton Rouge: Louisiana State University, 1989.

Deleuze, Gilles. *Nietzsche and Philosophy.* Translated by Hugh Tomlinson. New York: Columbia University Press, 1983.

Detwiler, Bruce. *Nietzsche and the Politics of Aristocratic Radicalism.* Chicago: University of Chicago Press, 1990.

Gillespie, Michael Allen, and Tracy B. Strong, eds. *Nietzsche's New Seas: Explorations in Philosophy, Aesthetics, and Politics.* Chicago: University of Chicago Press, 1988.

Golomb, Jacob. *Nietzsche's Enticing Psychology of Power.* Ames: Iowa State University Press, 1987.

Haar, Michel. *Nietzsche and Metaphysics.* Translated by Michael Gendre. Albany: State University of New York Press, 1996.

Hales, Steven D, and Rex Welshon. *Nietzsche's Perspectivism.* Urbana: University of Illinois Press, 2000.

Havas, Randall. *Nietzsche's Genealogy: Nihilism and the Will to Knowledge.* Ithaca, N.Y.: Cornell University Press, 1995.

Hayman, Ronald. *Nietzsche.* New York: Routledge, 1999.

———. *Nietzsche: A Critical Life.* New York: Penguin Books, 1982.

Heller, Eric. *The Importance of Nietzsche.* Chicago: University of Chicago Press, 1988.

Higgins, Kathleen Marie. *Nietzsche's* Zarathustra. Philadelphia: Temple University Press, 1987.

Hollingdale, R. J. *Nietzsche: The Man and His Philosophy.* Cambridge: Cambridge University Press, 1999.

Hunt, Lester H. *Nietzsche and the Origin of Virtue.* New York: Routledge, 1991.

Kaufmann, Walter. *Nietzsche: Philosopher, Psychologist, Antichrist.* Princeton, N.J.: Princeton University Press, 1974.

Krell, David Farrell. *Infectious Nietzsche.* Bloomington: Indiana University Press, 1996.

Krell, David Farrell, and David Wood, eds. *Exceedingly Nietzsche: Aspects of Contemporary Nietzsche Interpretation.* London: Routledge & Kegan Paul, 1988.

Lampert, Laurence. *Nietzsche and Modern Times.* New Haven, Conn.: Yale University Press, 1993.

Löwith, Karl. *From Hegel to Nietzsche.* Translated by David Green. Garden City, N.Y.: Doubleday, 1967.

———. *Nietzsche's Philosophy of the Eternal Recurrence of the Same.* Translated by J. Harvey Lomax. Berkeley: University of California Press, 1997.

Magnus, Bernd. *Nietzsche's Existential Imperative.* Bloomington: Indiana University Press, 1978.

Magnus, Bernd, and Kathleen M. Higgins, eds. *The Cambridge Companion to Nietzsche.* Cambridge: Cambridge University Press, 1996.

Magnus, Bernd, Stanley Stewart, and Jean-Pierre Mileur, eds. *Nietzsche's Case: Philosophy as/and Literature.* New York: Routledge, 1993.

Nehamas, Alexander. *Nietzsche: Life as Literature.* Cambridge, Mass.: Harvard University Press, 1985.

O'Hara, Daniel T., ed. *Why Nietzsche Now?* Bloomington: Indiana University Press, 1985.

Okonta, Ike. *Nietzsche: The Politics of Power.* New York: Lang, 1992.

Oliver, Kelly, and Marilyn Pearsall, eds. *Feminist Interpretations of Friedrich Nietzsche.* University Park: Pennsylvania State University Press, 1998.

Parkes, Graham. *Composing the Soul: Reaches of Nietzsche's Psychology.* Chicago: University of Chicago Press, 1994.

Pavur, Claude Nicholas. *Nietzsche Humanist.* Milwaukee, Wisc.: Marquette University Press, 1998.

Poellner, Peter. *Nietzsche and Metaphysics.* New York: Oxford University Press, 1995.

Rampley, Matthew. *Nietzsche, Aesthetics, and Modernity.* Cambridge: Cambridge University Press, 2000.

Richardson, John. *Nietzsche's System.* New York: Oxford University Press, 1996.

Rosen, Stanley. *Nihilism: A Philosophical Essay.* New Haven, Conn.: Yale University Press, 1969.

Safranski, Rüdiger. *Nietzsche: A Philosophical Biography.* Translated by Shelley Frisch. New York: W. W. Norton, 2001.

Sallis, John. *Crossings: Nietzsche and the Space of Tragedy.* Chicago: University of Chicago Press, 1991.

Schacht, Richard. *Making Sense of Nietzsche: Reflections Timely and Untimely.* Urbana: University of Illinois Press, 1995.

———. *Nietzsche.* London: Routledge & Kegan Paul, 1983.

———, ed. *Nietzsche, Genealogy, Morality: Essays on Nietzsche's* Genealogy of Morals. Berkeley: University of California Press, 1994.

Schrift, Alan D. *Nietzsche and the Question of Interpretation: Between Hermeneutics and Deconstruction.* New York: Routledge, 1990.

Schütte, Ofelia. *Beyond Nihilism: Nietzsche without Masks.* Chicago: University of Chicago Press, 1984.

Scott, Charles E. *The Question of Ethics: Nietzsche, Foucault, Heidegger.* Bloomington: Indiana University Press, 1990.

Sedgwick, Peter R., ed. *Nietzsche: A Critical Reader.* Cambridge: Blackwell, 1995.

Shapiro, Gary. *Alcyone: Nietzsche on Gifts, Noise, and Women.* Albany: State University of New York Press, 1991.

Simmel, Georg. *Schopenhauer and Nietzsche.* Translated by Helmut Loiskandl and Deena Weinstein. Amherst: University of Massachusetts Press, 1986.

Sleinis, Edgar E. *Nietzsche's Revaluation of Values: A Study in Strategies.* Urbana: University of Illinois Press, 1994.

Smith, Gregory B. *Nietzsche, Heidegger, and the Transition to Postmodernity.* Chicago: University of Chicago Press, 1996.

Solomon, Robert C., ed. *Nietzsche: A Collection of Critical Essays.* Garden City, N.Y.: Anchor Press, 1973.

Solomon, Robert C., and Kathleen M. Higgins, eds. *Reading Nietzsche.* New York: Oxford University Press, 1988.

Stambaugh, Joan. *Nietzsche's Thought of Eternal Return.* Baltimore: Johns Hopkins University Press, 1972.

———. *The Other Nietzsche.* Albany: State University of New York Press, 1994.

———. *The Problem of Time in Nietzsche.* Translated by John F. Humphrey. Lewisburg, Pa.: Bucknell University Press, 1987.

Staten, Henry. *Nietzsche's Voice.* Ithaca, N.Y.: Cornell University Press, 1990.

Stauth, Georg, and Bryan S. Turner. *Nietzsche's Dance: Resentment, Reciprocity and Resistance in Social Life.* Oxford: Blackwell, 1988.

Strong, Tracy. *Friedrich Nietzsche and the Politics of Transfiguration.* Berkeley: University of California Press, 1975.

Thiele, Leslie Paul. *Friedrich Nietzsche and the Politics of the Soul: A Study of Heroic Individualism.* Princeton, N.J.: Princeton University Press, 1990.

Vattimo, Gianni. *The Adventure of Difference: Philosophy after Nietzsche and Heidegger.* Translated by Cyprian Blamires and Thomas Harrison. Baltimore: Johns Hopkins University Press, 1993.

White, Alan. *Within Nietzsche's Labyrinth.* New York: Routledge, 1990.

Wilcox, John. *Truth and Value in Nietzsche.* Ann Arbor: University of Michigan Press, 1974.

Williams, Linda L. *Nietzsche's Mirror: The World as Will to Power.* Lanham, Md.: Rowman & Littlefield, 2001.

Winchester, James J. *Nietzsche's Aesthetic Turn: Reading Nietzsche after Heidegger, Deleuze, Derrida.* Albany: State University of New York Press, 1994.

Wininger, Kathleen J. *Nietzsche's Reclamation of Philosophy.* Amsterdam: Rodopi, 1997.

Young, Julian. *Nietzsche's Philosophy of Art.* Cambridge: Cambridge University Press, 1992.

Zeitlin, Irving M. *Nietzsche: A Re-examination.* Cambridge: Polity Press, 1994.

Works by Heidegger

Basic Problems of Phenomenology. Translated by Albert Hofstadter. Bloomington: Indiana University Press, 1982.
Basic Writings: From Being and Time *(1927) to* The Task of Thinking *(1964).* Edited by David Farrell Krell. San Francisco: Harper, 1993.
Being and Time. Translated by John Macquarrie and Edward Robinson. New York: Harper & Row, 1962.
Ontology: The Hermeneutics of Facticity. Translated by John van Buren. Bloomington: Indiana University Press, 1999.
The Concept of Time. Translated by William McNeill. Oxford: Blackwell, 1992.
The Fundamental Concepts of Metaphysics: World, Finitude, Solitude. Translated by William McNeill and Nicholas Walker. Bloomington: Indiana University Press, 1995.
Towards the Definition of Philosophy: With a Transcript of the Lecture Course "On the Nature of the University and Academic Study." Translated by Ted Sadler. New Brunswick, N. J.: Athlone Press, 2000.

Works on Heidegger

Carman, Taylor. *Heidegger's Analytic: Interpretation, Discourse, and Authenticity in* Being and Time. New York: Cambridge University Press, 2003.
Chanter, Tina. *Time, Death, and the Feminine: Levinas with Heidegger.* Stanford, Calif.: Stanford University Press, 2001.
Ciaffa, Jay A. "Toward an Understanding of Heidegger's Conception of the Inter-Relation Between Authentic and Inauthentic Existence." *Journal of the British Society for Phenomenology* 18 (January 1987): 49–59.
Cohn, Hans. *Heidegger and the Roots of Existential Psychotherapy.* London: Continuum, 2002.
Dreyfus, Hubert L. *Being-in-the-World: A Commentary on Heidegger's* Being and Time, *Division I.* Cambridge, Mass.: MIT Press, 1991.
Dreyfus, Hubert L., and Harrison Hall, eds. *Heidegger: A Critical Reader.* Oxford: Blackwell, 1992.
Dreyfus, Hubert L., and Mark A. Wrathall, eds. *Heidegger Reexamined.* 3 vols. New York: Routledge, 2002.
Fell, Joseph P. *Heidegger and Sartre: An Essay on Being and Place.* New York: Columbia University Press, 1979.
Gadamer, Hans-Georg. *Heidegger's Ways.* Translated by John W. Stanley. Albany: State University of New York Press, 1994.
Gorner, Paul. *Twentieth-Century German Philosophy.* Oxford: Oxford University Press, 2000.

Guignon, Charles, ed. *Cambridge Companion to Heidegger.* Cambridge: Cambridge University Press, 1993.

———. *Heidegger and the Problem of Knowledge.* Indianapolis, Ind.: Hackett, 1983.

———. "Heidegger's 'Authenticity' Revisited." *Review of Metaphysics* 38 (December 1984): 321–39.

Hall, Harrison. "Love and Death: Kierkegaard and Heidegger on Authentic and Inauthentic Human Existence." *Inquiry* 27 (July 1984): 179–97.

Hatab, Lawrence J. *Ethics and Finitude: Heideggerian Contributions to Moral Philosophy.* Lanham, Md.: Rowman & Littlefield, 2000.

Haugeland, John. "Heidegger on Being a Person." *Nous* 16 (March 1982): 6–26.

Holland, Nancy J., and Patricia Huntington, eds. *Feminist Interpretations of Martin Heidegger.* University Park: Pennsylvania State University Press, 2001.

Hopkins, Burt C. *Intentionality in Husserl and Heidegger: The Problem of the Original Method and Phenomenon of Phenomenology.* Dordrecht, Holland: Kluwer Academic Publishers, 1993.

Keller, Pierre. *Husserl and Heidegger on Human Experience.* Cambridge: Cambridge University Press, 1999.

Krell, David Farrell. *Intimations of Mortality: Time, Truth, and Finitude in Heidegger's Thinking of Being.* University Park: Pennsylvania State University Press, 1986.

Magnus, Bernd. *Heidegger's Metahistory of Philosophy.* The Hague: Martinus Nijhoff, 1970.

Malpas, Jeff, and Mark Wrathall, eds. *Heidegger, Authenticity, and Modernity: Essays in Honor of Hubert L. Dreyfus.* Vol. 1. Cambridge, Mass.: MIT Press, 2000.

Mansbach, Abraham. *Beyond Subjectivism: Heidegger on Language and the Human Being.* Westport, Conn.: Greenwood Press, 2002.

Mulhall, Stephen. *Routledge Philosophy Guidebook to Heidegger and* Being and Time. London: Routledge, 1996.

Olafson, Frederick A. *Heidegger and the Philosophy of Mind.* New Haven, Conn.: Yale University Press, 1987.

Polt, Richard. *Heidegger: An Introduction.* Ithaca, N.Y.: Cornell University Press, 1999.

Raffoul, François. *Heidegger and the Subject.* Translated by David Pettigrew and Gregory Recco. Atlantic Highlands, N.J.: Humanities Press, 1998.

Renaut, Alain. *The Era of the Individual: A Contribution to a History of Subjectivity.* Translated by M. B. DeBevoise and Franklin Philip. Princeton, N.J.: Princeton University Press, 1997.

Richardson, John. *Existential Epistemology: A Heideggerian Critique of the Cartesian Project.* Oxford: Clarendon Press, 1986.

Vogel, Lawrence. *The Fragile "We": Ethical Implications of Heidegger's* Being and Time. Evanston, Ill.: Northwestern University Press, 1994.

Zimmerman, Michael E. *Eclipse of the Self: The Development of Heidegger's Concept of Authenticity.* Rev. ed. Athens: Ohio University Press, 1986.

———. "Heidegger's 'Existentialism' Revisited." *International Philosophical Quarterly* 24 (September 1984): 219–36.

Works by Sartre

Being and Nothingness: An Essay on Phenomenological Ontology. Translated by Hazel E. Barnes. New York: Philosophical Library, 1956. Reprinted by Washington Square Press, 1972.
The Emotions: Outline of a Theory. Translated by Bernard Frechtman. New York: Philosophical Library, 1948.
Existentialism and Humanism. Translated by Philip Mairet. London: Methuen, 1957.
Nausea, or The Diary of Antoine Roquentin. Translated by Lloyd Alexander. New York: New Directions, 1949.
The Transcendence of the Ego; An Existentialist Theory of Consciousness. Translated by Forrest Williams and Robert Kirkpatrick. New York: Noonday Press, 1957.
The Words. Translated by Bernard Frechtman. New York: Brazilier, 1964.

Works on Sartre

Anderson, Thomas C. *The Foundation and Structure of Sartrean Ethics.* Lawrence, Kans.: Regents Press, 1979.
——— . *Sartre's Two Ethics: From Authenticity to Integral Humanity.* Chicago: Open Court, 1993.
Barnes, Hazel. *Sartre.* New York: J. B. Lippincott, 1973.
Bell, Linda A. *Sartre's Ethics of Authenticity.* Tuscaloosa: University of Alabama Press, 1989.
Busch, Thomas W. *The Power of Consciousness and the Force of Circumstances in Sartre's Philosophy.* Bloomington: Indiana University Press, 1990.
Catalano, Joseph S. *A Commentary on Sartre's* Being and Nothingness. New York: Harper & Row, 1974.
Caws, Peter. *Sartre.* London: Routledge & Kegan Paul, 1979.
Cumming, Robert., ed. *The Philosophy of Jean-Paul Sartre.* New York: Vintage, 1974.
Detmer, David. *Freedom as a Value: A Critique of the Ethical Theory of Jean-Paul Sartre.* La Salle, Ill.: Open Court, 1986.
Flynn, Thomas R. *Sartre and Marxist Existentialism.* Chicago: University of Chicago Press, 1984.
Greene, Norman. *Jean-Paul Sartre: The Existentialist Ethic.* Ann Arbor: University of Michigan Press, 1960.
Grene, Marjorie. *Sartre.* New York: New Viewpoints, 1973.
Hartmann, Klaus. *Sartre's Ontology: A Study of* Being and Nothingness *in the Light of Hegel's Logic.* Evanston, Ill.: Northwestern University Press, 1966.
Hayim, Gila J. *Existentialism and Sociology: The Contribution of Jean-Paul Sartre.* New Brunswick, N.J.: Transaction Publishers, 1996.
Hoffman, Piotr. *The Human Self and the Life and Death Struggle.* Gainesville: University Presses of Florida, 1983.

Howells, Christina, ed. *The Cambridge Companion to Sartre*. New York: Cambridge University Press, 1992.

———— . *Sartre: The Necessity of Freedom*. Cambridge: Cambridge University Press, 1988.

Jeanson, Francis. *Sartre and the Problem of Morality*. Bloomington: Indiana University Press, 1980.

McBride, William L. *Sartre's Political Theory*. Bloomington: Indiana University Press, 1991.

Murdoch, Iris. *Sartre, Romantic Rationalist*. New York: Viking, 1987.

Murphy, Julien S., ed. *Feminist Interpretations of Jean-Paul Sartre*. University Park: Pennsylvania State University Press, 1999.

Schilpp, Paul Arthur, ed. *The Philosophy of Jean-Paul Sartre*. La Salle, Ill.: Open Court 1981.

Silverman, Hugh J., and Frederick A. Elliston, eds. *Jean-Paul Sartre —Contemporary Approaches to His Philosophy*. Pittsburgh, Pa.: Duquesne University Press, 1980.

Warnock, Mary. *The Philosophy of Sartre*. London: Hutchinson, 1965.

Index

About the Editor and Contributors

CHARLES GUIGNON has taught at Berkeley, Princeton, the University of Vermont, and the University of Texas at Austin, and is currently professor of philosophy at the University of South Florida. He is author of *Heidegger and the Problem of Knowledge*; editor of *The Cambridge Companion to Heidegger, The Good Life*, and Dostoevsky's *The Grand Inquisitor*; coeditor of RICHARD RORTY (in the Cambridge "Philosophers in Focus" series) and *Existentialism: Basic Writings*; and coauthor of *Re-envisioning Psychology*.

ROBERT MERRIHEW ADAMS, professor of philosophy at Yale University, is the author of *Leibniz: Determinist, Theist, Idealist* (1994) and *Finite and Infinite Goods: A Framework for Ethics* (1999).

THOMAS C. ANDERSON, professor emeritus of philosophy at Marquette University, is author of *Foundation and Structure of Sartrean Ethics* (1979) and *Sartre's Two Ethics* (1993).

LOUIS DUPRÉ is emeritus professor of religious studies at Yale University. Among his books is *Passage to Modernity* (1993).

HARRISON HALL, professor of philosophy at the University of Delaware, author of several papers on phenomenology and existentialism, has also co-edited volumes on Husserl and Heidegger.

DOROTHY LELAND, Vice President and professor of philosophy at Florida Atlantic University, has written on existentialism and phenomenology.

ALEXANDER NEHAMAS is the Edmund N. Carpenter II Professor in the humanities and comparative literature department at Princeton University. His most recent books include *Virtues of Authenticity* (1998) and *The Art of Living* (2000).

ROBERT C. SOLOMON is professor of business and philosophy at The University of Texas at Austin. The most recent of his more than thirty books are *Spirituality for the Skeptic* (2002) and *The Joy of Philosophy* (2003).